JANE BUTEL'S

FREEZER COOKBOOK

Also by Jane Butel

FAVORITE MEXICAN FOODS

Food and Appliance Brochures for:

Con Edison
Edison Electric Institute
General Electric
Heublein
Hotpoint
Public Service Company of New Mexico

JANE BUTEL'S FREEZER COOKBOOK

Coward, McCann & Geoghegan, Inc. New York

SBN: 698-10727-6

Library of Congress Cataloging in Publication Data

Butel, Jane
    Jane Butel's freezer cookbook.
    Includes index.
    1. Cookery (Frozen foods)   2. Food, Frozen.
I. Title.   II. Title: Freezer Cookbook.
TX828.B87 1976   641.6'1'53   76-13656

Printed in the United States of America

To

Mother and Amy

Contents

Preface

No matter what are your interests, your lifestyle, or your means, you no doubt would like to eat better for less. This book has been developed to share insights on how you can put a freeze on your food costs, allowing you to eat better, yet spend less time fussing with food purchasing and preparation. A freezer, once you develop your own favorite system, gives you the most precious gift of all—more time to spend as you wish—doing things that please you and your loved ones.

Whether you're trying to decide if a freezer makes sense for you or are learning how to use it to gain the most benefits or frozen assets, this book should be an invaluable guide. A freezer is best thought of as a time bank rather than a money bank. The savings are in convenience. The cost of the freezer over an average life of twenty years (many last far longer), coupled with the cost of electricity, rarely allows a net savings. You can maximize your investment by smart use. Many new time- and labor-saving techniques have been developed that are guaranteed to be worthwhile. Tips for dieting and eating alone and how-tos based on the latest research for fresh foods of all types from game to fruit have been included.

I genuinely appreciate the unselfish help so many have given to make this book a reality. It's truly impossible to credit everyone. The enthusiastic encouragement from many of my fellow General Electric employees was outstanding, especially in the refrigeration products division, the library, and our communications group. Home economics research was so generously shared by all the state and national extension services and state universities; by General Electric's range home economists and home economists with food and packaging companies and trade associations; professional help from such great friends as Randall Smith, Frazier Clark, Harry Rosen, Helen Ayers Davis, Dr. Gertrude Armbruster, and my mother, Mrs. Dorothy Franz—plus the many dedicated helpers.

1
Choosing A Freezer

WHICH FREEZER?

Are you already convinced that you'd like to begin building your own storehouse of frozen assets? Or, are you dubious whether you'd really use your freezer once purchased? Do think it through very seriously—and for heaven's sake, don't invest in a great new or new-to-you freezer until you know how it will improve your life.

A freezer can allow for more free time at the most precious times— when family and friends are at hand and you'd like to feed them your very best! This can happen only if you take the time to fill your freezer as you shop and cook. I know you'll really enjoy having a well-stocked freezer . . . and it *does* take planning. But the planning is worthwhile, saving hours and hours of shopping and cooking time . . . to say nothing of the bargains and the seasonal and regional markets you can exploit.

I can't help but tell you the plight of a favorite secretary I had for several years who, through my enthusiasm for a freezer, decided to buy one. She had typed countless recipes and scripts for the freezer and the great idea had just rubbed off. But, I was never so disappointed as one evening when I was at her home for dinner and she said, "Jane, I've just got to show you something." She led me over to where her freezer was and opened the door. To my utter amazement, all she had in it was one long loaf of bakery bread. She certainly had no frozen assets, just a real liability. She said that somehow she never could get herself to think about her freezer when she shopped or cooked and wanted my advice on whether to keep it or not. You should never let that happen—and it won't, as long as you reorient your thinking to include bargain buys and extra batches when shopping and cooking.

My freezers have always been jammed full. For years I maintained an 18.5-cubic-foot upright frostless, plus two freezers over refrigerators— totaling about 30 cubic feet of freezer space. Of course, I'm a compulsive bargain buyer and cook. I love to prepare favorite dishes, such as cassoulet, beef Bourguignon, meat loaves, and Coq au Vin to have on constant call.

Personally, I like being able to prepare whatever dishes the mood and circumstances dictate without a lot of fuss or trips to the store. I like to keep on hand all the goodies I need to prepare any kind of food from Chi-

11

nese to Syrian to Mexican. To me, it's such an exciting and rewarding way to live—sharing my favorite specialties.

Now, once the questions of whether or not to buy a freezer are resolved, the next question is which one will be best for you? There are several basic questions to answer that are more pertinent to your own cooking, eating, and living habits.

Perhaps you will be somewhat surprised to know that there really is no magic formula—no basic set of questions which will definitely pinpoint the best size, style, and type for you. There are guidelines, though, that really help narrow down the choices.

Start by taking an in-depth look at yourself and/or your family, if you have one. Where are you in your life cycle? Have you just established your family—will it grow, or has it already grown, with children moving out, or soon to? The most basic issue is *how* you will use a freezer.

Along this line, you will want to consider whether both the husband and wife work (I feel freezers are indispensable for working wives or to anyone leading a busy, busy life); whether your family eats most of its meals together; whether one or both of you travels a lot; whether you are home or gone on weekends; whether you have a garden, hunt, or even enjoy cooking. Do you entertain frequently; do you give big or small parties; or do you just plain love to eat well?

A sizing guide that you can use is to allow 5 to 6 cubic feet for each family member. A family of four could use a 20- to 24-cubic-foot model. I feel, though, size is a very individual matter, based on living habits.

After narrowing down how a freezer can fit into your lifestyle, you must match the way you wish to you use it with the space available. Ideally, you should place the freezer as conveniently as possible, hopefully in the kitchen or nearby. If kitchen space just won't stretch to include a freezer, consider a pantry or utility room, a den, nearby bedroom, basement, or, as the least desirable, the garage.

A garage is the poorest choice because of the temperature extremes, especially during warm weather when the freezer will run more of the time. And, there is usually much more dust, meaning that frequent vacuuming of the condenser coils will be needed to maintain any degree of energy efficiency. (The compressor coils need to be vacuumed whenever they become covered with dust to allow the compressor to do its job of pulling heat out of the freezer. The more dusty they become, the longer the compressor works and the more energy is required.) In addition to its requiring more energy, the potential lifetime of the freezer could be shortened by locating it in the garage.

Once you've analyzed your needs for a freezer and matched them to the space available, you should know that freezers seem to just work and work. In my job I have often heard from consumers with thirty-year-old freezers. So take a very careful look at just how large a freezer you will efficiently use. Trends indicate that people are freezing more and more foods.

For example, a July 1974 University of Maryland study showed that grains, including rice, keep their nutritive values far longer when frozen, making for a whole new category of foods for the freezer.

As you and your family discover the improved flavor of frozen foods over canned or not-so-fresh-tasting leftover foods, you too will find yourselves wanting even more freezer space.

Freezers are sized by volume only, as the pounds per cubic foot measurement is too difficult to define and obviously dependent on whether you are freezing bones or spinach! (Just for your information, 35 pounds used to be allowed per cubic foot in the old sizing charts.) Most appliance and food experts agree that a minimum of 3 cubic feet and a maximum of 6 cubic feet per person should be planned when deciding what size of freezer to buy.

A final note about which size to buy: When I was just getting acquainted with each General Electric/Hotpoint model, Vice-President Chuck Griffin, then of Refrigeration Products, put the whole matter into a rather clever perspective. He said, "You know, each of us, if we are average, have only three opportunities in a lifetime [every fifteen years after a household is established] to buy a refrigerator—possibly less for a freezer—so the best consumer advice is to tell them to think as big as practical for them." He added, "I've yet to see a consumer complaining about a refrigerator or freezer that was too big—but I've seen thousands of complaint letters from disappointed consumers wishing they had gotten a bigger refrigerator or freezer." Once you know the approximate size of freezer you wish to buy, it's best to study the available types and sizes.

A freezer may be part of a refrigerator—on the top, bottom, or along one side. These days the proportion of freezer to refrigerator space is growing. Presently, true freezer sections range from just over 2 cubic feet to almost 9 cubic feet. Not all freezers on top of refrigerators are true 0° to 5°F freezers. Many are just cold storage compartments. Basically, you can tell the difference by noting whether the refrigerator has a separate outside freezer door. If you feel you will not need a large freezer space and that you need a new refrigerator too, consider getting a combination model to serve both your freezer and refrigerator needs—remember that operating one compressor is much more economical than running two, one for the refrigerator and another for the freezer.

If floor space is limited, large freezers generally can be obtained in top mounts. Top-mount floor dimensions range from 24 to 33 inches wide, 26¾ to 32 inches deep, and heights from 60 inches to 67¼ inches. Side-by-side floor-space dimensions range from 30 to 41 inches wide, 29 to 33⅛ inches deep, and heights from 64 to 67-7/16 inches. Some models require 4 inches above the top for air circulation.

Upright freezers come in sizes from 4½ to 31 cubic feet, in widths from 24 to 35 inches, depths from 25¾ to 32 inches, and heights from 36 to 72⅛. Some models require 4 inches on top and 2 inches on each side for

13

air circulation. They are equipped with various features such as three to six shelves, adjustable bins, door shelves for dispensing frozen food packages, temperature controls, inside lights, self-ejecting locks, defrost drain, and off-on signal lights. Some models have refrigerated shelves for fast freezing.

Many people prefer an upright because it takes less floor space, stored food is easier to locate, and it's easier to reach into. However, most uprights require more energy to operate. Due to differences among models, energy use can be checked most easily by looking at the energy fact tag on each model.

Chest freezers are sized from 5 to 28 cubic feet and measure from 22¼ to 72 inches wide, 22½ to 31 inches deep, and 34 to 36 inches high. Some features to look for are sliding or lift-out baskets, partitions for separating foods stored in the bottom, counter-balanced lid, temperature control, inside lights, outside drains for defrosting, and locks. Most people who buy chest freezers buy them because of their larger size and the fact they require less energy to operate. Statistically, 60 percent of the freezers sold are the chest type. Do check whether you are tall enough to reach to the bottom of the freezer, though, before buying. You'll be quite unhappy if you can't!

About one-third of all upright freezers sold are frostless. The frost is sublimated as it forms, keeping the interior clear of frost. Frostless freezers require more energy, although they have more continuously available space and the foods are much easier to recognize. For me, the convenience of not having to defrost has always been worth the higher costs, both in initial investment and in operating. However, generally, only uprights are frostless. They are available in widths from 28 to 35 inches and capacities from 13 to 30 cubic feet.

Manual defrost freezers should be defrosted every six months or as often as the inside frost layer builds to more than one-fourth inch. To assist defrosting a built-in drain tube is a big help and a feature to look for when buying a manual defrost freezer.

Other features I particularly like are the new thin wall insulation which reduces electricity costs and increases inside space, interior lights to help you see the foods, indicator lights to tell when the freezer is running, and magnetic gaskets for tighter door seals. For your own protection, look for a UL (Underwriters Laboratories) approval and a heavy-duty electrical cord with a three-prong grounding plug.

After carefully examining your personal preferences, be sure that the freezer of your choice will fit where you want it, or at worst, where it has to go. Like a pair of shoes or a dress, a freezer that doesn't fit is worse than none at all. Sometimes you can cleverly rearrange a closet or a back porch, if need be, to accommodate the freezer of your dreams. I'm a firm believer in the theory that where there's a will there's a way!

Know exactly the dimensions of the floor space—the height, width, and depth—before setting out to shop. If you want an upright, check to see which side the door opening should be on. A problem that arises especially in older homes is that some of the bigger freezers simply don't fit through the halls or doors without major dismantling of either the house or the freezer or both. Check any tight-looking corners or doorways. Measure them so that you know what the limitations are.

You should have a 110-volt electrical circuit available just for the freezer's use. With such a major investment in food, you should not risk an overloaded circuit. In almost any home, a 110-volt electric circuit can be added easily. Contact an electrician if you need the work done. You will, of course, want to factor this cost into your budget.

Before you shop, you may wish to consult consumer magazines and contact freezer dealers or manufacturers for their specification sheets and study them to determine which brands and models best suit your needs. This is always an excellent idea for gaining insight on the various features and dimensions available so that you won't be taken by a glib salesman and stuck with a freezer not well suited for *you*.

When studying the specification sheets or when shopping, be sure you look into the manufacturer's warranty. You should look for such assurances as:

- Does it cover repairs and for how long?
- If repairs are required, what kind of service will be available and on what terms—do they have a policy of quick service for freezers and will they make appointments for service, maybe even after hours?
- Is the warranty on the appliance or the owner? By that I mean, should you for any reason have to part with your beloved freezer within the warranty period, would the warranty be transferred with the appliance or does it stop with the first owner?
- Does the warranty cover food loss should there be a failure due to inoperation of the appliance?

Now that you're ready to buy, you should think through which dealer you wish to patronize. First evaluate his reputation. Is he a franchised dealer of a well-known brand? How long has he been in the appliance business? What sort of assistance will he provide? Does he have shopper's checklists? Does he provide specification sheets or aids for choosing? Or is he a buy-it-and-beat-it operator? Is he connected with a factory service operation staffed with trained appliance repairmen? Does the dealer enjoy a dependable reputation for consumer satisfaction? These are all very important considerations for a **happy, trouble-free appliance** purchase.

COSTS

The initial purchase price of a freezer is only the beginning of the costs. Electricity to keep it frigid must be considered along with the cost of packaging materials and the cost of food to be placed in the freezer. Electrical costs are becoming easier to determine. Manufacturers quote the average monthly cost of operation in a fact label attached to each freezer. Do look at your electric bill or check with your local utility to determine your average kilowatt-hour cost; multiply it by the average consumption listed on the freezer fact tag to estimate the cost of energy.

The location of the freezer, the number of door openings, and the food load affect the cost of operation. A constant temperature such as within a home or basement will keep the energy demand fairly consistent. The fewer the door openings and the fuller the freezer (air does not retain the cold as well as solid material), the lower the cost of operation.

The average monthly cost to operate the average freezer in use in a 1975 study was developed by Cornell University. The research revealed that a 15-cubic-foot manual defrost freezer with an average wattage of 341 watts uses 1165 KWH (kilowatt-hours) per year. The same size frostless model uses an average of 440 watts and approximately 1761 KWH per year. Figuring the electricity cost at four cents a KWH, the average monthly cost would be $3.86 for the manual defrost model and $5.87 for the frostless model.

The Cornell study stated that 0.1 kilowatt-hour is required to freeze a pound of food and lower its temperature to 0°F. The cost of packaging was determined to be four to six cents per pound. Freezer ownership averages were based on USDA information citing the average life to be twenty years and the cost of repairs to be 2 percent of the purchase price. The researchers used a total approach to computing the cost of owning the freezer based on an alternative investment in a 6 percent savings account.

The Cornell study lends insight to the need for planning and rotating the foods in the freezer. (See chart, next page.)

The annual cost of freezing each pound of food can be greatly reduced when you turn over each cubic foot by constantly using and replacing foods. The rate of at least three turnovers a year is most desirable.

On average, the cost of energy to operate a freezer is about halved when you turn over each cubic foot three times a year. Also, the relative cost of energy becomes less when you operate a larger freezer. In general, for each additional 6 cubic feet of capacity, the annual energy cost to freeze each pound is reduced by 10 percent or more. This means that the cost of freezing each cubic foot of a 12-cubic-foot freezer averages, say, 10.8 cents, while the cost of chilling each cubic foot of an 18-cubic-foot freezer would run about 10 percent less, or 8.8 cents per year (based on a 4 cent KWH rate at one turnover a year).

Example:

The cost to operate a 15-cubic-foot conventional chest-style freezer of 525-pound capacity, purchased new for $300.00, and anticipating a single turnover per year is as follows:

	Cost per pound
Cost of electrical energy:	
0.1 KWH per pound to freeze food	
2.3 KWH per pound to maintain 0°F	
2.4 KWH	7.2¢
Cost of Packaging	5.0¢
Cost of Repairs (figuring 2% of the purchase price)	
($300.00) 2%	
525 pounds	1.1¢
Depreciation (figuring an average life span of 20 years)	
($300.00)/20 years	
525 pounds	2.9¢
Interest from Alternate Investment	
Time deposit at 6%	
($300.00)/6%	
525 pounds	3.4¢
TOTAL COST PER POUND	19.6¢

Courtesy of Cornell University. From "Actual Costs of Home Food Preservation," June 1975.

Packaging costs can be cut by reusing materials and keeping economy in mind when purchasing them. However, don't take a penny-wise, pound-foolish approach and buy poor-quality materials which will not maintain an air- and moisture-proof seal.

Food costs are usually less when you own a freezer, considering bulk bargain buying versus single purchases. The only exception is buying produce to freeze—here the relative costs of buying fresh produce and freezing your own should be considered in light of the value of your time. All in all, the price of convenience and better eating are in the balance against the costs. The decision is very personal. I for one have felt very well paid for the frozen assets I've created.

CARE

Now that you are (or are about to become) the proud owner of a freezer, you will want to take the best care of it to be sure it gives you many, many years of frozen assets. Actually, its care is very simple. Keep the exterior attractive by periodic cleaning with a damp cloth, occasional sudsing and waxing with a good appliance wax. Ammonia is a big cleaning help for stubborn marks and stains.

Keep the interior organized with periodic rearranging so that the older foods are up front for first use. If you have a manual defrost model, you will want to defrost it whenever the frost accumulates to one-quarter inch or every six months. Keeping the frost at a very low level assures that the foods will keep at their best and gives you more storage space—plus the foods will be easier to find. Thick frost build-ups add to the cost of operation.

To defrost, first turn the freezer off. Then remove the packages to large cardboard cartons, using a different one for each shelf or type of food for easiest reloading. Keep foods frozen by lining the sides of each box with several layers of newspaper and topping the box with a thick layer of newspaper.

Remove the feathery frost with a wood or plastic scraper, then place a large pan or bowl of hot steamy water on each shelf or in each section and close the door. Check every few minutes to remove more frost and replace the cooled water with more hot.

When the frost is all removed, sponge out the interior with a solution of one teaspoon baking soda to each quart of water. Then sponge with clear water and towel dry with an absorbent cloth or towel.

Turn the freezer on to the coldest setting, close the door, and allow it to become chilled (about 15 to 30 minutes) before returning the food. Place the packages of food back in good order, keeping the like items together, with the older foods closest to the front center of each shelf. If packages are frosty, scrape each food package to remove any frost or moisture before placing in the freezer. An organizational hint I like to follow is to place all fruits in one area, all vegetables together, all baked goods in one place, all prepared main dishes and sauces in another, and all meats together. Place small packets and cartons in a large rigid container to keep them all together and easier to find. The amount of time spent organizing in this manner is more than repaid with the degree of convenience you will net. Packed this way, the freezer will not frost up as rapidly nor will it require as much energy, because you will be able to find things much more rapidly. Long door openings build frost.

Though you won't have to defrost a frostless, you should clean it out about once a year or whenever there is visible soil. To keep a frostless freezer clean, remove the food in the same way in separate boxes wrapped with newspapers. Turn off the freezer, and keep the door open. When the side walls and shelves warm slightly, clean with soda water, using one teaspoon baking soda to each quart of warm water. Rinse with clear water, and towel dry. Replace the foods when chilled as above.

A bonus that comes from defrosting or cleaning out your freezer is that you often find little goodies that accidentally got covered or hidden away. Sometimes it can be like finding a great treasure—once I found a long-lost package of yummy Maine blueberries; another time, some great venison steaks.

It is sensible to keep an eye on your freezer daily to make sure it's operating properly. If it fails for any reason, don't panic! Freezers rarely fail—but sometimes the door is accidentally left ajar, or the plug inadvertently loosened (to prevent this, have the plug installed about three feet above the floor or tape the plug in for extra assurance, especially if the plug is at floor height). The freezer could break down mechanically or there could be a power failure. A daily check can prevent a bad experience.

When you are gone for a period of time, in addition to having someone check that all is well at home—with the plants and with Tabby—ask them to be sure the freezer and the refrigerator are operating properly—the few seconds it takes is so worthwhile.

I've heard many sad freezer experiences from friends and consumers who have called me for advice. I'd like to steer you away from the same experiences. In fact, why not write the specific "what to do's" on a card and attach it on or near your freezer. The "what to do's" will follow, but first I'd like to share a couple of very memorable accidents.

Once my neighbors were gone on an extended vacation. Upon returning home, they found to their utter shock that their prized frozen goodies, which included lots of elk and expensive meats, had all spoiled to the point of putrefaction and their whole freezer was really a stinking mess. They hoped they could somehow get the terrible odor under control. That's why they called me. Unfortunately, the strong smell of spoilage had so thoroughly saturated the entire freezer liner and somehow seeped into the insulation that there was no remedy. This happened in the middle of summer in New Mexico. With the freezer latched shut, the smell had just increased with no relief. A regular check by a friend or neighbor could have prevented this.

Another time, some friends had gone on an extended weekend to the country. Their child, who had brought in some foods from the freezer while they were packing to go, somehow had not closed the door. Upon their return, they found the door open and much of the food warm and soggy. They called me to see what could be salvaged. She was rapidly pitching out everything and he thought it was unnecessary. I explained that if foods are still firm and have ice crystals, they are OK to refreeze but should be used as soon as possible, depending on what they are. Seafood, poultry, and pork spoil quickest, in that order. They all spoil uniformly throughout. Beef, however, spoils from the outside in and is slower to spoil. Game should really be treated as seafood because the storage conditions are usually a bit "iffy" from the time it is killed until it is frozen.

Your judgment will have to guide you in knowing how long meats have been thawed. If they are warm, it is risky to do anything but discard them. If they're still cool, you can cook the meats and then freeze, using them as soon afterward as possible. If icy, refreeze for use as soon as possible. Fruits, vegetables, and cooked main dishes can be refrozen if ice crystals still remain. If there are no ice crystals, cook and freeze, providing they haven't been thawed too long. In the case of baked main dishes, ones with cream sauce are an exception and should be discarded if they are not icy. Baked goods such as breads, cookies, and cakes are usually safe to refreeze unless they are made with some particularly fast-spoiling ingredient, such as custard filling. Fruit pies, if totally thawed, should be reheated until the filling is hot and used as soon as possible.

WHAT TO DO IF YOUR FREEZER FAILS

A full freezer will stay frozen for at least 48 hours. Some say a freezer should keep foods frozen up to 72 hours without power. Less full freezers warm faster, depending on circumstances such as location, weather, etc.

If for whatever the reason you cannot get the freezer repaired quickly—or the power cannot be restored immediately due to outages from a natural disaster—rather than risk losing a freezer-load of food, I recommend the following steps to save the food. After 24 to 48 hours, either move the food to a commercial locker or get a block of dry ice. About 50 pounds of dry ice will keep the average freezer full of food frozen for another 36 hours. To place the dry ice in the freezer, have it cut into thick slices (two to three inches thick) and place it on heavy cardboard or on a piece of wood. Never place dry ice directly on top of food. Be sure to handle dry ice with tongs or mitts.

Try to keep from opening the door if the freezer is not operating. Each second the door is open the chill will be leaving the freezer to be replaced by warmer air.

2
About Freezing

Have you ever thought much about just what freezing does to preserve food? Actually freezing just preserves food as it is—freezing does not kill any bacteria—it simply halts its multiplication. Frozen food that is contaminated will continue its rate of spoilage upon thawing. This is one of the reasons that highly perishable food such as seafood is best cooked after partial refrigerator thawing. More about the best thawing and cooking methods in the following chapters.

What to freeze is a personal question. You should use your valuable freezer space to preserve your very favorite foods—what else? You will want to give the priority of what to freeze some thought so that you will have a balance of varied foods on call. Don't overdo it with pastries, commercially frozen foods, or a whole cow. I'm sure you'll regret it. I have had so many dismayed consumers call or write after finding to their utter horror that the half of beef they bought filled their freezer, leaving little or no space for main dishes, fruit, vegetables, and so on.

For maximum pleasure without making filling the freezer hard work, reorient your thinking to buying bargain-priced family favorites when you see them. But restraint is needed. Buy only what you will use within the recommended storage period for each food (see the storage charts in the back of this book). When you're cooking, make double or triple recipes so that you can have one or two bonus meals. It really requires very little extra time and energy.

Buy in season, but don't be tempted to stock up on last-of-the-season bargain buys. There are some exceptions—extra-ripe fruits such as strawberries, peaches, or other favorite jam-making fruits can be bought, sugared, treated with ascorbic acid, and packaged in jam-making quantities for luscious fresh jam out of season. In general, most vegetables not at their peak of freshness will not be worth buying. The key point is to always buy the best quality available, remembering that freezing (with the exception of stale bread, which does moisturize) will not improve the quality of the food. Some argue that meats tenderize—the little that they do should not be factored in when buying.

21

FOODS THAT SUFFER WHEN FROZEN

There is considerable disagreement over whether some foods can be frozen or not. I am a very liberal freezer of most foods as I believe unfreezables such as lettuce and green onions are better frozen than thrown out. They can still be used for soups, vegetable medleys, and the like. In fact, a favorite use for frozen lettuce and green onions is French peas, combining the lettuce and onions with peas, mushrooms, tarragon, and sweet butter over a hot heat in a sauté pan to make a marvelous vegetable side dish.

In general, unfreezables are those foods that do not maintain their original consistency, but almost always are salvable for use in cooking.

Following is a list of foods that change consistency when frozen.

- Most salad greens lose their crispness when frozen.
- Radishes, tomatoes (except for stewed tomatoes and juice), and green onions become soft.
- Cured meats, frankfurters, bologna, and luncheon meat freeze poorly. (Salt speeds the rancidity of frozen meat.)
- Canned hams can become watery and change texture.
- Cooked egg white becomes tough and rubbery.
- Gelatin weeps when thawed, unless combined with a cream product such as cheese.
- Mayonnaise and salad dressings separate.
- Fried foods lose crispness, except French fries and onion rings (these can be crisped in hot oven).
- Milk sauces may curdle.
- Custard and cream pie fillings become watery and lumpy.
- Potatoes may darken, and texture changes occur when they are included in frozen soups and stews.
- Meringue toughens.

SEASONING TIPS

Seasonings can change in character. Many feel that the changes are so insignificant they can't notice them—but here are the more commonly agreed upon spice and flavor changes.

- Pepper, cloves, bay leaves, and synthetic vanilla tend to get strong and bitter.
- Fresh onion intensifies tremendously when frozen—use dried onion instead.

- Celery seasonings become strong.
- Curry may develop a musty off-flavor.
- Salt loses flavor and has the tendency to increase rancidity of any item containing fat.

A good rule of thumb is to underseason, then add seasoning to taste when heating for serving.

FOOD VALUE OF FROZEN FOODS

Freezing does not destroy nutrients. During the blanching or processing of foods for freezing, there can be some losses. Refreezing greatly destroys food quality and can destroy some of the nutrients if foods have been completely thawed. (See page 19 for more specific guidelines.)

NUTRIENT LOSS DURING FREEZING

Protein: Generally not affected. Some fish or shellfish may become less digestible if over-stored.

Fats: Those which have become rancid on meat, fish, or poultry as a result of poor packaging, over-storage, or too high a temperature, may lose the nutritive value of vitamin A.

Carbohydrates: No change with the exception of the sugar (sucrose) being reduced to simple sugars (glucose and fructose) during long storage . . . of no importance.

Minerals: Might be lost in solution during blanching and cooking of vegetables and by "drip" loss in thawing of meats, fish, and poultry. The loss by blanching and cooling is usually no greater than when cooking fresh vegetables.

Vitamin A: Loss through rancidity of fat and in vegetables which were not blanched.

B vitamins (such as thiamine and riboflavin): Lost by over-storage and through solution in blanching and cooling. However, a greater loss is suffered if the vegetable is not blanched. Some thiamine also is lost by the heat of cooking. Both thiamine and riboflavin will be lost through "drip" in thawing of meat, fish, and poultry.

23

Vitamin C (ascorbic acid)	Easily destroyed through solution as well as oxidation. Vegetables lose some of their vitamin C through blanching, but without this process, the loss would be much greater. The amount of vitamin C is greatest in fruits and vegetables at their peak of maturity— "just ripe stage." The time that elapses between harvesting and freezing is particularly important for retaining this vitamin in its largest amounts. Try to keep the time between harvest and freezing to an hour or two at most.

Courtesy, Cooperative Extension Service, North Dakota State University.

BIG OR SMALL PACKAGES

When freezing big or small packages—double and triple recipes of favorite casseroles, sauces, and the like—always package in family-sized quantities for easy use. The beauty of a freezer is that you need never have leftovers, so don't create them by freezing huge masses of each food in large packages. Though today's microwave ovens allow for rapid defrosting, why bother if part of the food must be refrozen? Without a microwave, you can really lose your cool with an ice pick and damage good containers by trying to chisel out small quantities from a too large frozen mass.

It's smart to package some single servings too, for when most of the family isn't home for a meal—it makes eating alone much simpler and more pleasurable too. Even if you are serving several people, two or more smaller quantities are always much faster to thaw than one large one. (For more information, see Chapter 14.) And assist those interested in weight loss by packaging some diet portions (see Chapter 15).

BUYING FOR YOUR FREEZER

When buying frozen foods—especially in quantity—take along a portable ice chest or some provision to keep the foods well frozen on the way home. Try to make frozen foods the last items on your shopping list.

When buying commercially frozen foods, be careful to select fresh, good-quality items. Examine the freezer storage cabinet in the store. Don't buy if the freezer cabinets are encrusted heavily with frost. Resist the temptation to buy foods that are frosty on the outside as this indicates not-so-fresh food. Foods should not be stacked so high that they are not solidly frozen. If any package is soft, you can be sure the quality of the food will be less than the best.

Frozen fruits and vegetables should rattle if individually frozen. If in a clear wrap, note the color, since more brightly colored foods have fresher flavor. Inspect the packaging too, as foods stored in damaged packages will have lost quality.

FOOD PLANS

Think more than twice before investing in a frozen food plan. My favorite advice is to give freezing your own foods a try first, and I'll bet you won't even be tempted to purchase a food plan once you discover the bliss of doing your own things. However, if you find that you don't have the time or inclination to prepare your own goodies, then really investigate the food plan before buying. Be certain that you will actually get food you or your family likes—that you won't be getting gobs and gobs of French fried potatoes which no one will eat. Be sure the quality will be excellent and that the delivery arrangement, whether at once or in installments, will suit your needs and available freezer space. More than one very unhappy consumer has spun a sad yarn to me about freezer plans that delivered less than expected. Do be sure you check the reputation and business ethics of the food plan purveyor. Your local Better Business Bureau would be a good place to check before buying.

HOW TO FREEZE

To preserve the peak of flavor and maximize your dollar and time investment, be sure to freeze each food properly, following the guidelines for that particular food. In general the guidelines are very easy—package it properly and be sure to freeze it quickly. Cool hot foods rapidly in ice water or the refrigerator. Quick freezing assures the best preserved flavor because small, rather than large ice crystals will form in the freezing process.

To quick-freeze in a chest freezer, place unfrozen foods close to the outside walls in a single layer if possible. In an upright freezer, place unfrozen foods on a shelf closest to the outside walls in a single layer. If your freezer has a quick-freeze shelf, place the unfrozen foods on it against the freezer walls. In all cases, allow for cold air to circulate around the packages. Leave for 24 hours before arranging. The best plan is to place the newest foods to the sides and back of the freezer so that the older ones will be used first.

In each 24-hour period, *never freeze more than 3 pounds of unfrozen food per cubic foot of freezer capacity.* For example, if you have a 16-

cubic-foot freezer, you should never freeze more than 48 pounds of un-frozen food every 24 hours.

The reason is that if foods are frozen slowly, the quality reduces and bacteria are allowed to multiply. Don't be like the enthusiastic new freezer owner who could not wait to stock his freezer with a side of beef. Wanting to get the best possible buy, he found a willing farmer who sold him a nice freshly butchered carcass. Not knowing any better, he packaged the meat and put it all in the freezer at once, jamming the entire space with warm meat. I can't honestly recall whether he got to use any of the meat or not—but some of it lost most or all of its freshness. Circulating cold air must be maintained to keep the foods solidly frozen. If you buy a large quantity of meat you can arrange to have a commercial locker plant or butcher shop quick-freeze the meat before you bring it home. Commercial freezers are just much bigger and have the capacity for air to circulate and quick-freeze large quantities.

Create your own freezer policy, with the guideline that you should aim at keeping the freezer at least two-thirds full most of the time. Perhaps less full right before the fruit and vegetable season, a special party, the holidays, etc. If you have a reserve of about one-third of the capacity, you will have space for special buys, party goodies, an extra good catch.

PLANNING AND STORAGE

Determine your freezer priorities and then divide your freezer into flexible sections or shelves for meats, vegetables and fruits, main dishes and sauces, and pastries. You may wish to have, say, half of the space reserved for meat, splitting the balance according to your own food preferences. Use baskets, dividers, or boxes for little items to keep your freezer well organized so that you can easily find the foods you are looking for. This will save both electrical energy and your own patience. With an organized storage system, you will find it easier to keep a balanced assortment of food on hand as you can see what your inventory is. It will remind you of what foods need to be used up too.

Always organize the oldest foods at the front or on top so that you will use them first. Some find that keeping a log or inventory helps to keep a tab on just what they have without wasting time and energy. It's a good idea, but my experience has been that I never really keep it up. With organized storage of like foods together, you can fare just about as well. A log, however, can save the frustration of a prolonged search for a package of special steaks that you've forgotten you used.

To keep foods best, 0°F is the recommended temperature. However, research has shown that between −6°F and +5°F, the rate of deterioration is approximately the same as if the food were held at a constant temperature of 0°F (according to Dr. D. K. Tressler, Wallace Van Arsdal, and Dr. Michael J. Copley in *Freezing Preservation of Foods*).

All in all, remember, for maximizing your investment in freezing, *use* your frozen assets; don't hoard them. To maximize the efficiency of your freezer space, you should turn the food over three times a year in order to net a reasonable return on your investments—the freezer, operating energy, and your time. Keep the freezer at least two-thirds full. Freeze foods as soon as possible after preparing them. Never cool for more than two hours before freezing.

When trying to assign priorities to foods for the freezer, think of the potential savings per cubic foot. For instance, a cubic foot of commercial bread bought at a bargain price will not net nearly the savings of a cubic foot of steak bought at a good price.

3
How To Wrap It Up

How you package your foods for the freezer makes the difference between great frozen foods and barely palatable ones. Freezer wraps must be airtight, vapor-proof, and moisture-proof to keep foods at their peak and prevent freezer burn. Freezer-burned foods are dried out, leathery, and unflavorful, if even edible. Also, tastes and odors can develop in poorly packaged foods, as they absorb odors from other foods.

Another factor about wraps is that the packaging you select will add to the cost of freezing. The average cost, according to the Cornell study, is five cents a package. You can beat that! You don't want to spend an arm and a leg on packaging materials, however, you have to use packaging of sufficient quality to preserve the food at its best. Try to select reusable or salvaged containers whenever possible. Buy materials at the best prices in bulk and, if possible, on sale. Always think of yourself too. Almost always one type of packaging will offer more convenience than another. I'm a great bagger, because bags are faster than packaging with paper, foil, or other flat wraps, but they're often hard to stack. Rigid plastic containers are another favorite because they are quick, easy, and reusable.

When packaging, always keep in mind the way the foods will stack up. Round and odd shapes make organizing a freezer like trying to stack round rocks. Sometimes in haste or for economy I've packaged vegetables, such as green chiles, in double refrigerator-type plastic bags and lived to regret the many times I had to restack them. Taking the extra time to place the bags in boxes such as used margarine containers or the bottoms of half-gallon milk cartons or other reusable boxes would have saved so much time later.

On the other hand, you can really go overboard spending lots of time and money on very neat boxes. A trick for organizing those lumpy, odd-shaped packages is to place them in a carton or open box within the freezer, placing like foods together. An important tip also is to think about storage when you select the packaging.

Recycle packaging as much as possible, rinsing it off and saving it in a box or deep drawer near the freezer for later use. Whenever you empty a potentially usable carton such as a margarine or milk carton, clean it out and save it. Organize the wraps, containers, tape, closures, and marking

28

pencil in one place as close to either the sink or the freezer as possible and you will save lots and lots of time.

WRAPS

Select the wrap best suited to airtight packaging of the food you are freezing. For most meats, baked goods, bulky vegetables such as corn on the cob, or casseroles, a flat wrapping material or a freezer-weight bag will work equally well. If you use the lightweight plastic bags, be sure to use them double for best protection of the food.

Type	Remarks
Laminated polyethylene paper	Can be written on for labeling Can be reused when cleaned with damp cloth.
Laminated or double waxed paper	Can be written on for labeling.
Heavy-strength or double cello or plio wrap	Molds easily, can be seen through, still needs labeling.
Heavy-duty aluminum foil or double thicknesses	Molds easily around odd shapes; sharp points such as bones should be padded with crumpled waxed paper; reusable if rinsed.
Freezer-weight plastic wrap or bags (if not freezer-weight, use double)	See-through; reusable. Bags are very timesaving.

There are two basic wrapping techniques—butcher's or druggist's. They are equally good and the choice is yours. I prefer the butcher's wrap for odd shapes such as chops or steaks. The druggist's wrap is my favorite for thin, flat foods such as pies. Always force out extra air by smoothing wrap firmly over the food. Seal all seams with freezer tape.

CONTAINERS

Containers serve two purposes—to form composite packages and make storage more compact, or to serve as the packaging. Select the type of container best suited to both the food and the way you will use it. For example, liquid foods are best packaged in a box, jar, or tin. Drier foods such as sliced meats, baked goods, and prepared foods are best placed in a foil tray, shallow carton, or tub.

Type	Remarks
Plastic cartons	Stack easily; reusable; available in many shapes and capacities.
Waxed tubs	Usually round, require more space, reusable.
Waxed boxes with plastic bags or liners	Commercially made; stack flat; reusable; form and protect the plastic bag.
Glass jars	Straight-sided ones best; allow double amount of head space (1½″ for pints, 2″ for quarts); handle with care; thaw foods before removing; require more freezer space.
Tin boxes or cans	Good for cookies or delicate foods easily mashed or crumbled; separate layers with waxed or other paper; can be used for stews, sauces, and main dishes; wash thoroughly —preferably in dishwasher to remove original odors such as coffee or other strong food flavor; seal with freezer tape.
Aluminum foil containers	Convenient; can be used for heating; stack well; can be salvaged from commercial products. Handle with care; they have a tendency to crumple when washing.
Improvised—"saved" boxes from milk, margarine, etc.	Economical; use with plastic bag insert. Milk cartons, well rinsed, can be used as is for soups and sauces.
Plastic-treated paper plates, cups, and bowls	Convenient, especially for microwave heating and serving. Place second plate over top and seal with freezer tape; best for short-term storage—do *not* leave in freezer over a month or two for best keeping quality. (If keeping longer, over-wrap with plastic wrap or bag.)

DRUGGIST'S WRAP

is one of the most useful and is ideally suited to square or rectangular-shaped packages and thin flat foods.

Place food in center of an oblong piece of heavy duty wrap large enough to go around the food and allow for folding at top and sides. Pad protruding bones with small crumpled pieces of foil.

Bring two sides up and over the food item, match the long ends and fold over about 1/2 inch. Make a crease the entire length.

Make one more tight fold to bring wrapping down to level of food surface. Press out air towards end.

Then, molding foil to contours of food item, fold short ends up and over again, continuing to press out air before sealing ends.

Press with the palms of your hands towards the ends to be sure the air is pushed out. This is important because air space can draw moisture from food, resulting in "freezer burn," those frosty white spots that indicate loss of flavor, texture and color.

BUTCHER'S WRAP

is great for those odd shapes that crop up and especially for semi-moist foods.

Place odd-shaped food on a square of heavy duty wrap large enough to permit adequate wrapping.

Bring four corners up together in a pyramid shape.

Squeeze and mold foil close to food.

Seal by folding over ends and pressing to package.

For round casseroles, line with foil having enough collar to cover filled dish adequately. Close and seal by bringing foil collar up in pyramid shape. Mold to surface of food. When frozen, the block of food is removed from dish, sealed as in Butcher's wrap and returned to freezer.

CASSEROLE WRAP

is most practical for square or rectangular casseroles and, combined with the Butcher's finish, for round and odd-shaped containers.

Tear off enough heavy duty wrap to line the casserole and leave a 1-1/2 inch collar all around top edges. Place casserole upside-down and mold foil over outside.

With casserole now turned upright, "drop" shaped foil into casserole and fit it to sides, letting collar extend over sides.

After food has been cooked and cooled, cover with a piece of foil the size of casserole and collar.

To seal all around, fold edges up and over, pressing lightly. Place in freezer until package is rigid enough to be lifted out of casserole dish. Return foil package to freezer. To serve, place foil package in the original casserole and reheat.

Isn't it nice that there is no scrubbing the casserole dish!

Credit: Reynolds Metals Company

LABELS

Label with as complete information as possible, using a wax marking pencil or crayon. Felt-tip pens are poor as the ink runs when wet. Mark the information on a piece of freezer tape or directly on the packaging if a paper wrap is used. If wrap is to be reused, mark a piece of freezer tape and place it on the package. It's easier than trying to mark out or remove old lettering.

LABEL "MUSTS"

Contents
Date
Type of preparation
Servings
Special notes (such as add cooked potatoes, brandy, sour cream, or any nonfreezable ingredient)

The few extra moments of labeling makes up for the frustration of thawing the wrong food or wrong quantity, or not knowing a key ingredient that you don't have on hand needs to be added.

PACKAGING: TIPS AND TECHNIQUES

Seal all packaging seams, loosely fitting lids, and any potential air leaks with freezer tape—available at most grocery, variety, and hardware stores.

Use a gooseneck twist to seal the top of any bag. To do this, exclude the air by pressing the bag against its contents from the bottom up. Twist the top firmly together for about one inch, double over and secure with a wire twist or freezer-quality rubber band. (Usually the twist or band closures are packaged and sold with the bags. They're reusable.)

Always allow head space at the top of any container. For pints, allow one-half inch; for quarts, one inch. For glass jars, add one more inch to each. When packaging a food such as a fruit that will darken if exposed to air, keep the tops of the pieces submerged in the acid-treated syrup by adding a piece of crumpled waxed paper or cello wrap before sealing.

For soups and rich sauces, freeze them first in an ice cube tray, then remove the cubes and store in a rigid carton or plastic bag. Individually freeze meatballs, shrimp, whole berries, or dollops of whipped cream. When firm, place in bags or rigid containers. For foods such as the whipped cream, place paper between dollops and store in rigid containers to keep them from being mashed or stuck together.

A final note—foods do not spoil in the freezer, but they can lose all flavor and texture because of poor packaging; or if freezer is not set at 0° to 5°F; or, if foods are kept too long. It's easy to avoid these poor practices and enjoy fine quality frozen foods.

4
Meat and Poultry

BEEF

Beef is the mainstay for most of us. We Americans rely more heavily on beef as our staple meat than any other. And meat in total takes one-third of our food dollars. Generally most people think of savings on bulk beef buying as the primary reason for buying a freezer. Personally, I list the main reason for owning a freezer as convenience. I relish having a storehouse of my favorite foods ready for eating.

Meat is the most valuable frozen asset—and probably one of the chief reasons you decided to buy your freezer. To maximize your food dollars and to add the most to your own personal convenience, a little thought and study really pay off in big dividends.

First, decide the amount of freezer space you wish to devote to beef. If you want to freeze other foods, you will want to know very early just how much of your freezer you'd like filled with beef.

Once you have decided the amount of freezer space you want to devote to beef, you will know how much you should buy. A general guide that may help is that each cubic foot of freezer space holds approximately 35 pounds. The amount of fat or bone will increase or decrease the storage volume required. Remember, all meats may be frozen successfully. Usually the higher the fat content, the more cut up the meat is, the more bone or seasoning there is, the shorter the storage life of frozen meats of any kind.

The first consideration is your family's taste and the availability of beef at a good price. If your family has a very distinct liking for steaks, roasts, and ground beef, you will want to direct your beef buying to these.

The more flexible your family's beef taste is, the more money you will be able to save, because you will be able to take advantage of the real bargains in meats as they occur. Usually only two meats are ever on special— really reduced for a good buy—on any given day in any one supermarket.

Explore the kind of special buying opportunities you can take advantage of—is there an excellent butcher shop you are familiar with, do you have access to beef on the hoof, or do you wish to just shop the specials for beef as you see them?

A half of beef will more than fill the average 16- to 20-cubic-foot freezer, depending of course on the weight of the half and packaging style. Some butchers are much more conscientious than others about how they package, trimming off excess fat and giving you the large bones separately for making stock. To help you decide whether to buy a half, a front quarter, or a hindquarter, perhaps some of the following guidelines will help: on average, a side of beef contains 25% steak, 25% roast, 25% hamburger and stewing meat, and 25% waste (fat and bone). A forequarter will dress out as about 76% usable cuts and a hindquarter about 70%. The forequarter contains a higher percentage of less tender cuts. (Note chart, page 37.)

When you are shopping for a beef quarter or half, there are a number of critical questions to ask the butcher. I once learned the hard way! I blithely ordered a half of beef without asking many questions other than making certain the quality was excellent. I knew the butcher was good and dependable for regular buying. Well, I ended up with a gross abundance—more than I ever thought a half of beef could yield—poorly packaged and barely labeled. The embarrassing part was that I was reared on a farm where we butchered our own beef and I had a degree in home economics. I should have known better! I thought, with my new 18.5-cubic-foot frostless freezer, that a half was the only way to go. For me it wasn't. First, all the beef would not fit. Then, even with my regular entertaining, I couldn't use it all up before the best-quality storage time had elapsed.

Getting the Best Butcher

To get the best buy for you, consider the following points carefully:

- How much beef can your family eat within the recommended storage periods for the cuts you wish to buy? (Study the recommended storage time chart for beef at the back of this book.)
- Shop carefully for a reputable butcher who makes a business of selling beef for freezing.
- Ask how long the beef is aged—usually five to seven days' aging at 34° F is best for beef.
- Will he flash-freeze the beef? Freezing in commercial freezers capable of flash-freezing at about −30° F makes the best quality beef for eating. The quicker the meat is frozen at very low temperatures, the finer the ice crystals and the juicier the meats will be when served. Their natural texture, color, flavor, and nutritive value are all maintained.
- Will he individually package the cuts of beef in the package sizes you prefer? Will he place double layers of freezer paper between steaks and chops? Will he label with precise information, listing the cut, amount, and date? (You may wish to weigh the roasts and label as you store them—or maybe he will.)

- Does he use good-quality freezer paper?
- Will he package the ground beef in a convenient way? Suggest forming the ground beef in patties, separated with double freezer paper. Or as an alternative, ask if he won't pat the ground beef flat and score at quarter pound points. You may wish to form the patties of at least part of it yourself before it is frozen. You can either package with a layer of double freezer paper between layers of patties, or freeze patties on a cookie sheet and place in bags or containers.
- Inquire about his butchering practices. Request that he trim the meat to your liking—you can ask for the suet trimmings if you like, for use in plum puddings or feeding the birds. Also, ask that he pack every cut as compactly as possible, trimming out the large bones. Large bones are great for simmering to make stock, which is a super time and space saver.
- If you are unable to accommodate the entire half or quarter, will he freeze and store the balance in a sealed carton? If so, for how long and will it be free or will he charge?
- You may wish to purchase a wholesale cut and cut it to your own liking. (Remember, you should freeze only 3 pounds per cubic foot of capacity every 24 hours.)
- Or, you may wish to butcher a large portion such as a quarter or a half. If so, either have a commercial butcher do the carving and packaging, using the above checklist for selecting a good butcher—or do the cutting and packaging and arrange for quick- or preferably flash-freezing with the butcher.

Buying Beef

Purchase the grade best for you and your family, remembering that even though freezing may tenderize slightly, the beef you will get out of your freezer will be of no better quality than that which you bought.

According to the National Live Stock and Meat Board, "Meat grading is a consumer service provided by the government but paid for by meat packers. Purpose of grading is to make sure customers get the quality meat they expect and pay for. That's why when you buy graded beef, veal or lamb, you can expect consistent eating qualities, depending on whether you buy U.S. PRIME, CHOICE, GOOD, STANDARD, etc. or comparable packer grades."

U.S. Prime is the "highest" grade. It is produced in limited quantities. Its principal market is the so-called tablecloth restaurant trade or the "carriage trade" in meat shops and gourmet stores.

Prime is most suitable for the natural "aging" process because it has a thick fat cover. (In aging, natural enzymes cause tenderizing and flavor development.)

Over the past 30 years, *U.S. Choice* has become the most popular grade in butcher shops and supermarkets. Choice also is widely distributed in the restaurant trade. As long as it has been economically feasible to produce it, due to abundant and inexpensive grain supplies, the customer demand for U.S. Choice quality has been filled. With scarce grain at high prices in 1974–75, there was less-than-usual Prime and Choice. Choice is leaner than Prime, but still can be aged moderately.

Both *U.S. Good* and *U.S. Standard,* respectively, fall below Choice on the grading scale. Normally they contain less fat, seldom are offered as graded beef, but are more apt to have the store brand on them as an "economy beef" where available. Good generally is not as flavorful, juicy, or tender as Choice and likewise, Standard falls below Good in these palatability characteristics. But they still have pleasing flavor though milder than Choice and Prime grades.

The *U.S. Commercial, Utility, Cutter* and *Canner* grades usually are not available in food stores. This meat normally is purchased by processors for conversion into ground beef or to be processed as sausage meats, cold cuts, canned stew, luncheon loaf, or other manufactured meat items. Though nutritious and wholesome, these grades lack the palatability characteristics of higher grades. However, this is not a problem since the cuts most always are ground or pre-cooked. The more tender cuts (ribs and loins) are featured in many popular low-cost "steakhouses."

Courtesy, National Livestock & Meat Board

At times, grass-fed or baby beef is sold, so do check to see if the beef you wish to buy is as mature as you like it.

Cured beef, such as corned beef and beef bacon, is not recommended for

BEEF CHART

RETAIL CUTS OF BEEF — WHERE THEY COME FROM AND HOW TO COOK THEM

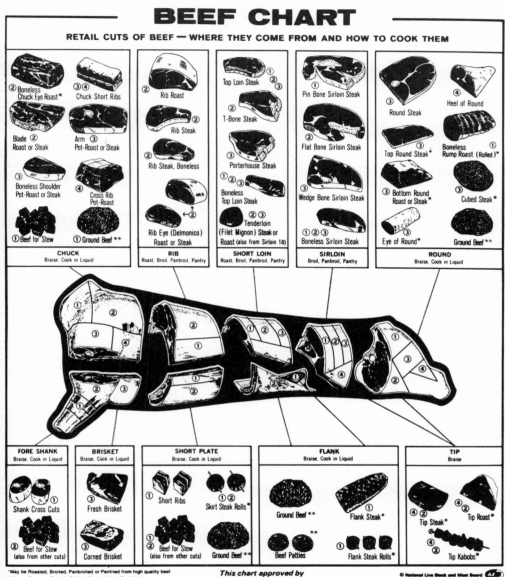

CHUCK
Braise, Cook in Liquid

- ② Boneless Chuck Eye Roast*
- ③④ Chuck Short Ribs
- ② Blade Roast or Steak
- ③ Arm Pot-Roast or Steak
- ③ Boneless Shoulder Pot-Roast or Steak
- ④ Cross Rib Pot-Roast
- ① Beef for Stew
- ① Ground Beef **

RIB
Roast, Broil, Panbroil, Panfry

- ② Rib Roast
- ② Rib Steak
- ② Rib Steak, Boneless
- Rib Eye (Delmonico) Roast or Steak

SHORT LOIN
Roast, Broil, Panbroil, Panfry

- ①②③ Top Loin Steak
- ② T-Bone Steak
- ③ Porterhouse Steak
- ①②③ Boneless Top Loin Steak
- ②③ Tenderloin (Filet Mignon) Steak or Roast (also from Sirloin 1a)

SIRLOIN
Broil, Panbroil, Panfry

- ① Pin Bone Sirloin Steak
- ② Flat Bone Sirloin Steak
- ③ Wedge Bone Sirloin Steak
- ①②③ Boneless Sirloin Steak

ROUND
Braise, Cook in Liquid

- ③ Round Steak
- ④ Heel of Round
- ③ Top Round Steak*
- ① Boneless Rump Roast (Rolled)*
- ③ Bottom Round Roast or Steak*
- Cubed Steak*
- Eye of Round*
- Ground Beef **

FORE SHANK
Braise, Cook in Liquid

- ① Shank Cross Cuts
- ② Beef for Stew (also from other cuts)

BRISKET
Braise, Cook in Liquid

- ③ Fresh Brisket
- ③ Corned Brisket

SHORT PLATE
Braise, Cook in Liquid

- ① Short Ribs
- ①② Skirt Steak Rolls*
- ①② Beef for Stew (also from other cuts)
- Ground Beef **

FLANK
Braise, Cook in Liquid

- Ground Beef **
- ① Flank Steak*
- ** Beef Patties
- ① Flank Steak Rolls*

TIP
Braise

- ④② Tip Roast*
- Tip Steak*
- ④② Tip Kabobs*

*May be Roasted, Broiled, Panbroiled or Panfried from high quality beef.
**May be Roasted, (Baked), Broiled, Panbroiled or Panfried.

This chart approved by
National Live Stock and Meat Board

© National Live Stock and Meat Board

37

freezing; however, I've found that short-term freezing for a few weeks works satisfactorily.

As another helpful insight, a good choice-grade beef weighing 1,000 pounds on the hoof will dress out to about 600 pounds, yielding 57% to 63% of the original carcass. The final cutting of the beef to package for freezing or table use will yield about 450 pounds of beef or 66% to 76% of the dressed carcass. In essence, 2.15 to 2.30 pounds of live-weight beef are required to net each pound of ready to eat beef.

Packaging

If you do your own beef packaging, you will need a foil, heavy plastic, or waxed or plastic-laminated freezer-weight paper. Package each cut as compactly as possible, eliminating big bones. Simmer the bones for stock and freeze it in ice cube trays, then bag the cubes for greatest convenience.

Place a double layer of freezer wrap between layers of chops, steaks, and hamburger patties. Package in quantities most frequently used in freezer wrap or bags.

Freeze ground beef several different ways. According to your family's preference, freeze a portion in one-pound packages or the size you generally use, a portion in patties, a portion in seasoned meatballs, a portion in meat loaves molded different ways—even some in individual servings—and perhaps some stuffed peppers or the like. There are two different packaging techniques for patties and meatballs: either use a double layer of freezer paper between layers or freeze solidly each patty and package in a bag or container. When freezing several meatballs or patties together, place a note on paper in the container listing the total number. Keep track of the amount remaining by adjusting the number each time you use some. Remember that seasonings shorten the freezer storage life of ground beef, so do not prepare more than can be used in two to three months.

After removing the drain tray, always repackage or overwrap any commercially bought beef with recommended freezing wrap. Store wraps are not air-, moisture-, and vapor-proof.

When packaging individual steaks or chops, you may wish to wrap individually or to quick-freeze on a cookie sheet and bag or box as hamburgers. If weight loss is a concern, package smaller portions for diet times (a guide to the amounts is listed in the chart in Chapter 15).

Always label each package as completely as possible. Include the information suggested on page 32.

Basic Beef-Freezing Tips

Before freezing a large amount of beef fresh from the butcher, turn your freezer to the lowest setting for about 24 hours as an extra safeguard to assure deep chilling. (See page 25 for more information.)

Seasoning greatly shortens the recommended freezer storage life of beef. Therefore season only what you will easily use within two to three months. Also, remember that a few seasonings change in the freezing process. (See page 22.)

To Thaw or Not to Thaw?

It is a much debated question whether meat has more flavor when defrosted and cooked or when cooked frozen. Basically, there is no difference in the palatability, nutritive value, or losses from evaporation when meat is thawed during cooking or before cooking.

If you decide to thaw, do allow time for thawing in the refrigerator. Leave the package wrapped, placing it on a platter or dish of some kind to keep any drippings from messing up your refrigerator. Refrigerator thawing allows the meat to absorb the thawed ice crystals, retaining flavor and moistness. Also there is less chance of spoilage.

To thaw in the refrigerator, allow about 4 to 7 hours per pound for thick steak or beef roasts of over 4 pounds; allow 3 to 5 hours per pound for roasts under 4 pounds, thinly cut steak, or ground beef patties. A pound package of ground beef or stew meat will require about 3 hours. When cooking thawed meats, begin cooking while there are still some ice crystals remaining. Many people like to cook thin steaks, chops, or patties while frozen. Allow about one-third more cooking time for frozen meats or approximately 15 to 20 minutes more per pound.

The quickest way to thaw is with a microwave oven, following the manufacturer's instructions. Some models have a special defrost feature that allows foods to thaw beautifully—or you can continue with the cooking process and be ready to serve in record time.

Steaks that you want well done—especially if over one and one-half inches thick—should be thawed before broiling. If some in your family like steak especially rare and others want only well done, start broiling with the ones to be well done at room temperature, the medium ones at refrigerator temperature, and the rare ones frozen. They all turn out right about the same time with considerably less clock watching and turning.

To be sure the roasts you cook are done just to your liking, always use a meat thermometer. If cooking a frozen roast, wait until it is thawed before inserting the thermometer.

To get the best browning on the outside of a meat cut before cooking it, thaw the meat first.

Refreezing Beef

If a package of beef still contains ice crystals, it is safe to refreeze—but plan to use it as soon as possible. If the meat is completely thawed but the temperature of the meat is still under 50°F, it is probably still in good condition. Beef spoils from the outside in and less quickly. If the temperature is above 50°F, the test for measuring eating quality is its odor—if it still smells fresh, cook it thoroughly and freeze again. Use as soon as possible.

PORK

A preference for pork seems to be regional, with the highest regard for it in the South, the Ohio valley, and the Midwest. You should determine the amount and types of pork cuts you wish to turn into your own frozen assets. Remember that your freezer does have capacity limitations—so if pork in quantity is your desire, there will be less room for other foods.

Many times if your family "likes everything," a good tip is to freeze more pork when pork prices are lower, changing to other meats as the prices fluctuate.

You will want to determine whether you wish to buy pork in bulk or just select specials as they are offered. The same pointers apply to determining the amount and the most preferable place to purchase a side or quarter of pork as with beef. Also, the same guidelines apply to selecting a butcher and the care in packaging.

Buying Pork

Pork is not graded in the same way as beef, lamb, or veal. The wholesale cuts are judged on their individual desirability. Look for cuts that are protected by some fat and trim off any excess as fat becomes stale or even rancid over a period of time. Too little fat will yield dry, less-flavorful pork.

Pork is ready to package for freezing after thorough chilling—about 48 hours. Aging, as for beef, is not necessary. Preferably arrange for flash-freezing at a super low temperature of −30°F, when freezing a quantity. (See pages 34–5 for more information.)

PORK CHART

RETAIL CUTS OF PORK — WHERE THEY COME FROM AND HOW TO COOK THEM

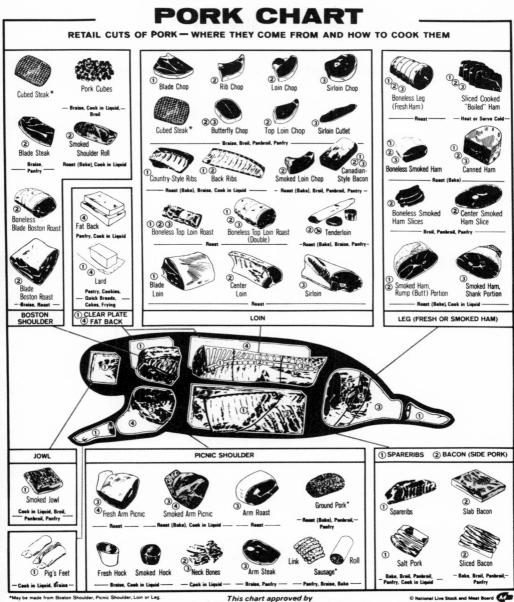

BOSTON SHOULDER

Cubed Steak*

Pork Cubes

— Braise, Cook in Liquid, —
Broil

② Blade Steak
Braise,
Panfry

② Smoked
Shoulder Roll
Roast (Bake), Cook in Liquid

② Boneless
Blade Boston Roast

② Blade
Boston Roast
— Braise, Roast —

① CLEAR PLATE
④ FAT BACK

④ Fat Back
Pantry, Cook in Liquid

④ Lard
Pastry, Cookies,
— Quick Breads, —
Cakes, Frying

LOIN

① Blade Chop
② Rib Chop
③ Loin Chop
④ Sirloin Chop

Cubed Steak*
②③ Butterfly Chop
②③ Top Loin Chop
Sirloin Cutlet

— Braise, Broil, Panbroil, Panfry —

① Country-Style Ribs
①② Back Ribs
② Smoked Loin Chop
②③① Canadian-Style Bacon

— Roast (Bake), Braise, Cook in Liquid —   — Roast (Bake), Broil, Panbroil, Panfry —

①②③ Boneless Top Loin Roast
① Boneless Top Loin Roast (Double)
②③④ Tenderloin

— Roast —   — Roast (Bake), Braise, Panfry —

① Blade Loin
② Center Loin
③ Sirloin

— Roast —

LEG (FRESH OR SMOKED HAM)

①②③ Boneless Leg (Fresh Ham)
①②③ Sliced Cooked "Boiled" Ham

— Roast —   — Heat or Serve Cold —

①②③ Boneless Smoked Ham
①②③ Canned Ham

— Roast (Bake) —

① Boneless Smoked Ham Slices
② Center Smoked Ham Slice

— Broil, Panbroil, Panfry —

①② Smoked Ham, Rump (Butt) Portion
③ Smoked Ham, Shank Portion

— Roast (Bake), Cook in Liquid —

JOWL

① Smoked Jowl
Cook in Liquid, Broil,
Panbroil, Panfry

① Pig's Feet
— Cook in Liquid, Braise —

PICNIC SHOULDER

③ Fresh Arm Picnic
③④ Smoked Arm Picnic
③ Arm Roast
Ground Pork*

— Roast —   — Roast (Bake), Cook in Liquid —   — Roast —
— Roast (Bake), Panbroil, — Panfry

Fresh Hock
Smoked Hock
②③ Neck Bones
③ Arm Steak
Link   Roll
Sausage*

— Braise, Cook in Liquid —   — Cook in Liquid —   — Braise, Panfry —   — Panfry, Braise, Bake —

① SPARERIBS   ② BACON (SIDE PORK)

① Spareribs
② Slab Bacon

① Salt Pork
② Sliced Bacon

— Bake, Broil, Panbroil, — Panfry, Cook in Liquid   — Bake, Broil, Panbroil, — Panfry

*May be made from Boston Shoulder, Picnic Shoulder, Loin or Leg.

This chart approved by
National Live Stock and Meat Board

© National Live Stock and Meat Board

41

Cured pork can be frozen; however, the storage time should be short as the fat becomes rancid if stored too long. Bacon should not be frozen longer than a month for optimum quality. Ham can be frozen up to two months; however, the flavor and color may become more bland and the texture more grainy than when served not frozen.

Sausage should be at least three parts lean to one part fat for best results. The salt and seasonings hasten rancidity, hence sausage should be frozen only in quantities you will be able to use within one to three months.

Franks, bologna, and prepared luncheon meats of various kinds contain salt and seasonings, meaning they should not be stored longer than three months at most. And, often the texture changes somewhat.

Lard can be frozen if tightly sealed. When freezing in quantities, check with your druggist or butcher for an antioxidant to prevent rancidity and follow the recommended directions.

A U.S. No. 1 pig weighing 200 pounds on the hoof will dress out to about 140 pounds yielding 68% to 73% of the original carcass. The final cutting of the pork to package for freezing or table use will yield about 140 pounds of pork, or 72% to 82% of the dressed carcass. So, 1.75 to 1.90 pounds of live-weight pork are required to net each pound of ready-to-eat pork.

Packaging

If you decide to buy a bulk quantity of pork, follow the recommended packaging tips listed in the beef section. The pork should be well trimmed and compactly packaged. Stew the boney cuts and freeze in family-sized servings or make stock and freeze in cubes for convenient use.

Sausage is most convenient packaged either in patties prefrozen and placed in a plastic bag or container or else frozen in chunks of the quantity you usually use for a meal.

For convenience, bacon can be frozen either in layers separated with double freezer paper or packaged in family-sized portions—all of which are placed in a large bag or container.

For sausage or bacon, keep a listing on paper in the bag or box for marking off the packages as you use them, to have an idea of the amount left.

Though many meat packers say no, hams *can* be frozen whole or, more preferably, in family-sized roasts or slices. Never freeze a whole ham in the can in which it is sold. Separate slices with double layers of freezer wrap.

Always repackage or overwrap any commercially bought pork, removing the drain tray from the package. Store wraps do not provide a freezer-proof seal.

To Thaw or Not to Thaw

See the beef thawing section for general hints and information.

I prefer to cook hams, sausage, and bacon from the frozen state because it seems to me they keep their fresh flavor better. Thawing too long can produce stale-tasting bacon or sausage and watery ham. Some people prefer refrigerator thawing—allow 3 hours per pound for bacon and sausage. Thaw ham according to the form—whole or in slices—as indicated under beef.

I prefer to thaw all fresh pork in the refrigerator before cooking, because pork must be cooked well-done to avoid trichinosis. Pork chops generally thaw in the refrigerator in about 4 to 5 hours. Breading and batters cling better to chops when thawed. (See beef thawing.)

Refreezing Pork

Pork can be refrozen if ice crystals remain and the meat is still very firm. Use as soon as possible. Do not refreeze if completely thawed. Instead, cook it if the temperature of the meat is still very cold, 50°F or below, and the meat has a good fresh odor. After cooking, either use immediately, refrigerate a short period of a day or two before using, or refreeze and use as soon as convenient.

LAMB AND VEAL

Lamb purchased by the half or in large wholesale quantities is one of my favorite meat bargains. I must admit I am very partial to lamb, dearly loving everything from stews of varying ethnic origins to roasts, shish kabobs, and broiled chops. Don't overlook the potential bargains in buying large quantities of lamb—if you like lamb, that is.

Veal purchased on sale or in large amounts usually makes it more accessible than when paying the average price per pound. My favorite veal-buying technique is to look at the veal counter and select bargains when offered. Usually supermarkets periodically offer legs of veal or an entire breast, both of which are splendid eating, prepared numerous different ways.

Both lamb and veal tend to be special foods with most families. The priority you place on the amount you wish to freeze is a personal determination.

When buying either in quantity, check the beef buying criteria listed on pages 34–5.

LAMB CHART

RETAIL CUTS OF LAMB — WHERE THEY COME FROM AND HOW TO COOK THEM

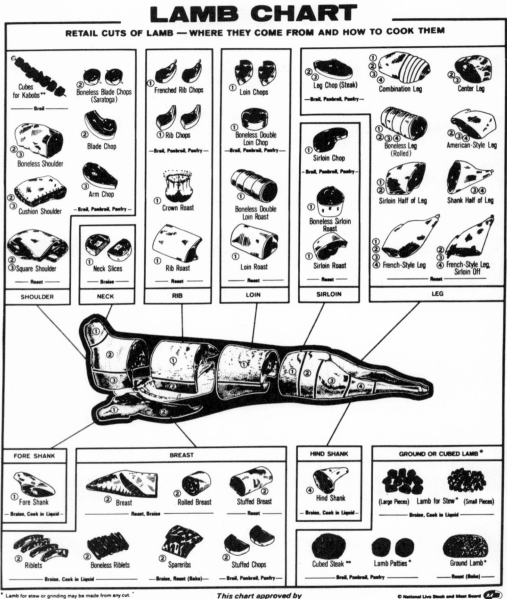

SHOULDER

Cubes for Kabobs**
② Boneless Blade Chops (Saratoga)
— Broil —
Boneless Shoulder
②③
② Blade Chop
Cushion Shoulder ②③
③ Arm Chop
— Broil, Panbroil, Panfry —
③ Square Shoulder
— Roast —

NECK

Neck Slices
— Braise —

RIB

① Frenched Rib Chops
① Rib Chops
— Broil, Panbroil, Panfry —
① Crown Roast
① Rib Roast
— Roast —

LOIN

① Loin Chops
① Boneless Double Loin Chop
— Broil, Panbroil, Panfry —
① Boneless Double Loin Roast
① Loin Roast
— Roast —

SIRLOIN

② Leg Chop (Steak)
— Broil, Panbroil, Panfry —
① Sirloin Chop
— Broil, Panbroil, Panfry —
① Boneless Sirloin Roast
① Sirloin Roast
— Roast —

LEG

① ② ③ ④ Combination Leg
② ③ Center Leg
① ② ③ ④ Boneless Leg (Rolled)
③ ④ American-Style Leg
① ② ③ ④ Sirloin Half of Leg
③ ④ Shank Half of Leg
① ② ④ French-Style Leg
① ② ④ French-Style Leg, Sirloin Off
— Roast —

FORE SHANK

① Fore Shank
— Braise, Cook in Liquid —

BREAST

② Breast
② Rolled Breast
② Stuffed Breast
— Roast, Braise —   — Roast —
② Riblets
② Boneless Riblets
② Spareribs
— Braise, Cook in Liquid —   — Braise, Roast (Bake) —
② Stuffed Chops
— Broil, Panbroil, Panfry —

HIND SHANK

④ Hind Shank
— Braise, Cook in Liquid —

GROUND OR CUBED LAMB*

(Large Pieces)   Lamb for Stew *   (Small Pieces)
— Braise, Cook in Liquid —
Cubed Steak **
Lamb Patties *
Ground Lamb *
— Broil, Panbroil, Panfry —   — Roast (Bake) —

* Lamb for stew or grinding may be made from any cut.
**Kabobs or cube steaks may be made from any thick solid piece of boneless Lamb.

This chart approved by
National Live Stock and Meat Board

© National Live Stock and Meat Board

44

VEAL CHART

RETAIL CUTS OF VEAL — WHERE THEY COME FROM AND HOW TO COOK THEM

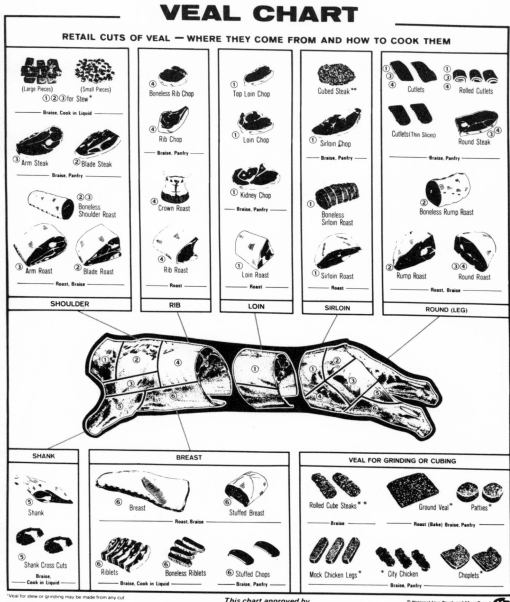

SHOULDER

(Large Pieces) (Small Pieces)
①②③for Stew*

— Braise, Cook in Liquid —

③ Arm Steak   ② Blade Steak

— Braise, Panfry —

②③ Boneless Shoulder Roast

③ Arm Roast   ② Blade Roast

— Roast, Braise —

RIB

④ Boneless Rib Chop

④ Rib Chop

— Braise, Panfry —

Crown Roast

④ Rib Roast

— Roast —

LOIN

① Top Loin Chop

① Loin Chop

① Kidney Chop

— Braise, Panfry —

① Loin Roast

— Roast —

SIRLOIN

Cubed Steak **

① Sirloin Chop

— Braise, Panfry —

① Boneless Sirloin Roast

① Sirloin Roast

— Roast —

ROUND (LEG)

①③④ Cutlets   ①③④ Rolled Cutlets

Cutlets(Thin Slices)   ③④ Round Steak

— Braise, Panfry —

② Boneless Rump Roast

② Rump Roast   ③④ Round Roast

— Roast, Braise —

SHANK

⑤ Shank

⑤ Shank Cross Cuts

— Braise, Cook in Liquid —

BREAST

⑥ Breast   ⑥ Stuffed Breast

— Roast, Braise —

⑥ Riblets   ⑥ Boneless Riblets   ⑥ Stuffed Chops

— Braise, Cook in Liquid —   — Braise, Panfry —

VEAL FOR GRINDING OR CUBING

Rolled Cube Steaks **   Ground Veal*   Patties*

— Braise —   — Roast (Bake) Braise, Panfry —

Mock Chicken Legs*   * City Chicken   Choplets*

— Braise, Panfry —

*Veal for stew or grinding may be made from any cut
**Cube steaks may be made from any thick solid piece of boneless veal

This chart approved by
National Live Stock and Meat Board

© National Live Stock and Meat Board

45

Selecting Lamb or Veal

Lamb and veal are graded in much the same way as beef. Usually only U.S. Prime or Choice is available. Look for meatiness with a moderate degree of fat. Veal by nature will have very little fat; lamb has more. Trim off excess fat, especially at the ends of chops and on the breast and shoulder.

Both should be frozen as soon as chilled—about 48 hours after slaughter or immediately upon returning home if store-bought. If you buy a half or very large quantity, arrange for flash-freezing at −30°F. (Reminder: A home freezer should not be loaded with more than 3 pounds per cubic foot within each 24-hour period.)

A final thought on buying good to choice lamb is that a live-weight lamb of 100 pounds will dress out to about 50 pounds, yielding 48% to 52%. Butchering for table use and/or packaging for the freezer will yield about 41 pounds, or 76% to 86% of the carcass. In total 2.35 to 2.50 pounds of live-weight lamb are needed to yield one pound of table-ready lamb.

Packaging

Generally the same hints and techniques apply to lamb and veal as to beef.

You may wish to have the butcher prepare a crown rack of the lamb ribs or French the leg of lamb (stripping the shank bone clean), for extra-special serving. I always like to chunk some of the leg or shoulder roasts into shish-kabob-sized pieces and place them for two hours in favorite marinades at room temperature. Marinate in the freezer containers, then seal, label, and freeze for very convenient shish kabob dining. Just thaw in the refrigerator for a day before broiling.

To Thaw or Not to Thaw

The same hints for beef apply to lamb and veal. See page 39.

Refreezing

Lamb and veal can be refrozen only if still very icy and firm. Use as soon as possible. Do not refreeze if completely thawed.

If still mostly icy, cook immediately, then use or refreeze and use as soon as possible. If thawed meat is warm, discard it.

POULTRY

Chicken is one of the most versatile and economic meats. From the most elegant entrees such as Chicken Kiev or Coq au Vin to fried or broiled, chicken makes for a true frozen asset.

Turkey has become a year-round popular meat too, as the varieties and availability have increased. Capons, Cornish hens, ducks, geese, and other less popular fowl are generally not available at good prices. To freeze them, follow the same directions given for chicken and turkey in this chapter.

Poultry freezes well, and for the greatest convenience and eating versatility, you will want to freeze it a number of ways—whole, cut-up, and cooked. The way you buy and package should be determined by your family's tastes.

Usually the best buys come from buying whole birds. You can then package to suit your family's favored serving ways. For example, if breast meat is by far the general favorite—freeze the breasts separately. Package the other pieces together for saucy or stewed dishes—or cook, bone, and freeze. Breast meat can be a good buy if you don't pay more than about one-third extra per pound.

Depending on where you live and what sort of buying opportunities are available, you will need to decide the best way to buy poultry. Usually the amount of time you have available for butchering the live birds is the main issue. When time is limited, it is best to watch for bargain buys at supermarkets or butcher shops.

Buying Poultry

Select fresh birds that have few skin blemishes and firm, well-fleshed bodies with well-formed breasts and evenly distributed fat. Chickens are quality-graded as A, B, or C. "A" quality is highest and best for most eating. Lesser grades are acceptable for stewing.

Live chickens weigh about one-third more than their dressed weight. Live turkeys weigh about one-fourth more when under 13 pounds and up to one-fifth more when larger—25 pounds and over. For help in planning: a chicken ready to cook dresses out about as follows:

Breast	28%–30%
Legs and thighs	32%
Wings	11%–12%
Back and neck	19%–20%
Gizzard and heart	4%
Liver	3%

Courtesy, Ohio Extension Bulletin #344

Broiler chickens should weigh about 2½ pounds, fryers about 3 to 3½, roasters about 5 pounds or more. For roasting, buy young, plump birds. The heavier the bird, the higher the percentage of meat there will be to bone. Allow about one pound per person when purchasing chickens, capons, and turkeys for roasting. For ducks and geese, allow about 1½ pounds.

Older, fatter birds usually labeled "hens" are better for fricasseeing or stewing and can be packaged fresh or stewed.

Chill birds as soon as butchered in ice water or refrigerator, then package and freeze. Some prefer to chill birds for 12 hours in the refrigerator before freezing, feeling that this makes the birds more tender.

Packaging

Package poultry several different ways for greatest convenience and versatility in serving. Always label with complete information, listing weight, date, and expected use (remembering younger, lighter birds are better for frying; older ones for fricasseeing).

Commercially bought poultry, if purchased frozen, should be overwrapped. If bought fresh, remove from bags and clean before packaging.

First, clean the inside cavity and remove any extra membranes. Pluck out remaining pinfeathers, and clean the skin and drain. Do not season fresh birds. Always package giblets and liver separately, not inside or in same wrap with the chicken.

Whole birds: Make the body as compact as possible by locking the wings and folding the neck skin over the wingtips. Press the legs firmly back against the body and tie together. Pad the leg ends with freezer paper or foil to prevent puncturing the packaging. Freeze the giblets and liver separately. *Do not stuff.* The easiest packaging is in freezer-weight plastic bags or you may wish to package in foil, freezer paper, or plastic, using druggist's wrap. When bagging, place the bird in bag neck first, then lower the bag into warm water, pulling it firmly over the bird. Smooth out any extra air and twist top tightly into a one-inch-long twist—double over, twist, and secure closed. Label the package.

Halves: Split broilers in two, cutting through the breast and down the back. Place double layer of freezer wrap between halves and place together. Pad ends and legs and package as directed for whole birds. Label.

Pieces of poultry: Cut poultry into serving pieces. You may wish to wrap some entire cut-up birds, packaging the giblets separately. Keep some like parts together, such as breasts, legs, or bony pieces. You may even wish to stew the bony pieces first, freezing stock and meat separately for greatest space-saving and serving convenience.

Flatten or pat each piece firmly together. Either package fresh or freeze individual pieces first on a cookie tray and then package. You may wish to

48

flour or crumb-coat some pieces of chicken before freezing so that they can be cooked without thawing—especially great for busy days and microwave ovens. Pack into bags, cartons, or flat wrap. Label.

Giblets: Package giblets and livers separately as they have shorter storage lives. Use giblets within three months and livers within one month for best flavor. Label.

Cooked poultry: A very good idea for space saving and convenience is to cook bony pieces before freezing. After deboning, place meat on foil trays or in rigid containers. You may wish to freeze some or all of the stock separately.

Cooked chicken dishes such as Coq au Vin seem to be more flavorful after freezing. Leftovers can be frozen as is, sliced, or in meals with the vegetables alongside. If freezing a roasted bird, save space by slicing the meat and stewing the carcass for stock. Package in meal- or recipe-sized quantities. Label.

To Thaw or Not to Thaw

Poultry can be cooked while frozen but will require one-third to one-half longer cooking time. When fowl is frozen, coatings will not stick well and browning will not be as even. Therefore, for frying, birds should be thawed first. However, for convenience, pieces *can* be coated before freezing. Even doneness when broiling is also difficult with frozen poultry. An important point is to cook poultry as soon as defrosted and while still cold—do not allow it to warm as it will be less juicy and could possibly develop contamination if allowed to stand thawed at room temperature.

Refrigerator thawing is best as it yields juicier meat and is safer. To thaw, leave in packaging. Allow 5 to 6 hours per pound. For ducks and geese, allow 3 to 4 hours per pound. For turkeys, allow 2 to 3 days if over 18 pounds, 2 days or less if under 18 pounds. At room temperature, allow about one hour per pound for any poultry.

To thaw under cold running water—a method recommended only for whole birds—allow 2 to 3 hours for most birds, 4 to 6 hours for turkeys.

Microwave ovens are the fastest, most convenient way to thaw. Birds will thaw in minutes. Just follow manufacturer's instructions.

Cooked chicken can be heated without defrosting. If thawing, do not allow it to become warm before heating and serving.

Refreezing

Poultry can be refrozen only if still very icy and firm. Use as soon as possible. Do not refreeze if completely thawed; discard instead. If still mostly icy, cook immediately, then use or refreeze and use as soon as possible.

VARIETY MEATS

Variety meats offer some of the best values going in nutrition—but the opportunity to use them varies widely, depending on the venturesome nature of the appetites you're serving. Many people never outgrow their childhood "ugh" reactions to liver, brains, and the like.

I for one like them—and I feel nearly everyone would, given half a chance to taste how delicious various sauces and preparations can make them. Serving variety meats offers a pleasant change of pace from regular meats and an opportunity for real money-saving frozen assets.

You should get at least a portion of the liver when you purchase a quarter or half of an animal. And, perhaps you'll even be able to get the heart, kidneys, sweetbreads, and brains. Probably you will have to make your liking for tripe known ahead of time as it generally has only a regional or ethnic appeal. Many butchers actually assume people won't want "the innards" unless they say so.

You can almost always get bargain buys on variety meats. Check with your favorite butcher and make your likes known because he may have had trouble selling them in the past and would happily give you a good price on a large amount of any one of them. One word of caution: all variety meats are very perishable and require more preparation to ready them for the freezer than muscle meat. When buying, never purchase more than you can handle in a day or two. Don't buy more than your family will eat in one to four months. (Check the Appendix for specific keeping recommendations.) Basically, the most perishable variety meats are brains and sweetbreads, which keep their freshness in the freezer for only a month. Liver keeps quite well up to four months.

Variety meats are all quite similar. The size will be consistent with the size of the animal. As an example, beef will have the biggest innards, lamb the smallest, and the size of veal and pork organs will fall in between. Because all variety meats are highly perishable, select only the sturdiest, heaviest-quality packaging materials.

Buying and Packaging

Liver: For the best buy, pork liver usually cannot be beat. Since the nutritive values are relatively the same for beef, pork, or lamb, why not economize and spend less on the pork liver? The most popular liver is usually calf's liver, which is much more costly and somewhat less nutritious. Whichever you buy, either have it sliced or slice it yourself into one-half-inch-thick slices. Some like it thinner for frying, others prefer it thicker for broiling. Chill or refrigerate, then package in meal-sized quantities

50

with the slices separated by double layers of freezer paper. Or, if desired, the slices can be individually wrapped and a large quantity bagged together. Then the needed number of slices can be removed each time. Keep track of the remaining balance.

Package in heavy freezer-weight wrap if freezing meal-sized quantities. Package individually wrapped slices in heavy-weight plastic bags or cartons if freezing a quantity. Label with type of liver, quantity, date, and intended use, such as frying or broiling.

Heart: Somehow people tend not to think of the heart as a meat. I often find it difficult to buy. Though heart is tough and requires long, slow cooking, absolutely marvelous stuffings and sauces transform it into a very nice meat trade-off. Trim off any hard muscular spots and remove large arteries; rinse and drain. Package whole in freezer-weight packaging materials. Label with weight of heart and the date.

Kidneys: Unless raised in a somewhat Continental environment, many Americans find it difficult to "adjust" to kidney as an entree. My family was not fond of it and claimed you could never rinse or soak kidneys adequately to get a good flavor. When visiting England, I just had to try beefsteak and kidney pie and I loved it! Also, I have enjoyed kidneys in London mixed grills. In fixing them for freezing, I have learned some tricks—a few the regrettable way. First, trim off fat and tubules, then soak kidneys in salt water for 30 minutes before freezing. This way the kidney has a far better flavor when served. Be sure to soak the kidneys before preparing a dish such as beefsteak and kidney pie as strong undesirable flavor develops, really taking the enjoyment out of an otherwise pleasurable dish. I leave the kidneys whole when freezing, although some like to cut beef kidneys into squares as for a casserole. For my taste, I prefer the size and flavor of lamb kidneys. Package in meal-sized quantities using freezer wrap. Label with the type of kidneys, how they are prepared, and the date.

Brains: Brains are a very delicately flavored organ meat—absolutely marvelous when freshly prepared by sauteing in brown butter, drizzled with lemon juice, and garnished with capers. You must buy only the freshest of the fresh from a very reputable butcher. Beef, pork, lamb, and veal have fine-flavored brains. As soon as you've bought them, rush home and trim off excess membrane and blood clots. Simmer in 1 quart of water with 1 teaspoon salt and 1 tablespoon lemon juice. Either leave whole or split, dice, or slice. Package in heavy-weight freezer packaging and label with the type of preparation, quantity, date, and any other specifics.

Sweetbreads: Sweetbreads also have a very mild flavor and are found only in very young animals. Beef supply most sweetbreads, which are the two lobes of the thymus gland. The gland disappears as the animal ages. Sweetbreads are as highly perishable as brains and should be pretreated in the same lemon-flavored brine. Remove extra membrane and trim into

51

the size pieces you wish for the intended recipe. Package in heavy-weight paper, label with the intended use and the date.

Tongue: Beef tongues are the largest and can be frozen fresh, cooked, corned, or smoked. Pork and lamb tongues are sometimes pickled in brine. I prefer to freeze the tongue whole, roots and all. Then, after cooking, I sometimes package small serving-size cartons of sliced tongue. Package in good heavy freezer packaging and label.

Tripe: An interesting observation about tripe is that it is usually enjoyed only by the very highest and lowest strata of our society. Sometime give it a try, if you haven't already. It is usually extremely inexpensive and there are a number of varied ways to prepare and serve it—grilled, in soups, or as the famous tripe à la mode. Honeycomb tripe is the muscular lining of a beef's second stomach. The smoother type is the stomach's wall. Freezing is the easiest way to preserve tripe, although it is frequently pickled or canned.

Tripe is one of the tougher variety meats and requires long, slow cooking. It is partially cooked before it is sold; however, further cooking is almost always necessary (unless it is sold fully cooked). Precooking in salted water, using 1 teaspoon salt to each quart of water, for a minimum of 2 hours is usually required before it is ready to prepare in a recipe for serving. Herbs, other seasonings, and wines may be desired and can be added to the salted water. If preparing a variety of batches for various uses, be sure to label each accurately with as complete information as possible. Package in recipe-sized quantities using heavy-weight freezer wrapping.

To Thaw or Not to Thaw

Since these are the most delicate of all meats, I prefer to thaw in the refrigerator or cook them frozen. Thaw in the packaging in a bowl or on a plate. Allow about 5 hours per pound. If cooking frozen, allow about one-third to one-half more cooking time.

Refreezing

Variety meats can be refrozen only if still very icy and firm. Use as soon as possible. Do not refreeze if completely thawed; discard instead. If still icy, cook immediately; then use or refreeze and use as soon as possible.

BASTES AND MARINADES

Bastes and marinades go a long ways toward enhancing the flavor and texture of meats and are a favorite trick for disguising the flavor of not so great meat—say, a forgotten frozen package that accidentally got hidden. Very candidly, I've used them just as the cooks did in the Middle Ages. Then they did not have refrigeration or freezing, so they used spices to hide stale, even rotten flavors caused by keeping their meats too long. Of course, none of us would consider the latter, but what's to stop us from sparking the flavor of a tired piece of meat?

When meat is not so fresh or tender, bastes and marinades can make a delicious, even elegant, dish out of what might otherwise have been a miserable failure. Bastes are best chosen for their ability to add moisture as well as to add flavor.

Marinades make a more dramatic flavor change. They are the greater salvager of not so good meat and they also tenderize. For convenience, I like to freeze meats in marinades—it works beautifully. Recipes for some of my favorites are included in this chapter—steak siciliano, hula steak, sauerbraten, and shashlik shish kabob.

Bastes and marinades can be simmered and served as a sauce or they can be frozen and reused. If freezing, freshen them before reuse with some more seasonings, wine, etc. Do not store for more than three or four uses or over a year.

Bastes

Bastes are for brushing on the meat as it cooks and are almost always more oily than marinades, often containing one part oil to one part wine or vinegar or fruit juice. A combination of acidic liquids can be used if desired; also a combination of various oils. With practice, you will know what you like and don't like, flavorwise.

The oil makes the meat more moist. Strong-flavored oils such as olive and sesame should be diluted with vegetable oil unless the strong flavor is preferred. Wine or other acidic ingredients tenderize the meat. Never use salt as a baste seasoning; always use soy sauce to provide the flavor—it doesn't toughen the meat. Ginger or dry mustard provides a hot, spicy flavor in a more gentle way than ground black pepper. Of course, whole black pepper or red peppers can be used.

Certain rules of thumb can be employed: red wine complements dark meats, white wine complements lighter meats. However, you will find many famous dishes that violate these rules. For example, the famous French chicken dish Coq au Vin uses red wine.

53

Marinades

Marinades are for soaking meat prior to cooking, and are generally less oily and more spicy than bastes. The same suggestions about ingredients listed under bastes apply to marinades. Often, people like to brush the marinade on the meat as it cooks, but don't overdo it—the meat has already absorbed most of this flavor.

Since the purpose of the marinade is to flavor and tenderize the meat, a 24- to 72-hour soaking is generally preferred. For long marinating, meat should be placed in the refrigerator. (If time is short, leave the marinating meat at room temperature to gain maximum flavor.) To freeze meat in a marinade, soak meat in marinade in a freezer carton at room temperature for about two hours. Seal and label. Be sure only fresh meat is frozen in marinade. Thawed meat must not be refrozen without cooking.

RECIPES

NOTE: More meat recipes are included in the microwave recipe section, page 221. To convert to conventional cooking, increase the cooking time by approximately two-thirds—after first checking the timing and cooking process in a similar conventional recipe.

SAUERKRAUT BALLS

Three types of meat, sauerkraut, and spices make this a great appetizer. These sauerkraut balls require quite a bit of work, so plan to prepare them ahead of time and freeze, because the raves you receive will make them well worth the effort.

Temperature: 370°F hot fat
Cooking time: 2 to 4 minutes each
Yield: 90 to 100

½ pound lean, boneless ham	1 teaspoon dry mustard
½ pound lean, boneless pork	1 teaspoon salt
½ pound corned beef	2 cups milk
1 medium-sized onion	2 pounds sauerkraut, cooked
1 teaspoon minced parsley	and drained
3 tablespoons shortening	2 eggs, slightly beaten
2 cups all-purpose flour	Dry bread crumbs

1. Put meats and onion through food grinder; add parsley. Blend well.
2. Sauté in shortening until browned.
3. Add flour, mustard, salt, and milk. Blend.
4. Cook, stirring constantly, until thick.
5. Add sauerkraut and put entire mixture through food chopper.
6. Mix thoroughly. Return to skillet and cook, stirring constantly until very thick.
7. Cool. Form into balls about the size of a walnut.
8. Roll in flour, dip in eggs, roll in bread crumbs, and fry in hot, deep fat 370° F until browned.
9. Serve hot as an appetizer with a pot of mustard, if desired.

FREEZING HINTS: Freeze on cookie sheets until firm. Then place in rigid cartons.

MAXIMUM RECOMMENDED FREEZER STORAGE: 2 months

GRAPELEAF ROLLS

Close friends from Beirut shared this recipe with me. I liked them so well, I planted a grape arbor just so I could have the leaves for making them. You can serve them as an appetizer or a meat course.

Temperature: Simmer
Baking Time: 30 minutes
Yield: 3–4 dozen small to 2 dozen large

1 small jar grapeleaves—fresh or wilted	½ teaspoon cinnamon
	1 teaspoon salt
	½ teaspoon black pepper
Several lamb bones	Juice of 1 lemon
3 cloves fresh garlic	1 #303 can whole tomatoes,
1 pound ground lamb	optional
½ cup rice	

1. Soak leaves in water. Place lamb bones and garlic in bottom of large saucepan.
2. Mix ground lamb with rice, cinnamon, salt, pepper, and lemon juice. Place a spoonful of mixture on each leaf and roll, tucking the ends in.
3. Place the rolled leaves in bottom of saucepan on top of bones. Pour tomatoes over top. Then add water until it comes to just below the tops of the rolls. Bring mixture to boil using high heat.
4. Cook until rice in filling is tender, about 30 minutes.

FREEZING HINTS: Package sauce and rolls in separate freezer cartons. Serve warm with the sauce.

NOTE: If grapeleaves are unobtainable, one large head of cabbage may be substituted. Wilt the leaves and use as grapeleaves. If lamb bones are not obtainable, place rolls on a trivet.

MAXIMUM RECOMMENDED FREEZER STORAGE: 3 months

CURRY CHICKEN BALLS

Chicken curry in miniature. This exotic appetizer not only tastes good but looks interesting as well. Adjust the amount of curry to your own taste.

Yield: 3 dozen

¼ pound cream cheeze	1 tablespoon chopped
2 tablespoons cream or	chutney
mayonnaise	½ teaspoon salt
1 cup chopped chicken	⅓ to 1 tablespoon curry
1 cup chopped blanched almonds	½ cup grated coconut

1. Beat together cream cheese and cream (or mayonnaise).
2. Add the chicken, almonds, chutney, salt, and curry powder.
3. Shape into walnut-sized balls. Roll in coconut. Chill before serving.

FREEZING HINTS: Place on cookie sheets covered with waxed or cello paper and freeze until firm. Place in rigid cartons, separating layers of balls with cello or waxed paper. Coffee cans, well rinsed, are good freezing containers for these.

MAXIMUM RECOMMENDED FREEZER STORAGE: 3 months

NOTE: For more meat and poultry recipes, see chapters 15 and 16 .

ELEGANT PATÉ

No hors d'oeuvres tray is complete without a liver paté and this one is excellent. Serve it in aspic with a fancy garnish for a very impressive and professional appearance.

Temperature: 350°F
Cooking time: 2 hours
Will keep one week refrigerated
Yield: 3 cups

½ pound chicken livers	1 small onion, coarsely diced
2 tablespoons butter	1 clove garlic
2 eggs	¼ cup rum

1 pound pork, ground twice	sage, marjoram, basil, salt,
2 tablespoons flour	freshly ground black
½ teaspoon allspice	pepper
¼ teaspoon each of thyme,	Salt pork strips

1. Sauté chicken livers in butter until just partly cooked.

2. Put in the blender with the eggs and blend until smooth. Add the onion, garlic, and rum and blend again.

3. Mix the chicken liver puree with the ground pork (be sure the pork is lean, without gristle and finely ground) and add the flour and seasonings. Beat together thoroughly.

4. Line a bread loaf pan with strips of salt pork and fill with the meat mixture.

5. Cover with aluminum foil and place in a deep pan of hot water so that water comes to within an inch of the top of the loaf pan. Bake in a 350°F oven for 2 hours. (Be sure you do not run out of water.)

6. Chill thoroughly. Unmold, cut away the salt pork.

7. Several hours or the day before serving, pour ½ inch beef or chicken aspic* flavored with sherry in the bottom of the loaf pan used for cooking it and arrange a garnish of tarragon, hard-cooked egg, or whatever. Place in refrigerator until set. Put liver pate on top of aspic and pour remaining aspic around sides. Chill. When firmly set, unmold and serve with crackers or breads. Extra aspic can be poured in a cookie sheet, scored with a meat fork at right angles into tiny squares, and arranged around the paté on the serving plate. Silver platters are extra pretty for serving paté.

*Make aspic by thickening flavored chicken stock with unflavored gelatin. One pint chicken stock to one envelope gelatin is usually enough.

FREEZING HINTS: Package in a plastic bag, foil, or other freezer wrap. Seal and label.

MAXIMUM RECOMMENDED FREEZER STORAGE: 2 to 3 months

STEAK DIANE

This is a quick-as-a-wink way to prepare succulent frozen sirloin or loin steaks. If using this dish for entertaining, measure and set out the seasonings so you can prepare the steak at the last minute while adding the last touches to the other foods and the table. Or you can prepare it at the table in a chafing dish or electric skillet.

Preparation time: 15 minutes
Cooking time: 7 minutes
Serves: 4

2 boneless sirloin steaks or 4 loin steaks ¾ inch thick (thawed for 5 hours or more, if frozen)	3 tablespoons sweet butter
¼ cup sweet butter	4 teaspoons Worcestershire sauce
2 teaspoons dry mustard	1 fresh lemon
½ teaspoon onion salt	2 tablespoons chopped parsley
2 tablespoons olive oil	¼ cup dry brandy, optional
1 teaspoon freshly ground black pepper	2 tablespoons capers, optional

1. Cut each sirloin steak in half to make 4 pieces. Place either kind of steak between pieces of waxed paper and pound to ½ inch thick. Warm dinner plates in 200° F oven.

2. Melt ¼ cup butter in large skillet or griddle (use an electric skillet or chafing dish for table preparation). Stir in mustard and onion salt. Drizzle one tablespoon olive oil over steaks. Sprinkle with half the pepper, then rub oil and pepper into steaks with the bowl of a spoon. If cooking at the table, take to table now.

3. Cook steaks with oil-pepper side down for 2 minutes; spoon pan juices over steaks occasionally. Rub remaining oil and pepper on unseasoned side of steaks; turn over; cook 2 minutes longer. Steaks will be rare.

4. Remove from pan; keep warm on warmed dinner plates. Remove pan from heat; add three tablespoons butter and Worcestershire sauce. Cut lemon into quarters, squeeze juice into skillet. Spear one piece of meat on fork and use as a stirrer. Continue with each steak, stirring into sauce, then placing sauce side down on each warm plate.

5. Warm brandy in skillet, if you wish to flame steaks, just until it almost bubbles. Meanwhile, be certain your guests are seated. Add warm brandy and parsley to pan juices, which must still be warm. Ignite and immediately sauce the top of each steak. Garnish with capers and serve.

Steaks taste best freshly cooked.

MAXIMUM RECOMMENDED FREEZER STORAGE FOR STEAK: 12 months

STEAK SICILIANO

A favorite quick and easy steak salvager—for not-so-tender or not-so-fresh steak. Great for entertaining because it needs no pot watching and if frozen ahead in the marinade, simply thaw that day in the refrigerator and proceed with the last preparation steps. Remember, you cannot thaw, marinate, and then refreeze meat. If you wish to freeze in the marinade, use only fresh meat. Frozen meat can be marinated, but must be cooked immediately after the soaking.

Temperature: low
Cooking time: 20 to 30 minutes
Yield: 6 servings

1 cup Burgundy wine	2 teaspoons minced parsley
1 small clove garlic, crushed	2 teaspoons prepared
1 teaspoon Worcestershire	mustard
sauce	1 teaspoon sugar
¼ teaspoon oregano	Unseasoned meat
1 small onion, minced	tenderizer
1 teaspoon salt	2 teaspoons butter, melted
¼ teaspoon pepper	2½ pounds round steak
2 teaspoons prepared	(thawed for 5 hours or
horseradish	more, if frozen)

1. Combine the first 11 ingredients, placing them in a shallow baking dish.
2. Pierce the steak with a fork and dash on the tenderizer following the package instructions.
3. Allow steak to marinate for 1 hour at room temperature; then 6 to 8 hours or more, refrigerated.

FREEZING HINT: Or, freeze in marinade, sealing and labeling. Thaw overnight in the refrigerator before proceeding with recipe. Leftover prepared steak freezes well too.

4. Melt the butter in skillet, using low heat setting. Drain the meat from the marinade and quickly pan-fry, slightly browning the sides, using medium heat.
5. Add the marinade to the meat and let simmer on low heat, covered. Spoon sauce over the top every few minutes. The longer the steak sits in the sauce, the better it is. So if the guests arrive late or if for any reason dinner has to wait, this dish is great for that!

MAXIMUM RECOMMENDED FREEZER STORAGE: 6 months

SUKIYAKI

Though this recipe is best fresh, the meat is much easier to slice if frozen almost solid. I like to freeze a nice sirloin or thick top round—say about 4 to 6 pounds—then go on a slicing binge. Having frozen, thinly sliced beef on hand makes sukiyaki a really fun participation party dish. I've often assigned each of my guests or family a vegetable to prepare Japanese style, start to finish. When the cooking begins they are responsible for adding their "charges" and it makes the whole preparation a fun event, especially if you request they they use chopsticks for adding, stirring, removing, and eating.

Temperature: medium
Cooking time: 30 minutes
Yield: 4 to 6 servings

2 pounds beef round steak, sliced thinly
2 onions, sliced thinly
1 cup celery, cut in diagonal strips
2 cups sliced fresh mushrooms (or drained canned)
1 pound fresh spinach (can substitute 1 10-ounce package of frozen spinach

or 1 pound Romaine lettuce cut in 1-inch strips)
6 scallions, chopped
2 cups canned bean sprouts, drained
½ cup beef bouillon
¼ cup soy sauce
1 teaspoon sugar
Freshly ground black pepper
Steamed rice

1. Heat large skillet with beef trimmings. Render out fat and discard solid part remaining. If preferred, substitute about one tablespoon of oil.

2. Meanwhile slice partially frozen meat paper thin or use thawed frozen sliced meat and chop or slice vegetables. When fat is rendered out, add onions and cook for 5 minutes.

3. *Add celery, mushrooms, spinach, scallions, and bean sprouts and cook over high heat for 5 minutes, stirring frequently.

4. Push vegetables to one side of pan, add beef, and fry for 3 minutes.

5. Stir beef and vegetables together. Add bouillon, soy sauce, sugar, and lots of black pepper and cook for about 5 more minutes, stirring frequently. Serve with rice.

NOTE: *For a more traditional Sukiyaki, add each ingredient separately and leave it in its own spot in the pan, stirring each in place. Do not stir the ingredients together.

I DON'T RECOMMEND FREEZING SUKIYAKI, ONCE MADE.

MAXIMUM RECOMMENDED FREEZER STORAGE: 12 months for the beef

HULA STEAK

Created to win an outdoor barbecue cooking contest, this recipe has always been a winner with all my guests or family. I always make it as the featured attraction of a Polynesian menu. It's great for steak that may have stayed too long in the freezer too. Hawaiian hors d'oeuvres such as bacon-wrapped, soy-soaked water chestnuts that have been swirled in sugar and secured with a toothpick (rumaki), banana or coconut chips, macadamia nuts, or any other of an endless variety of nibbles and Hawaiian drinks such as scorpions or mai tais are great beginnings for the meal. Serve an embellished rice dish and oriental-style sliced and seasoned vegetables. For drama, garnish the hula steak with a lei of any blooming plant such as petunias, roses, or any other colorful, not too strong-smelling flower.

Temperature: broil or high
Yield: 4 servings

3–4 *fingers finely chopped fresh ginger root or 1 teaspoon ground ginger*
2 *cloves fresh garlic or ½ teaspoon garlic powder*
2 *cups soy sauce*
¼ *cup brown sugar*

¼ *cup brandy (or bourbon)*
4 *pounds 1-inch steak—fresh or thawed frozen—round, sirloin, or lean boneless steak*
Additional ground ginger, if desired

1. Mix together all ingredients for marinade in a shallow dish just large enough to hold the meat.
2. Place meat in marinade for 1 hour, turning frequently.

FREEZING HINTS: Freeze in a rigid carton, if fresh meat was used. Thaw about ½ day in the refrigerator before cooking. Leftover marinade can be frozen.

3. To cook, preheat barbecue and brush grill with a piece of meat fat. Or preheat broiler.
4. Before cooking steak, rub a thin layer of ground ginger on both sides for a more pungent, spicy steak. Broil to desired doneness.
5. Remove steak to heated platter and garnish, if desired, with a ring of flowers or squares of fresh green pepper and pineapple.

MAXIMUM RECOMMENDED FREEZER STORAGE: 4 months

SAUERBRATEN

An authentic German pot roast with a richly flavored gingersnap sauce! It's one of those creations that keeps on improving with reheating—just getting more tender and flavorful each time.

Temperature: simmer
Cooking time: 3½ hours
Yield: 8 servings

1 large 3-pound frozen or fresh beef roast (can be arm, chuck, or bottom of the round)
1 tablespoon salt
Freshly ground black pepper
2 onions, chopped
1 carrot, chopped
1 celery stalk, chopped
2 bay leaves
6 peppercorns

6 cloves
½ pint wine vinegar
2 pints water
1 tablespoon butter
2 tablespoons bacon drippings
4 tablespoons butter
4 tablespoons flour
2 tablespoons sugar
12 gingersnaps, crushed (use electric blender for crushing)

1. Place the meat in a large casserole or stainless steel pan. Sprinkle with salt and pepper

2. Add the chopped vegetables, bay leaves, peppercorns, cloves, vinegar, and water. If liquid does not cover the meat, add more water and vinegar, keeping the same proportion.

3. Marinate roast 4 days in refrigerator.

FREEZING HINTS: The meat, if fresh, can be frozen in the marinade (after 4-day marination), if desired, and kept for 4 to 6 months in a sealed carton. Label. Leftover cooked sauerbraten can also be frozen.

4. Drain the meat and reserve the liquid.

5. Using a heavy-weight large pan, brown the roast in a mixture of 1 tablespoon butter and 2 tablespoons bacon drippings.

6. When well browned, cover with the reserved marinade and simmer over low heat for about 3 hours.

7. In a small skillet melt 4 tablespoons of butter, add flour, and stir to a smooth paste. Stir in the sugar and cook until dark brown, stirring to prevent scorching.

8. Add above mixture to the meat sauce, cover, and simmer ½ hour longer. Place meat on a heated platter. Add crushed gingersnaps to sauce,

simmer a few minutes, then pour the sauce over the meat. Garnish with sour cream, if desired. Serve with potato pancakes.

MAXIMUM RECOMMENDED FREEZER STORAGE: 4 to 6 months

BEEF BOURGUIGNON
(Beef in Red Wine, Stewed)

Don't let the length of this recipe scare you! This heady beef stew is somehow worth the effort. I like to use this recipe for leftover cubed beef. I simply save extra tads (in small plastic bags) from each time we have beef fondue and when I have enough, I make this bourguignon. Of course, you can make it from any lean frozen or fresh beef.

Temperature: 350° F
Cooking time: 3 to 4 hours
Yield: 6 to 8 servings

¼ cup or ½ stick butter
20 small white onions
1 teaspoon salt or to taste
3 tablespoons butter
1 pound fresh small or quartered large mushrooms or 1 #303 can button mushrooms
3 pounds lean beef from a good cut—can be arm or rump
1 tablespoon parsley
1 bay leaf
1 carrot, very finely chopped
4 finely chopped shallots or

1 green onion, finely chopped
¼ cup flour
1 cup beef stock or consommé
2½ cups Burgundy or other good dry red wine
1 tablespoon tomato paste
4 garlic cloves, minced
1½ teaspoons thyme, crushed—double the amount fresh if available
Freshly ground black pepper
Minced fresh parsley

1. Heat the butter in a large, heavy skillet while rinsing and peeling the onions. Brown onions until uniformly browned, seasoning with salt and stirring frequently. Place on a pie plate in 350° F oven for about 30 minutes.

2. Add the additional 3 tablespoons butter to the same skillet and set aside while preparing the mushrooms, cleaning and trimming them and quartering large ones. Heat the butter over medium heat and sauté the mushrooms until lightly golden, seasoning with salt and a few grinds of black pepper. Remove mushrooms and set aside.

63

3. Pour remaining butter into a cup, leaving just a thin film in the skillet. Brown the beef, a few cubes at a time, browning evenly on all sides. Place browned beef cubes in a heavy baking casserole, 4- to 6-quart capacity. Continue browning beef cubes until all are done, adding more butter as needed.

4. Add the tablespoon of parsley and the bay leaf, pushing into beef cubes. Cook the carrots and shallots lightly in the remaining butter. Add the flour and stir constantly over medium heat until the flour and vegetables become lightly browned. Pour in the beef stock and deglaze the pan, stirring constantly until thick and smooth.

5. Stir in the wine, tomato paste, garlic, thyme, several grinds of black pepper, and about 1 teaspoon salt. When well blended, pour over beef. Sauce should almost cover beef—if not, add more stock and wine using one part stock to two parts wine. Stir to moisten beef uniformly.

6. Bring mixture to a bubble on high heat on surface of range. Place in oven covered. Cook for 2 to 3 hours or until beef is very tender when forked.

7. Add onions and mushrooms and any drippings in the pan or bowl they've been waiting in and return to oven for about 15 minutes. Serve at this point, or chill for serving in a day or two, or freeze.

FREEZING HINTS: Cool, then freeze in casserole if it can be spared, or place in large rigid container or bowl; seal and label.

8. To serve, thaw overnight or for a day in refrigerator and heat until bubbly, about 30 minutes in a 350° F oven. Serve right from the casserole, garnishing each serving with minced parsley.

MAXIMUM RECOMMENDED FREEZER STORAGE: 3 months

CARBONADES WITH DUMPLINGS

A special stew-like casserole that is tremendous for early fall days, after a football game or leaf raking or other rigorous outdoor activity. It's a splendid follow-up for a beer keg party too. (It uses up stale beer very well.) There are several tricks to assure marvelous flavor which I've tucked into the directions. A critical one is to crisply brown the outside of the beef cubes, a few at a time, to create a rich brown sauce. You can either freeze a whole casserole ahead or prepare it a day or several hours before and leave it simmering while you're out. This great stew originated in Belgium.

Temperature: 325° F
Cooking time: 3 hours or more
Yield: 6 to 8 servings

½ cup or more cooking oil
½ cup flour
4 pounds lean roasting beef such as round, arm, or rump cut into 1-inch cubes
6 large onions, thickly sliced
1 teaspoon garlic chips
¼ cup dark brown sugar or molasses
½ cup dry red wine

⅓ cup chopped fresh parsley
1 tablespoon fresh thyme, chopped, or 2 teaspoons dried leaves, crushed
1 tablespoon salt or to taste
Freshly ground black pepper
1 pint beef stock (fresh, canned, or beef bouillon)
1 quart beer or 2 12-ounce bottles or cans plus water

1. Heat oil in large heavy frying pan and brown floured beef cubes a few at a time until each is well browned. A medium-high heat works best. Add more oil if necessary.

2. As cubes are browned, place in bottom of 6-quart or larger Dutch oven or other heavy casserole with a tight-fitting cover. Lightly brown onion slices.

3. Preheat oven to 325° F. Add onion slices to top of casserole. Add garlic, sugar, half of wine, herbs and seasonings.

4. Pour off excess oil, then deglaze frying pan with the beef stock and add to beef-onion mixture. Stir casserole together lightly and skim off extra oil.

5. Add beer and cover casserole. Bake until meat is tender—at least 2 hours. Add remaining half of wine and cool, if planning to freeze.

FREEZING HINTS: Package in rigid cartons or a very large bowl. Thaw stew, if frozen, overnight or for a day in the refrigerator.

6. To serve, bring carbonades to a simmer while preparing dumpling dough. Taste and adjust seasoning if necessary. Do not freeze with dumplings. If you wish to freeze leftovers, freeze the dumplings separately from the carbonades.

MAXIMUM RECOMMENDED FREEZER STORAGE: 3 months

DUMPLINGS

1½ cups flour
2 teaspoons baking powder
½ teaspoon salt
1 teaspoon dried, minced chives

1 tablespoon parsley flakes
2 tablespoons soft butter or margarine
½ cup milk or enough to make soft dough

1. Mix all ingredients together, being certain butter is well distributed.

2. When stew is at a bubble—but only simmering, never boiling—add

dumpling dough by first rinsing a metal tablespoon in hot stew, then dipping out a spoonful of batter and holding batter-filled spoon in stew just long enough to release dumpling. Repeat until all batter is used. Make certain stew is barely bubbling.

3. Cover tightly and cook for 15 minutes without peeking. Test to see if done by pricking with a tester or fork. If no dough clings to tester—serve it up!

Serve with cold beer, a simple vegetable, and light salad. The cooking pot is the best serving container for the stew as it will maintain heat best—critical for fluffy dumplings.

PORK CHOPS MARTINI

A great way with vermouth!

Cooking time: 1 hour
Yield: 4 servings

8 double-thick pork chops	1½ teaspoons dill weed
Salt and pepper to taste	1 teaspoon cornstarch mixed
1 tablespoon shortening	with ¼ cup water
1 cup dry vermouth	

1. Rub salt and pepper into both sides of the chops and brown in the shortening in a heavy skillet.

2. Reduce heat, add the vermouth and dill weed, and simmer for 1 hour.

3. To serve, remove the chops from heat. Add the cornstarch water and boil up for 2 or 3 minutes. Glaze the chops and serve.

FREEZING HINTS: Freeze with juice in well-sealed carton and label.

MAXIMUM RECOMMENDED FREEZER STORAGE: 3 months

SWEET AND SOUR PORK

My all-time favorite way to prepare Sweet and Sour . . . so special with this crunchy crust.

Cooking time: 1 hour
Yield: 3 or 4 servings

1 pound of pork (lean), cut	½ cup flour
into 1-inch cubes	2 eggs, slightly beaten

½ teaspoon salt	1 clove garlic, chopped fine
Oil for frying	1 cup water
1 cup pineapple chunks	2 tablespoons vinegar
6 small sweet pickles, sliced	1½ tablespoons sugar
1 green pepper, cut into	1 tablespoon Chinese
1-inch squares	molasses
3 small carrots, sliced	1 tablespoon cornstarch

1. Mix flour, eggs, and salt to make a batter.

2. Dip the cubed pork into batter. Fry in deep hot oil for 10 minutes. Remove and drain on absorbent paper. If freezing, freeze at this point in well-sealed freezer carton. Label.

3. To serve, put freshly cooked or thawed pork cubes into frying pan, add pineapple, sweet pickles, green pepper, carrots, garlic, and ½ cup of water. Cook covered for 10 minutes.

4. Combine the vinegar, sugar, molasses, cornstarch, and ½ cup water and blend thoroughly.

5. Mix well with the meat and cook for another 5 minutes.

FREEZING HINTS: Freeze sauce and fried pork in separate rigid cartons.

MAXIMUM RECOMMENDED FREEZER STORAGE: 3 months

TAMALES

Tamales are tantalizing when you make them yourself! In just one long session you can make a year's supply and store them in your freezer. On tamale-doing day, invite at least one, preferably two helpers to really lighten your work and add to the fun. I always like to prepare the filling the night before. By the way, the filling and/or masa mixture freezes well individually if you run short of one ingredient or just run out of time or "steam" while making them.

Cooking time: 45 minutes or 20
minutes at 15 pounds pressure
Yield: 5 to 6 dozen

CHILE CON CARNE FILLING

1½ pounds round steak or lean	cup ground red chile
stewing beef, pork, or	1 teaspoon salt
chicken	Pinch of oregano
2 tablespoons bacon	1 clove garlic, minced
drippings	1 to 2 cups meat stock—to be
1 tablespoon flour	added little by little as
1 cup red chile sauce or ½	needed to make a thick filling

1. Simmer meat in water to cover, using medium to low heat. Cook until tender.

2. Cut meat into very tiny cubes or chop using low speed of the electric blender. Heat the fat in a large skillet and add the meat and brown.

3. Add the flour and, stirring constantly, lightly brown the flour. Remove the pan from the heat; when slightly cooled, add the chile sauce or powder; stir.

4. Season with salt, oregano, and garlic. Add a scant cup of meat stock if using the chile sauce, more if using the powder, and continue adding more as the mixture simmers, stirring constantly. Cook for at least 30 minutes to blend the flavors. The sauce should be very thick and smooth.

NOTE: To prepare the sauce for topping the tamales when serving, use coarser chopped meat and thin the sauce more. The tamales are best served with this sauce and to save time a double recipe of the above can be prepared. After stuffing the tamales the remaining half of the filling can be thinned for use as a sauce.

MAXIMUM RECOMMENDED FREEZER STORAGE: 1 year

TAMALE MASA

6 cups masa	2 teaspoons salt
3½ cups water, approximately	5 to 6 dozen rinsed and
2 cups lard	trimmed corn husks

1. Add warm water to the masa; allow to stand. Beat the lard, using an electric mixer at medium speed, until it is quite fluffy and creamy. Add the salt. Then combine the lard with the masa, mixing well.

2. Meanwhile, soak the corn husks in warm water until soft.

3. Spread each husk with about two tablespoons of the masa mixture, then add filling down the center of the masa. (If desired, more masa may be added to the top of the filling.) Then fold over one side of the husk and tie both ends with strips of corn husk or just leave them folded. If you plan to freeze the tamales, freeze them at this point, steaming them just before serving for best flavor.

FREEZING HINTS: Package tamales in plastic bags of a dozen each or any suitable quantity. If packaging large quantities, keep track of the remaining inventory on a card. Package chile mixture or masa in rigid cartons, seal, and label.

4. Otherwise, steam tamales by placing them in a pressure cooker, deep-fat cooker, or a large kettle, standing them upright. Steam them for 45 minutes or under pressure for 20 minutes at 15 pounds pressure. For frozen ones, increase the cooking time by one-half. Serve as indicated.

MAXIMUM RECOMMENDED FREEZER STORAGE: 1 year

SHASHLIK SHISH KABOB

My own shish kabob marinade is based on samplings from many fine chefs. For the best control of doneness, do not alternate meat and the various vegetables. Instead, thread skewers each with the same kind of food— do not mix meats and vegetables since they require different amounts of cooking time. For example, onion, eggplant, and green pepper require longer cooking than the meat and other vegetables. Onions take the longest, whereas tomatoes burst quickly. Mushrooms are best sautéed to a golden turn in butter. The platter can be very attractively arranged with the meat skewers in the center surrounded by the vegetables. Push the pieces of meat close together for rare meat and do not cook long on each side. For well done, separate the meat cubes and leave longer on each side before rotating. For a traditional Syrian meal, serve a pilaf, warmed pita bread halved or quartered, and a salad made of cucumbers marinated in tarragon, vinegar, and sour cream and topped with dill weed.

Temperature: broil or high heat
Cooking time: 3 to 4 minutes a side for rare, 5 to 6 minutes for medium, 7 to 8 minutes for well done
Yield: several servings, from 6 to 16, depending on whether it's a main course or appetizer

4 pounds lean lamb, cut from leg into 2-inch squares
2 cups Burgundy wine
½ cup minced onion (green onion is fine)
2 bay leaves
1 tablespoon Worcestershire sauce
2 crushed garlic cloves or ¼ teaspoon powdered garlic
2 to 4 tablespoons soy sauce, depending on saltiness preferred
6 tablespoons olive oil (part melted butter is fine)
½ teaspoon dry mustard
½ teaspoon rosemary
½ teaspoon thyme
½ teaspoon basil
½ teaspoon tarragon
½ teaspoon marjoram
Vegetables such as:
6 tomatoes cut in wedges or 1 pint cherry tomatoes
2 large green bell peppers, cut in wedges
12 small onions
1 pint fresh mushrooms
1 medium eggplant, unpeeled, or 2 medium zucchini, unpeeled and chunked
Butter

1. It is easiest to have a butcher cut up the meat—but do find a good butcher and tell him specifically that it is for shish kabob. Have the butch

69

er save the bones and you can boil them in water to make stock for soups and stews, or even use it as a broth for making Bull Shots.

2. Combine all the marinade ingredients from the Burgundy through the marjoram. Mix well and place all the meat chunks to soak. Cover and refrigerate for 24 to 72 hours, or freeze, if meat is fresh, in marinade after 2-hour countertop soak.

FREEZING HINT: Freeze in sealed carton. Label. Leftover marinade can also be frozen.

3. Cook each vegetable separately on its own skewer and brush with oil a few times. Tomatoes can be served raw in wedges, encircling the serving platter. Parboil the onions for 3 to 5 minutes. (Easiest way is to put the whole onion into boiling salted water and trim off both ends. Pop each onion out of its skin easily.) Or use canned onions, freshened by draining liquid and allowing to set 5 minutes in cold water.

4. Fry the mushrooms in a bit of butter only until they turn barely brown if planning to skewer. (As mentioned, I prefer to cook them in a skillet until done.) If preferred, thread the onions, pepper wedges, and mushrooms in any order you like alternating vegetables with meat, or thread each separately. Broil to preferred doneness. Serve shish kabob on small individual skewers on tomato-garnished platter. Flame, if desired, using at least a 50% alcohol that has been warmed. Pour the warm liquor over the meat and ignite. Or, if desired, a large ball of cotton in the center of platter can be doused in alcohol and ignited—this method is preferred by some because it keeps flame and liquor flavor in one place. The most important fact to remember when flaming is to have a hot plate or platter, hot food and warm liquor that has not boiled.

MAXIMUM RECOMMENDED FREEZER STORAGE: 6 months

LAMB CHOPS À LA ROQUEFORT

A surprising and savory way to prepare lamb. Shoulder chops or not-so-tender chops of any sort are very good prepared this way.

Temperature: 350° F
Cooking time: 1 to 1½ hours
Yield: 6 servings

6 *thick lamb chops*	½ *teaspoon black pepper*
6 *ounces Roquefort or Bleu cheese*	1½ *cups beef bouillon*
1 *medium-sized can whole potatoes*	1 *teaspoon salt*

1. Season chops and place in a shallow baking pan. Preheat oven to 350° F.

2. Crumble the cheese over the top of all the chops. Add the beef bouillon.

70

3. Bake in 350°F oven 1 to 1½ hours or until done, turning each chop about every half-hour.

4. Add drained potatoes and bake for about 10 minutes.

FREEZING HINTS: Can be prepared from fresh or frozen lamb and freezes well once prepared.

MAXIMUM RECOMMENDED FREEZER STORAGE: 3 to 4 months

PAELLA À LA VALENCIANA

Paella seems to be the national dish of Spain—recipes abound for varying combinations of saffron-seasoned rice, meat, seafood, and vegetable concoctions. Though this looks like one of those "more is better" recipes, I feel it has just the right blend to make for a very special Spanish experience.

Preparation time: 2½ hours
Yield: 6 to 8 servings

2 2- to 3-pound frying chickens, cut up
1 carrot, thinly sliced
1 small onion, sliced
2 sprigs fresh parsley
2 bay leaves
½ teaspoon salt
6 whole, black pepper berries
3 cups water
1 1½-pound fresh lobster, 2 frozen tails, or 1 6-ounce can
¼ cup olive oil
4 garlic cloves, minced
1 chorizo or Spanish sausage, thinly sliced
3 green peppers, sliced in rings
3 fresh red peppers cut in strips (or 1 4-ounce can pimiento)
¼ cup finely diced salt pork*
4 medium-sized onions, sliced and separated into rings
1½ cups raw, long grain rice,
   rinsed 3 times (use more, if desired)
2 teaspoons saffron, soaked in a little chicken stock
15 fresh mussels or clams in the shell, well scrubbed, or 1 11½-ounce can clams in shell
15 cooked and shelled medium-sized fresh or frozen shrimp
2 cups fresh or frozen peas
2 medium artichokes, trimmed and cut into eighths, or 1 package cooked frozen artichokes, quartered
6 medium-sized peeled tomatoes, cut into wedges
   Salt to taste
   Freshly ground black pepper
2 tablespoons coarsely chopped fresh parsley

NOTE: ★If desired, omit the salt pork and add 2½ teaspoons salt instead.

71

1. In a large covered pan such as a Dutch oven, stew the chicken giblets, carrot, 1 onion, 2 sprigs of parsley, 2 bay leaves, ½ teaspoon salt, 6 whole black pepper berries, and 3 cups water. Bring to a boil using high heat, then reduce heat to low and simmer covered for 45 minutes. Strain stock and reserve.

2. Meanwhile, cook lobster if serving (if freezing, delay cooking until serving day); if using a fresh one, cook by plunging it into hot boiling water until it becomes red (no more than 5 minutes). Remove meat from body and tail and cut in large chunks, but only crack the claws and reserve. Use same water to cook shrimp, reserving stock for later.

3. In a paella pan, wok, or large deep frying pan, heat the olive oil and garlic using medium heat. Brown the pieces of chicken rapidly and evenly. As pieces are browned, set aside and add more until all are well browned. Remove all pieces and set aside. Preheat oven to 350°F.

4. In same oil, add the chorizo, green pepper, fresh red pepper (if using canned, add it with the artichokes), salt pork, and 4 sliced onions. Cook and stir gently for about 5 minutes using medium heat.

5. Add the rinsed rice and saffron and stir gently to combine well. (Add more rice if desired.) Arranged chicken on top of rice. Measure stock, adding fish stock (from lobster, shrimp, etc.) or bouillon to measure 3 cups. Pour stock over rice mixture; cover. Bring to a boil using high surface heat, then place in a preheated oven.

6. Cook until rice is tender or about 1 hour. Stir mixture every 20 minutes while cooking.

FREEZING HINTS: If you wish to freeze, package in sealed, labeled carton at this point. Finish cooking the frozen paella by first thawing in refrigerator for a day. Then place paella in paella pan or wok and heat in a 350°F oven until hot—about 20 to 30 minutes.

7. Using a large bowl, combine the lobster meat and claws, mussels or clams, shrimp, peas, artichokes, and tomatoes. Add to rice mixture, being careful to stir very gently so as to not break up the chicken and vegetables. Add salt and pepper to taste.

8. To serve, arrange rice and vegetable mixture in the paella pan or a warm, large, shallow bowl. Insert the mussel or clam shells and lobster claws at random across the top of the rice. Arrange hot chicken around the edge. Sprinkle with parsley, and if canned pimiento is used, arrange it in strips on top. Serve warm on warm plates.

MAXIMUM RECOMMENDED FREEZER STORAGE: 6 months (leftovers may be frozen up to 3 months)

EGGS À LA TURK

An eating experience!

Temperature: 350° F
Cooking time: 20 to 30 minutes
Yield: 4 servings

1 ½ sticks butter
 ½ cup coarsely chopped
      chicken livers
 ½ cup finely chopped
      shallots (green onions)
 ¾ cup sliced mushrooms
 ¼ cup flour

 ¾ cup beef stock
 ½ teaspoon salt
 ½ teaspoon white pepper
 ½ cup red wine
 8 eggs
      Chopped parsley

1. Sauté chicken livers, shallots, and mushrooms in butter for about 5 minutes. Add flour, stirring constantly over low heat until flour is very brown.

2. Blend in stock, salt, pepper, and wine, and simmer 15–20 minutes. Freeze.

3. To serve, put 2 tablespoons of this sauce in each of 4 shirred egg dishes. Break 2 eggs into each dish and bake at 350°F until eggs are firm. Cover eggs in each dish with 2 more tablespoons of sauce, sprinkle with parsley, and serve.

MAXIMUM RECOMMENDED FREEZER STORAGE: 1 month

BEEFSTEAK AND KIDNEY PIE

This authentic recipe from the theater district of London has been a special favorite ever since I sampled it many years ago.

Temperature: 325°F
Baking time: 1 hour 45 minutes
Yield: 6 servings

1 ½ pounds cubed stewing beef
 6 ounces trimmed and
      soaked kidney, sliced
 ½ pound mushrooms, sliced
 1 cup chopped onion
 ¼ cup parsley, minced

 ½ bay leaf, crumbled
 1 teaspoon salt
 1 cup butter
 3 cups flour
 1 tablespoon baking powder
 ½ teaspoon salt

1. Place beef, kidneys, mushrooms, onion, parsley, bay leaf, and 1 teaspoon salt in greased baking dish. Add 2 cups water and set aside.

2. Prepare pastry by cutting butter into flour combined with baking powder and ½ teaspoon salt.

3. When well combined, add milk and mix lightly to form soft pastry dough.

4. Roll onto floured surface to about ⅛ inch thickness. Place on top of casserole, trim off excess, and prepare edging. Cut a pattern of holes in top creating any desired pattern.

5. If fresh meats were used, casserole can be frozen or baked immediately. If thawed meats were used, it must be baked before freezing. When baking, place in 325° F oven and bake for 1 hour 45 minutes. Add 1 hour if baking while frozen.

FREEZING HINTS: Freeze pie until solid before packaging.

MAXIMUM RECOMMENDED FREEZER STORAGE: 3 months

FRENCH COUNTRY SWEETBREADS

Sweetbreads are one of those dishes you love to discover—once you learn how delightful and delicately flavored they are they can easily become a habit. For French flair, create this dish at the table in a chafing dish.

Yield: 6 servings

3 pair sweetbreads, thawed
1 ½ cups beef or veal stock
¼ cup white or sherry wine
Pinch each of thyme and
cayenne

1 teaspoon salt
Bouquet garni composed of
1 sprig parsley, 1 bay leaf,
and several leaves of celery
8 peppercorns

1. Braise sweetbreads in rest of ingredients until tender, or about 35 minutes before dinnertime, using a tightly covered cooking pot. Drain and keep warm.

2. Set up tray with the following for dinner table chafing dish preparation (or proceed with the following in the kitchen, if desired):

⅓ cup sweet butter
¾ cup strained stock from
cooking sweetbreads
Lemon juice, salt, and

pepper to taste
2 tablespoons Dijon mustard
(or ordinary mustard)
Salt and pepper to taste

3. Melt butter in chafing dish. Add remaining ingredients and stir until well blended.

4. Add sliced sweetbreads, one whole sliced sweetbread at a time. If desired, coarsely grate black pepper onto each. Then, baste each with sauce. When thoroughly coated, remove each to a warm dinner plate garnished with asparagus tips and puree of fresh mushrooms.

FREEZING HINT: Best not to freeze after preparing.

MAXIMUM RECOMMENDED FREEZER STORAGE: 2 to 3 months for sweetbreads prior to preparation.

5
Wild Game

If you have a hunter in the family, game is one of the most precious frozen assets. Perhaps you'll want to share this chapter with him or her to get a coordinated "systems approach" to your game freezing. Game can be great or absolutely terrible depending on just how you go about caring for the carcasses as soon as the animal is shot. I'd like to share with you the know-how I've gleaned from the many hunters in my family and representatives of the fish and wildlife services.

If you like game and don't either hunt yourself or have a hunter among your family or friends, contact your local fish and wildlife service. You may just luck out as I have, though not often enough. In many states, you can request that your name be added to the list of recipients for penalty game—that shot either out of season or out of age or gender. The only regrettable but completely understandable policy they have is that when the game department "bags" an animal or fowl, the official gets to keep part of it. And their pick is usually the most choice—one of the hindquarters for example.

One of my especially fond memories is the young doe I got in New Mexico. It had been shot out of season and was fantastic—very tender and tasty! I got only one of the hindquarters. But I was truly fortunate, considering that the man who so carefully dressed it after illegally shooting it had only a cancelled check for his fine of $240.

To avoid any unpleasant experiences, check the game laws in your state to find the amount you can legally store and the maximum amount of time you can store it. The State Conservation Office or Provincial Government will be able to tell you the restrictions and may have additional game-preserving information.

The type of care given to game after killing will determine the quality of the meat. Flavor and keeping quality are highly dependent on good butchering and care between field and home. If animals are hunted great distances from home, explore having the animal butchered, packaged, and quick-frozen near the hunting site then shipped on dry ice. About 25 pounds of dry ice are needed to freeze 75 pounds of game for five days. (Be sure to handle the dry ice with gloved hands.)

The simplest way to ship packaged game is in styrofoam coolers. Lacking that, use heavy cardboard cartons—preferably ones made for meat shipping—and place on the bottom crumpled newspaper, then a layer of freezer paper (cut with ends long enough to fold over at the top), a layer of dry ice slices, another layer of freezer paper, and finally the game. Top with another series of freezer paper and dry ice layers. The ends of the freezer paper should be brought around to the top and folded together with the layer of dry ice in between. Another solution might be to use two boxes, one bigger than the other, placing an insulation layer of crumpled newspaper in between the two boxes. Add the layers of freezer paper and dry ice for extra protection.

I prefer to do my own butchering—with help of course! Only you know how you like the meat best and how extra-special care is needed for good flavor. No one else cares as much as you do. I carefully trim and rinse the meat, then package it in freezer-weight packaging. I like to remove as much of the bone as possible. I either scrape and save the scraps or take them to a butcher shop that makes ground meat, sausages, and salamis; I also stew the bones for stew and mincemeat. Package the meat in cuts the way you like them and in the portions you like. If you use a lot of steak, for example, package mostly steak cuts—or if you like roasts, then cut and package accordingly.

BIG GAME FIELD CARE

Proper care as soon after shooting as possible is extremely important. Don't delay! If you do, you are risking absolutely awful flavor, maybe even ruined meat, an unforgivable sin to me. As soon as the animal is shot, bleed it, then remove the entrails and cool the carcass. (Rapid removal of the entrails is critical as the shot can penetrate an intestine and cause spreading of bacteria.) Clean the blood from the cavity and trim off any parts damaged by gunshot. Cooling is necessary to keep damage from the shot from spreading in the muscles as muscles are the best eating.

Cleanliness is extremely important in order to keep the meat fresh tasting. Spoilage takes place fast when the shot is not immediately removed. If the weather is warm, sprinkle the cavity with pepper to keep the flies away. (By the way, this is how Indians make jerky. They sprinkle jerked strips of venison with pepper and hang them up to dry in the cool breeze.) Always hang the carcass in as cool and breezy a place as can be found. Sometimes it is desirable to spread the ribs apart with a stick to allow cold air to circulate.

Leave the hide intact, since it serves as a natural protection for the meat. In some states, where it's warm during hunting season, antelope must be skinned promptly to prevent spoilage.

Loosely wrap the meat when carrying it home to keep dust and other contaminants out. Carry game home in the coolest possible place—never in a hot trunk or on the hood of a car.

If the game is in good condition when you arrive home, you can age it for a total of five to six days from the killing in a cool dark place such as a cellar, basement, or commercial locker plant. If it's not in good condition, cut, trim, and package immediately, then quick-freeze.

SMALL GAME FIELD CARE

Rabbits, squirrels, and other small game should be dressed, cooled, and then skinned as soon as possible after killing. Wash very carefully, removing any shot. Either cut into serving pieces or leave whole, whichever way you will want the meat for serving. Wrap and package in freezer-weight material as soon as possible.

GAME BIRDS

Game birds should also be cared for immediately after shooting. First draw or bleed the birds, just as you would chickens. Chill them out in the open, if at all possible, rather than stuffing them into a hunting bag.

Pluck feathers from pheasants as you would from chicken. Pluck quail and ducks dry. To do this, melt about two pounds of paraffin and roll the birds in melted wax after first pulling out all large feathers. Let the wax stand until set, then peel off and the rest of the feathers should come off. Keep the birds cool, allowing chilling in the refrigerator for at least 24 hours before freezing. If the hunting is done a long way from home, the birds should ideally be cleaned, chilled, and frozen by a local locker plant for best flavor.

Remove all visible fat from geese as it becomes strong and easily rancid upon freezing. Always be sure to draw ducks quickly. They feed on strongly flavored water plants and the strong flavor seems tó set in more intensely if not immediately drawn.

Packaging

All forms of game are packaged basically in the same manner as their domestic counterparts. For venison, elk, antelope, or bear, follow the beef or lamb and veal instructions, being sure to package well in good-quality heavy freezer wrap and in family-sized servings. If at all possible, do the packaging yourself. Trim almost all the fat, as the fat is where the strong flavors lie and rancidity begins.

To Thaw or Not to Thaw

Thawing is also the same as for the domestic counterparts. Refrigerator thawing is best, right in the packaging, set on a plate. Or game can be cooked frozen, adding about one-third to one-half as much cooking time. If absolutely necessary, countertop thawing is feasible but never recommended because of the high incidence of contamination of game due to its precarious beginnings.

Refreezing

Wild game can be refrozen only if still very icy and firm. Use as soon as possible. Do not refreeze if completely thawed; discard instead. If still mostly icy, cook immediately; then use or refreeze and use as soon as possible.

RECIPES

What could be more fun than serving a hunter a fine dinner featuring his own game? That is, if you have discovered the excitement of well-prepared game dishes. If you should be so lucky, do prepare the game carefully. Perhaps one of the following recipes will please you.

Game dishes can be no better than the manner in which the game was treated after killing. As discussed above, field and freezer preparation care are vital to well-flavored game. Assuming that you have great-tasting game, here are a few tips:

Gamey flavors in venison, elk, etc., can be substantially reduced by first soaking the meat at room temperature in a solution of half vinegar and half water for 3 to 5 hours, then marinating it in any desired marinade.

Dilute the flavor of game, if it is too strong, with marinades and seasonings, but do not try to mask the flavor entirely by too long and strong soaking in such mixtures as vinegar water. You will end with very sour, vinegary meat—worse than the game flavor could ever have been.

Game flavor is strongest in the fat, so if a milder flavor is desired, trim off the fat and substitute a milder one such as beef suet.

Do not overcook—you will ruin the flavor and texture of the meat.

Venison is a lot like beef, only leaner and drier. Elk is considered by many to be the game meat most similar to beef in flavor, texture, and fat distribution and content. Both elk and venison can be prepared the same as any similar cut of beef. Antelope is leaner than either and needs basting with fat or larding.

Outdoor barbecue grilling complements the flavor of game. The secret to juicy, delicious steaks is to cut them thick and cook only to rare doneness or, at most, medium. If lean, lard the meat with beef fat and serve with a complementary butter such as rosemary butter, made by crushing rosemary (preferably fresh) with butter. Garlic and tarragon are both good too.

VENISON ROAST WITH WINE MARINADE

A rather basic way to roast and create a toothsome, tasty flavor.

Marinating time: 12 hours in
refrigerator
Temperature: 450° F to sear; 325° F
to roast
Roasting time: 45 minutes to 1
hour
Yield: 4 to 6 servings

1½ cups Burgundy	¼ teaspoon garlic powder
1½ teaspoons ginger	1 tablespoon minced onion
2 teaspoons salt	3–4 pound venison roast
½ teaspoon pepper	6 strips bacon

1. Combine first six ingredients; pour over roast. Cover and refrigerate overnight or longer, turning meat several times. If desired, you can allow meat to set in marinade in freezer carton for 2 hours on the counter, then seal, label, and freeze. Do not refreeze thawed meat.

2. Preheat oven to 450° F. Drain marinade from meat. Arrange strips of bacon across meat. Pour one half cup water in bottom of roasting pan.

3. Sear meat at 450°F in preheated oven for 15 minutes or until brown. Reduce heat to 325°F and roast till desired doneness is reached. Meat is more tender and juicy when cooked only to rare or medium stage. Allow about 12 minutes per pound or use a meat thermometer.

4. As meat roasts, baste with marinade. Allow to sit about 15 to 20 minutes before carving. Marinade can be simmered and served as a sauce.

FREEZING HINTS: Freeze leftover roast in the marinade in sealed, labeled carton.

MAXIMUM RECOMMENDED FREEZER STORAGE: 12 months

VENISON STEAK IN MIREPOIX

Venison with a bouquet—and beautiful too!

Temperature: medium or 325° F
Cooking time: 1 to 1½ hours
Yield: 4 to 6 servings

½ cup carrots	2 pounds venison round
½ cup celery	steak, cut ½ inch thick,
½ cup onion	thawed or frozen
3 tablespoons butter or	Salt
margarine	Pepper, freshly ground
¼ bay leaf	Garlic powder
2 cups beef broth	¼ cup flour

1. Dice carrots, celery, and onion very carefully into tiny, even squares of less than ¼ inch.

2. Melt 1 tablespoon butter using low heat in a saucepan and sauté the vegetables slowly until limp, then add bay leaf and beef broth and simmer this mirepoix gently for 5 minutes.

3. Trim excess fat from sides of meat, slash sides to prevent curling. Sprinkle the steak with salt, pepper, and garlic powder, and dredge the seasoned steak in flour.

4. Melt 2 tablespoons of butter in a heavy skillet using medium heat. Brown the steak on both sides. Add the mirepoix; cover skillet with tight-fitting lid and simmer over low heat until tender, usually 1 to 1½ hours. Allow at least ½ hour longer for cooking frozen steaks.

5. Serve in large pieces, with some of the vegetables and sauce spooned on top of each piece.

Variation: Substitute dry red wine for half the broth in the mirepoix and you'll have Venison Bourguignon.

NOTE: Mirepoix is a classic mixture of vegetables and liquid, used in French cooking as a flavor enhancer. Cut vegetables exactly as directed in step 1 as they form a built-in garnish.

FREEZING HINTS: Freeze leftover meat and sauce together in rigid cartons.

MAXIMUM RECOMMENDED FREEZER STORAGE: 8 months

VENISON BURGERS au BLEU

Bleu cheese makes a perfect filler for these scrumptiously flavored burgers. For a fantastic burger feast, especially on your patio, broil fresh tomato halves topped with Parmesan cheese after turning the patties the first time. When the tomatoes are done, top them with a tablespoon of butter and serve garnished with parsley. If desired, serve with a dish of wine-mushroom sauce. A pilaf of rice, wheat, or barley or eggplant patties and tossed green salad are nice with this.

Other uses for ground venison are: tacos, chile con carne, stroganoff, and spaghetti sauce.

Temperature: broil
Cooking time: 10 minutes
Yield: 2 to 4 servings

1 pound ground lean venison, thawed	1 tablespoon dry onion flakes
1 cup toasted croutons	1 teaspoon basil
1 teaspoon soy sauce	1 crushed bay leaf
½ teaspoon Worcestershire sauce	4 tablespoons dry red wine
	2 ounces Bleu cheese
½ teaspoon ground sage	4 strips bacon
1 clove garlic, minced	4 tablespoons butter

1. Combine the venison with the croutons, seasonings, and wine and mix well.

2. Divide into 8 portions and shape into flat patties.

3. On the top of 4 of the patties, place ½ ounce of Bleu cheese, crumbled, allowing about ¾ inch margin around the edge of the patty where there is no cheese. Top the 4 cheese-topped patties with the other four patties, pressing them firmly together.

4. Encircle each patty with a strip of bacon and secure with a toothpick. Broil about 5 minutes on each side to medium doneness. Top each with 1 tablespoon butter to serve.

FREEZING HINTS: Freeze any leftover patties individually packaged in foil or plastic bags. Seal and label.

MAXIMUM RECOMMENDED FREEZER STORAGE FOR GROUND VENISON: 3 months

VENISON KABOBS

Venison's singularly strong flavor makes this marinade a perfect complement for great shish kabob. Lamb and milder meats lend themselves to more complex seasoning mixtures. Try this one for venison—I think you'll like it.

Temperature: high (550° F) or broil
Cooking time: 12 minutes
Yield: 6 to 8 servings

2 pounds venison, cut in 1½-inch cubes (thawed)
Tiny whole onions or 2 medium onions, cut into wedges
12 cherry tomatoes or 2 medium tomatoes, cut into quarters
3 green peppers, quartered
12 mushrooms
2 zucchini, sliced ½ inch thick

MARINADE

½ cup olive oil
¼ cup red wine
¼ cup lemon juice
½ teaspoon salt
⅛ teaspoon pepper
⅛ teaspoon garlic powder
1 teaspoon soy sauce
½ teaspoon Worcestershire sauce

1. Combine marinade ingredients; mix until blended. Place venison cubes in mixture; marinate for 4 to 6 hours or overnight in the refrigerator, or for real frozen convenience, place marinade and meat in a freezer carton. Set on counter for 2 hours, then seal, label, and freeze. Do not refreeze if thawed.

2. Alternate meat and vegetables on skewers, or better yet, prepare separate kabobs of each (see page 69 for more information). Grill over high heat or broil approximately 12 minutes, turning frequently. Baste with marinade as kabobs cook.

For rare kabobs, push foods closely together on skewer; for medium or well-done, leave a little space between.

Grease skewer before threading meat and vegetables on it to make it easy to remove the food when the kabobs are done.

For extra flavor, run the skewers through a garlic clove before skewering foods.

FREEZING HINTS: Freeze remaining marinade; it can be used over and over. Before reusing, freshen with a little more wine and herbs. Leftover cooked kabobs can be frozen in foil or plastic bags. Seal and label.

MAXIMUM RECOMMENDED FREEZER STORAGE: 4 months in marinade, 6 months cooked

JUGGED HARE (or HASENPFEFFER)

This recipe is an old country favorite. Germans for generations have been noted for the amount of game they catch and the many traditional recipes they have innovated for game cookery. Here's one of my favorites. Don't let the length of the recipe scare you. For a real hunter's dinner, serve with potato pancakes or dumplings. Barley or bulgur pilaf is an excellent side dish.

Temperature: 350°F
Cooking time: 1½ to 2 hours
Yield: 6 servings

1 6-pound hare (thawed)	12 peppercorns
3¼ cups dry red wine	Salt
1 teaspoon thyme	½ cup bacon drippings or oil
12 pearl onions	⅓ cup flour
2 cloves garlic	1 cup sliced mushrooms
2 stalks celery	3 cups consommé or bouillon
2 carrots	18 small, whole mushroom caps
2 bay leaves	1 ¼ cups salt pork

1. Cut the hare into serving pieces and reserve its liver and blood, if available, to thicken sauce, freezing them if you are freezing the meat in marinade.

2. Combine two cups of wine and half of the thyme, onion, garlic, celery, and carrots, all chopped fine. Add bay leaves and peppercorns. Sprinkle with a little salt and add to the cut-up hare. Let marinate for 24 hours in refrigerator—or the meat can be frozen in the marinade if hare is fresh.

3. Drain hare and wipe dry. Heat the fat until nearly smoking; brown meat. Add remaining seasonings and vegetables, all finely chopped.

4. When all is well colored, add the remaining wine and sliced mushrooms. Reduce heat and add the consommé. Cover and bake in a 350°F oven until nearly tender, about one hour.

5. Transfer the meat to a serving casserole. Strain the sauce over it. Add the onions and mushroom caps and return to oven for 20 to 30 minutes.

6. Meanwhile, simmer the pork, drain, and sauté slices in a skillet until browned. Arrange slices around the dish. Finish cooking until the vegetables are done and the meat is very tender. Thicken the sauce with the minced liver and reserved blood or make a roux of butter and flour and gradually stir into the sauce. Serve, arranged in the casserole you cooked it in, with some sauce drizzled over hare. Serve rest of sauce on side—it's excellent over potato pancakes or pilaf.

FREEZING HINTS: Freeze leftover hare deboned in the sauce using rigid cartons, seal, and label.

MAXIMUM RECOMMENDED FREEZER STORAGE: 6 months

BRANDIED DUCK

Wild duck, if bled properly, makes nicely flavored entrees. It is best prepared with the benefit of a strong-flavored seasoning mix such as this recipe provides.

Temperature: high and simmer
Cooking time: 1 hour 12 minutes
Yield: 4 to 6 servings

1 6-pound duck (thawed)	1 clove garlic
Salt and pepper to taste	6 ounces cognac
2 large onions, chopped	1 pint claret
2 teaspoons chopped parsley	¼ cup olive oil
1 bay leaf	½ pound sliced mushrooms
Pinch of thyme	

1. Clean duck, cut into serving pieces, and sprinkle lightly with salt and pepper.
2. Place in an enamel or glass dish.
3. Add onions, parsley, bay leaf, thyme, garlic, cognac, and claret. Marinate for 4 hours at room temperature, or if fresh, freeze in marinade, after 4 hours' soaking. Seal and label.
4. Put oil in earthenware casserole; heat over high heat. Brown duck in oil for about 12 minutes.
5. Add liquid and sliced mushrooms. Cover; simmer over low heat for 1 hour or until duck is tender.

FREEZING HINTS: In addition to freezing fresh duck in marinade, cooked duck can be frozen in sealed cartons with the sauce. Seal and label.

MAXIMUM RECOMMENDED FREEZER STORAGE: 8 months

PHEASANT CRÈME DE BRANDY

Whenever I can lay my hands on a nice pheasant, such as from my father's Kansas farm, I prepare this fabulously festive bird. In fact, more than once I've served it instead of turkey for Thanksgiving. It's really a must to pop the wild rice for the platter garnish—it's so much fun and tasty too.

Temperature: 375° F
Cooking time: 1 hour
Yield: 6 servings

8 green onions, thinly sliced	*Freshly ground black*
¼ cup butter	*pepper*
3 pheasants (thawed)	*Pinch of thyme*
½ cup brandy	6 slices bacon
½ cups chicken bouillon	2 cups heavy cream
1 teaspoon salt	¼ cup horseradish

1. Preheat oven to 375° F. Sauté onions in butter in roasting pan 5 minutes, using medium-low heat. Add pheasants and sauté, using medium-high heat for 15 minutes or until brown on all sides.

2. Warm the brandy, using medium heat; pour over the pheasants quickly and flame the pheasants. When the flame dies, add bouillon, salt, pepper, and thyme.

3. Put bacon over pheasants' breasts and roast uncovered in a preheated oven at 375° F for 45 minutes, basting frequently.

4. Stir cream and horseradish into pan juices and roast 15 minutes more, basting frequently.

5. Serve pheasants on platter encircled with popped wild rice. Pop as for popcorn. Pour sauce into gravy boat and generously sauce pheasant as you serve it.

FREEZING HINTS: Freeze leftovers in rigid cartons. Separate the sauce from the meat.

MAXIMUM RECOMMENDED FREEZER STORAGE: 8 months

6
Fish and Shellfish

Fish and shellfish in your freezer—especially those caught yourself or bought at good prices—are a frozen asset of the highest order in my opinion. Freezing is really the best way to preserve fish and seafood. The flavor, when properly prepared and packaged, should be about the same as fresh cooked.

The key point when freezing fish and shellfish is not to overdo on quantity as most should be kept only about three to four months (some say even less) for optimum flavor. Lean fish will stay fresh tasting longer—up to six months—while crab and shrimp keep well up to almost a year. (For more specific recommended storage times, see the Appendix.)

Careful handling and packaging are musts. All forms of fish and shellfish are highly perishable and should be cleaned, shucked, and prepared for freezing as quickly as possible. If fish or shellfish must be kept for any reason before freezing, place on ice until ready to prepare. Package in the best air- and vapor-proof packaging materials available to insure maintaining highest quality.

I prefer very heavy freezer-weight packaging and sometimes guarantee freshness for extra-large fish by glazing. Sportsmen generally like to glaze their fish and then package them in plastic for "show-off" sessions (see section on fish packaging).

As with the other meats, you will want to have a general idea of how much space you wish to devote to fish and seafood before shopping. Now if there is a fisherman in the family, you will undoubtedly have less control and simply be pleased whenever the catch is good. Some of the tips in this chapter might be helpful to pass along to him or her for best quality and your own convenience. There's no reason the fish and seafood shouldn't be freezer ready when brought home.

BUYING FISH

The most important point is to buy the freshest fish you can get. Try to freeze within as short a time as possible, meaning you should buy what you have time to immediately care for and also what will fit in the freezer within the 3 pounds per cubic foot capacity guideline.

Determining a good buy will be very dependent on local conditions. If, for example, you live near the sea, you can be the lucky buyer of seasonal bargains and stock up on what you like.

Fresh fish should be icy cold with firm, elastic flesh that resists pressing. The eyes should look clear, the gills bright red, and the skin shiny with scales that adhere closely. Odor should not be strong.

BUYING SHELLFISH

Shellfish should also be the freshest possible—just recently harvested. Do not buy bargain shellfish that is not extremely fresh—it's no bargain at all and can even make you sick! Shellfish should be icy when you buy it. If buying frozen, be certain it will stay frozen all the way to your freezer. Some markets sell thawed seafood and don't bother to tell you it has been frozen. Always check, especially if you are thinking about buying a lot for your freezer. Refreezing seafood is just too risky and the flavor and texture are greatly impaired. It should always be cooked before refreezing.

PACKAGING FISH

Prepare the fish as for table use. Scrape off scales, using a fish scaler or the back of a heavy knife. Using a very sharp knife or lobster or kitchen shears, make a slit down the body cavity, removing the entrails. Scrape the backbone clean. Remove the gills, fins, and head and trim the tail or remove it if it is large. Wash the fish thoroughly inside and out and pat dry.

Fatty fish such as trout, pink salmon, tuna, or mackerel will keep fresh longer if treated briefly in an ascorbic acid mixture. To do this, prepare a solution of 2 tablespoons ascorbic acid to 1 quart cold water and dip each fish or fish part into it for 20 seconds. Drain and package.

Lean fish such as sole, bass, pompano, and flounder will keep better if dipped in a brine made of ½ cup salt to 1 quart cold water for 20 seconds. Drain and package.

Small fish are best frozen whole, placed in heavy freezer wrap, and packaged with either the druggist's or butcher's wrap. Or place family-sized quantities in rigid containers, adding water to cover. I often place a heavy plastic bag in a large carton such as a milk carton. I fill it with water, then tightly twist bag closed and double over and secure to make a gooseneck twist. Freezing in ice keeps the small fish fresh longer. Label.

Medium-sized fish to be served pan-fried or broiled should be prepared by removing the head, tail, and fins and packaged either in family-sized quantities or individually wrapped. Package in heavy-weight freezer paper, sealing tightly, using either the butcher's or druggist's wrap. Label.

Large fish can be cut into steaks or fillets depending on your family's preference and the way you wish to serve the fish. Here's a handy guide to fish butchering. Package as above in meal-sized quantities and label.

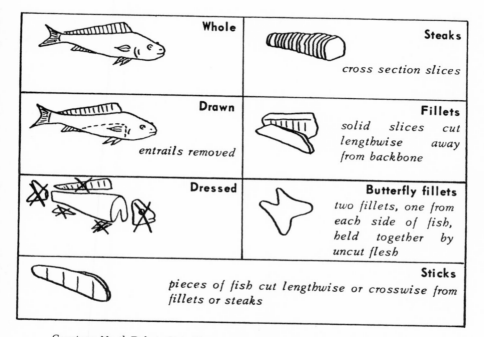

Whole	**Steaks**
	cross section slices
Drawn *entrails removed*	**Fillets** *solid slices cut lengthwise away from backbone*
Dressed	**Butterfly fillets** *two fillets, one from each side of fish, held together by uncut flesh*
Sticks *pieces of fish cut lengthwise or crosswise from fillets or steaks*	

Courtesy, North Dakota State Extension Service, *Food Freezing Guide.*

As previously mentioned, glazing fish adds an extra ice coating for protecting large fish you wish to freeze whole.

To glaze, freeze the fish quickly, unwrapped, then dip quickly in ice-cold water. A film of ice will form over the fish. Repeat the dipping as many times as necessary to make a glaze at least ⅛ inch thick. Place back in freezer between dippings if necessary to set a good hard glaze. Package in moisture- and vapor-proof material or large plastic bag. Label and freeze. The disadvantage of glazing alone as protection for the fish is that it can chip or crack and allow freezer burn, which will impair the flavor and texture. Therefore, the fish should be overwrapped.

PACKAGING SHELLFISH

Shrimp will be most tender if packaged very fresh, uncooked. To prepare for packaging, remove the head and sand veins. If desired, remove the entire shell, or just the tail. Rinse very well and drain. Pack in freezer-weight plastic bags. (Cartons, jars, or cans may be used—however, trying to reuse them later, I have found the pervasive odor very difficult to remove). Label with shrimp size, quantity, intended use, and date.

If for some reason you wish to freeze cooked shrimp, cook in boiling water until barely tender—10 minutes or less depending on the size and quantity, so it pays to watch carefully and stop the cooking as soon as they become pink. Drain and chill, then package as for raw shrimp.

Crab and Lobster are best cooked for long storage as they are for table use, drained and shelled. Pack the dry meat in heavy-weight plastic bags or rigid containers. Raw, whole lobsters can be kept up to 2 months—no longer for good eating quality.

Clams, Oysters, and Scallops are best frozen uncooked. Clams and oysters should be shucked and, for freshest flavor, packed in their own liquid or in brine made from 1 cup salt to 1 quart of water. It is best to use the liquid, adding only enough brine to come to the tops of the clams or oysters in the container. Scallops are usually purchased freezer ready. Just pack in enough brine to barely cover them in a rigid container.

To Thaw or Not to Thaw

Except when cooking in a microwave oven, I prefer to partially refrigerator thaw fish and shellfish in the freezer wrap. Because of their high moisture content and perishability, partial refrigerator thawing assures the most flavor and best texture. Partial thawing is the best method because the fish is great tasting and flavorful, yet it cooks more uniformly than when cooked frozen. The average medium-sized package (up to 2 pounds) will refrigerator thaw in its original packaging in about 4 to 6 hours. Allow more time for larger quantities. Cooked shellfish is best slightly thawed in the refrigerator before using. Allow about 4 hours for most quantities.

Refreezing

Shellfish and fish can be frozen only if still very icy and firm. Use as soon as possible. Do not refreeze if completely thawed; discard instead. If still mostly icy, cook immediately; then use or refreeze and use as soon as possible.

RECIPES

CIOPPINO

Laced with wine, and heady with a bouquet of herbs and garlic, this Pacific Coast delight is often a first for my guests. I keep the menu simple so that this dramatic-looking stew really takes the star role it should have. A tart creamy dressing on crisp lettuce, lots of garlic bread, red wine, and a fruity dessert are ideal accompaniments.

Temperature: simmer
Cooking time: approximately 1½ hours
Yield: 4 servings

1	large onion, cut in wedges	⅓	cup chopped parsley
6-8	green onions, finely chopped	1½	teaspoons salt
1	green pepper, seeded and diced	1½	teaspoons sugar
2	teaspoons fresh garlic, crushed	1	large Dungeness crab, uncooked, or 1 pound frozen King crab legs
¼	cup olive oil	1	dozen medium-hard shell clams in shells, well scrubbed
1½	cups Burgundy wine	1	to 1½-pound lobster or lobster tails, cut in chunks with shell
1	1-pound can tomato puree		
2	cups water		
1	bay leaf		
1½	teaspoons oregano	12	mussels, optional
1	small unpeeled lemon, thinly sliced	18	large shrimp in shells
¾	teaspoon basil	1	pound halibut, cut into chunks

1. Sauté onion, green onions, green pepper, and garlic in olive oil for 5 minutes in large pot or electric skillet.

2. Add wine, tomato puree, water, bay leaf, oregano, lemon, basil, half of parsley, salt, and sugar. Simmer for 1 hour. Taste and adjust seasoning.

FREEZING HINT: If freezing, freeze at this point in rigid containers. To serve, thaw, heat, and proceed with recipe.

3. Clean and crack crab and place meat in sauce. Top with well-scrubbed clams, lobster, and de-bearded mussels (if using) in the shell.

4. Remove shells and sand veins from shrimp and add to mixture. Add chunks of halibut and spoon sauce over the top of seafood. Cover.

5. Simmer 20 to 30 minutes more or until clams and mussels open.

NOTE: A microwave oven is super for this, especially the last step. Just follow manufacturer's instructions for timing.

MAXIMUM RECOMMENDED FREEZER STORAGE: 3 months for sauce

OYSTERS ROCKEFELLER

Prepare bunches of these and freeze on a cookie sheet!

Temperature: broil
Yield: 6 dozen oysters

8 ounces finely chopped bacon	1 bunch parsley, chopped fine
6 cloves garlic, chopped	1 stalk celery
1 stick butter	¼ teaspoon cayenne pepper
1 bunch shallots (green onions), finely chopped	2 teaspoons salt
	1 cup oyster liquid
6 cups finely chopped frozen spinach with juice	4 ounces absinthe
	Bread crumbs
	6 dozen oysters with shells

1. Brown bacon; add garlic and nearly brown. Add butter and shallots and after cooking a few minutes, add spinach and all other ingredients except oysters.
2. Place ingredients in blender and process until creamy, adding bread or bread crumbs to thicken.
3. If freezing, place shucked oysters on a cookie sheet, top with sauce, and freeze until firm. Then package in layers in a rigid carton. Seal and label.
4. To serve, place oyster shells in pie pans half filled with rock salt. Arrange six oyster shells in each pie pan and place oysters and sauce on the shells. Broil 6 inches from heat until heated through and browned on top.

MAXIMUM RECOMMENDED FREEZER STORAGE: 4 months

HOT CRAB BITES

A hot seafood canapé practically everyone likes.

Temperature: broil
Cooking time: about 15 minutes
Yield: 16 snacks

4 thin slices white bread or 4 English muffins	1½ cups crab meat (shrimp or other seafood can be substituted)

1 tablespoon lime or lemon juice	1 teaspoon Worcestershire sauce
½ teaspoon grated lime or lemon rind	1 teaspoon prepared mustard
	Generous dash of Tabasco
2 teaspoons minced green onion	2 tablespoons melted butter or margarine
2 tablespoons minced fresh parsley	½ cup grated sharp Cheddar or Swiss cheese

1. Quarter bread slices or cut English muffin halves in half again. Broil until golden on both sides.

2. Combine the crab meat, lemon juice and rind, onion, parsley, Worcestershire sauce, mustard, and Tabasco, breaking up the crab meat with a fork as you mix the ingredients.

3. Place toast squares on a cookie sheet and brush each with melted butter. Top with the crab mixture and the Cheddar cheese. Broil until bubbly or freeze as directed.

FREEZING HINT: Freeze them right on the cookie sheet, sealing them in a package of foil, a carton, or other wrap after they are solidly frozen.

4. To serve, thaw, then broil until the cheese is hot and bubbly—about 5 minutes.

MAXIMUM RECOMMENDED FREEZER STORAGE: 3 months

SAVORY STUFFED FISH

Frozen fresh fish stuffed with this delightful pickle stuffing—or frozen already cooked—is a good repast for getting or staying skinny.

Temperature: 350°F
Baking time: 20 minutes
Yield: 6 servings

	2 tablespoons onion, finely chopped
1 tablespoon lemon juice	1 3-pound dressed whole fish (striped bass, trout, etc.)
½ teaspoon salt	
½ teaspoon savory	
½ teaspoon thyme	Salt and pepper
½ cup minced dill pickle	1 lemon, thinly sliced

1. In a bowl, mix lemon juice, ½ teaspoon salt, pepper, savory, and thyme.

2. Add pickle and onion; toss lightly.

3. Rinse cavity of fish, pat it dry, and rub with salt.

4. Pile stuffing into fish lightly. To close cavity, fasten with skewers and lace with cord.

FREEZING HINT: Freeze now if desired. Package in freezer wrap, seal, and label.

5. To serve, place fish in a baking dish. Sprinkle with salt and pepper. Top with lemon slices.
6. Bake at 350°F for 45 to 50 minutes or until fish flakes with a fork. If preferred, fish can be frozen now before serving.
7. Remove laces and skewers; place on platter and garnish with parsley and lemon wedges. Good served either hot or cold.

MAXIMUM RECOMMENDED FREEZER STORAGE: 3 months

RED SNAPPER STUFFED WITH SHRIMP
À LA NANTUA SAUCE

I've prepared this special fish creation many times since savoring it first in Hermosillo, Mexico, in a rustic little hotel. Because of the sauce and stuffing, frozen snapper seems as good as fresh to me.

Temperature: 350°F
Cooking time: 35 to 40 minutes
Yield: 4 to 6 servings

1 *3-4 pound fresh or frozen red snapper*	2 *stalks celery, chopped*
1½ *cups fresh shrimp*	1 *teaspoon tarragon*
1 *cup sliced mushrooms*	1 *teaspoon basil*
2 *tablespoons butter*	1 *teaspoon savory*
2 *green onions, finely chopped*	1 *teaspoon thyme*
	Salt and pepper
	Dry white wine

1. Rinse out red snapper and set aside. Shell shrimp and coarsely slice mushrooms.
2. Add shrimp and mushrooms to melted butter in a skillet. Add green onions, celery, and herbs. Season to taste with salt and pepper. Sauté.
3. Stuff mixture into cavity of red snapper and skewer closed. Place in large roaster with lid. Just before popping into preheated oven, drizzle with wine and cover. Baste frequently with wine in roaster as it bakes, about 30 minutes or until done.

FREEZING HINTS: You can freeze a fresh red snapper after it is stuffed if you flash-freeze it in the coldest part of the freezer. Place on a cookie sheet, freeze until firm, and package in good-quality freezer wrap. For convenience, use foil if planning to cook conventionally, plastic wrap if planning to cook in a microwave oven. Reserve wine drippings from pan and use in Nantua Sauce or freezer for making sauce later. If desired, you can make the Nantua Sauce and freeze ahead too, as it freezes well and would eliminate any last-minute fussing. To serve, thaw the frozen stuffed fish in the refrigerator overnight or for a day on large platter or in roaster. Bake until hot or for about 30 minutes in a 350°F oven if previously cooked. If uncooked, bake 40 minutes or until hot and fish flakes near the bone. Heat sauce if previously prepared or make as follows.

NANTUA SAUCE

Prepare Nantua Sauce in the same frying pan the stuffing was made in. Add 1 chopped green onion and 2 tablespoons butter to pan. As onion starts cooking, add ¼ cup flour to pan and let brown. Add enough hot water to make smooth gravy. Then add ½ can of cream of mushroom soup, a tablespoon of sherry, pinch of thyme, salt and pepper to taste, and 1 teaspoon beef stock base. When fish is done, add wine in pan to sauce; boil up and serve.

MAXIMUM RECOMMENDED FREEZER STORAGE: 3 months

TREMENDOUS TROUT

I developed this recipe in my New Mexico days when we had quantities of trout from the babbling streams and rocky lakes. Either fresh or frozen trout is great this way.

Temperature: broil
Cooking time: 10 to 15 minutes
Yield: 4 servings

4 trout, 10 to 12 inches long (thawed)	Salt and freshly ground black pepper
¼ cup melted butter	1 lemon, cut in thin rounds
2 teaspoons mixed herbs (or mixture of tarragon and basil)	3 green onions, finely chopped (including tops)

1. Heat barbecue or broiler while preparing trout.
2. Rinse trout, dry, and then brush cavities with melted butter. Sprinkle with salt, pepper, and herbs. Place lemon slices and chopped onion in cavities and secure with skewers.
3. Brush one side of the trout with butter; sprinkle with salt, pepper, and herbs. Grill seasoned side down. When brown, brush second side with butter, herbs, and salt; turn, and grill remaining side. Trout is done when golden and flesh is soft to the touch, or when a skewer inserted near

the spine reveals juicy, flaky flesh. Serve immediately garnished with wedges of lemon and sprigs of fresh parsley.

NOTE: Salmon can be substituted for trout. When preparing salmon, remove skin before serving and serve with a pitcher of smoked butter. Make smoked butter by adding a few drops of liquid smoke to melted butter.

FREEZING HINT: Though I can't imagine freezing the cooked trout, it would work well. Package individually in foil or plastic bags.

MAXIMUM RECOMMENDED FREEZER STORAGE: 3 to 6 months (shorter time for cooked trout)

HAWAIIAN SESAME SALMON

A special way to make frozen salmon more tasty and moist—a rather simple dish, but the fact that it's salmon makes it company fare.

Temperature: broil
Cooking time: 30 minutes
Yield: 4 servings

4 eggs	thawed or fresh
Salt	Sesame seeds
Pepper	1 small jar tiny sweet pickles
Monosodium glutamate,	and pickle liquid
optional	Melted butter
4 center-cut salmon steaks,	Lemon slices

1. Beat eggs lightly; add salt, pepper, and monosodium glutamate (not necessary, but does make salmon moister).
2. Dip thawed salmon steak into egg mixture and press into sesame seeds until completely covered.
3. Sprinkle steaks generously with liquid from pickles and arrange each on a sheet of foil. Fold loosely to cover.
4. Broil 15 minutes on each side or until salmon tests flaky.
5. Just before steaks are completely cooked, carefully fold foil back and let them brown.
6. Serve on a warm platter. Garnish with melted butter, lemon slices, and whole sweet pickles.

I would not recommend freezing this once it is made, unless in a crisis—and then freeze only a short time.

MAXIMUM RECOMMENDED FREEZER STORAGE: 2 months for uncooked

7
Eggs, Cheese, and Other Dairy Products

EGGS

Never hesitate to invest in bargain eggs as long as they are fresh. They really can bring the country to your kitchen while adding convenience and saving money.

Amazingly, shelled eggs freeze quite well. (If you really feel compulsive about trying a whole egg frozen in the shell, experiment with limited numbers—like one or two. I'm sure you will agree that the gummy yolk and tough rubbery white aren't much of a bargain. Do not freeze hard-cooked eggs either, as they become rubbery also.)

Shelled eggs can be frozen whole or separated into yolks and whites. (Before breaking the shells, clean them with lukewarm water if dirty.) Decide how you most often use eggs—or perhaps how you'd really like to use eggs. For example, do you hesitate to thicken sauces the French way with egg yolk because you hate to waste the whites, or do you yen to make a fresh "from scratch" angel food cake but hate to try to use up all the yolks? These specialties and more are easily arranged with a storehouse of frozen eggs, both yolks and whites ready for the thawing and using.

Always freeze eggs in the amount you will use at one time. It's too messy and risky to attempt chiseling some egg off a block of frozen eggs. Never refreeze; eggs spoil very easily.

Eggs have dependable equivalents:

> 1½ tablespoons yolk   = 1 egg yolk
> 2 tablespoons whites   = 1 egg white
> 3 tablespoons whole egg = 1 egg

Egg cubes are one of the handiest ways to freeze eggs—whole, yolks, or whites. Just use an ice cube tray and freeze egg until solid—about 2 hours. Each cube will equal approximately one whole egg, two egg whites, or two egg yolks. When frozen, place in a freezer container or plastic bag and

97

label. Keep a running inventory of the remaining balance on a card in the bag or on the label.

Package large amounts in jars or cartons, allowing ½ inch head space. Label with the intended use, the quantity, and the date.

Packaging Eggs

Freeze shelled whole eggs in cubes or in the quantities you will usually use. Stir with a fork to break up the yolk and blend the white and yolk together. Do not incorporate air. If using in scrambled eggs, omelets, soufflés, and the like, add one teaspoon salt for each cup and freeze in rigid containers or jars allowing ½ inch head space for expansion. If using for cakes, desserts, or anything sweet, combine one cup mixed egg with one tablespoon sugar and place in jar or carton. When freezing egg cubes, the sugar or salt still needs to be added in the above proportions. Always remember to label whether sugar or salt was added and the intended use. Adjust the recipe to compensate for the slight amount of sugar and salt in the eggs.

Freeze egg whites by simply stirring them together and packaging as desired in cubes or in the quantities most usable for favorite recipes for angel food cake, meringues, etc. A delightful benefit that never ceases to amaze me whenever I use frozen egg whites is that the thawed whites always seem to beat up more quickly and to higher heights, especially if allowed to come to room temperature before beating.

Freeze egg yolks by beating slightly with a fork and treating as for whole eggs. Yolks freeze least satisfactorily. For many uses such as thickening sauces, egg cubes are handiest.

Thawing Eggs

Since eggs are so perishable, always thaw in closed containers in the refrigerator for 6 to 8 hours and use immediately. To thaw the cubes, place in a small covered dish. When using, adjust the seasoning or sweetening to allow for the salt or sugar added. To speed up thawing, place container in bowl of cold water. Use immediately. Thawed whites can be saved for 2 to 3 days in the refrigerator—but it's best to use them immediately. *Do not refreeze!*

CHEESE

Almost every kind of cheese freezes. Some people say that the slight texture changes prevent their freezing it. I say nonsense! The flavor is not affected at all. You might note that the outside may be slightly mottled—this comes from moisture that froze on the outside of the cheese. Airtight packaging should prevent this. The color should actually become uniform when the cheese completely thaws. The cheese may be slightly more crumbly in the case of hard cheese. Veined cheeses are decidedly more crumbly. Soft cheeses may be too grainy for some uses, but are fine for dips, sauces, frostings, and as an ingredient.

Packaging Cheese

Freeze cheese in the unbroken package or carefully wrap it in good-quality freezer wrap, pressing the wrapping as close to the cheese as possible. This will force the air out and prevent drying through evaporation. The more airtight the packaging, the better quality the cheese will be when used. Foil, plastic wrap, or cartons are the packaging I usually select. Jars or small containers are good for grated cheese or for cottage cheese. Do allow at least ½ inch expansion space for cottage cheese. Be sure to clearly label, stating the type of cheese, the amount, and any special treatment such as grated or cubed. Perhaps label also with the intended use. Freeze as quickly as possible, placing the packages in a single layer near the walls until frozen; then stack after about 24 hours.

Authorities do not agree on the length of time cheese can be stored. The USDA states cheeses may be frozen satisfactorily for up to 6 months. The American Dairy Association (ADA) recommends maximum freezer storage of 2 months for cheese in its original package but only 6 weeks for rewrapped cheese. Pasteurized process cheese is recommended for up to 4 months' freezer storage. The ADA states that only Neufchâtel cheese cannot be frozen. I am personally more liberal with cheese freezing. I find that well-wrapped cheeses will keep *at least* 6 months and longer for cooking uses. For best flavor for serving plain, store only 6 to 8 weeks. See Appendix for recommended maximum freezer storage periods.

Freeze hard cheeses in chunks of about ½ pound or the size you normally use for either serving or cooking. Slice no thicker when 1 inch for greatest convenience and freeze no more than 1 pound in a package. You may prefer to thinly slice, cube, or grate for use in cooking or serving. The USDA recommends brick, Cheddar, Edam, Gouda, Muenster, Port du Salut, Swiss, provolone, and mozzarella as best for freezing. However, I think you'll agree—hard cheeses all freeze well.

Soft cheeses can be frozen in the packaging if no larger than the 8-ounce size. Be sure to overwrap for greatest keeping quality. Camembert is the only soft cheese recommended by the USDA for its freezing quality.

Cottage cheese made of pasteurized or skimmed milk freezes fine right in the cartons you buy it in unless they're filled brim full—in that case remove about ½ inch before freezing. The creamed varieties do not freeze as

99

well. You may wish to freeze in smaller quantities. The best system is to freeze only the amount you will use in a day. There may be some slight water separation, but I have never found this objectionable. Always add the cream, if you serve it that way, just before serving.

Cheese food products such as sauces, dips, processed cheese—flavored or plain—usually freeze fine. If in real doubt, freeze a small quantity and check after 24 hours by thawing it. If you're pleased with the results, freeze the rest! Otherwise do not freeze.

Thawing Cheese

For most attractive serving of blocks of cheese, thaw 24 hours in the refrigerator. Small chunks or cubes thaw overnight in the refrigerator.

Grated cheese needs no thawing. All but cottage cheese can be thawed on the counter, if time is short, or in cold water. Cottage cheese is more perishable and should be refrigerator thawed.

If you are the lucky owner of a microwave range, check the instruction book for the quickest way to thaw cheese. It's my favorite method since it takes only seconds. Cheese for serving should be allowed to warm at room temperature, once thawed, for about an hour for greatest flavor. Cheese may be refrozen.

BUTTER AND MARGARINE

Freezing these is apple-pie easy—just overwrap with good-quality freezer wrap and label. A plastic bag is convenient—then all you have to do is date the package because the contents are easily visible. Thaw in the refrigerator about 2 to 3 hours in the wrapping before using. Butter and margarine can be refrozen.

MILK AND CREAM

Unless you are oversupplied or you bought milk at a fantastic price, freezing it is not entirely satisfactory. Milk loses its homogenization. Skimmed milk of course will not undergo that change. The nutritive value stays the same, the milk just seems less smooth.

Cream for use in cooking is okay to freeze. Whipping cream won't whip very well. I prefer to whip it first and freeze in a container or in dollops on a cookie sheet and then package in layers with waxed paper in between in a rigid container. Thinner cream is not satisfactory for table use but can be used in cooking.

Package cream or milk in air- and vapor-proof containers. Allow 1 to 2 inches head space depending on the quantity or whether you use glass. For large quantities of a quart or over, or when freezing in glass, allow 2 inches or more. Always thaw in the refrigerator. Do not refreeze.

SOUR CREAM, YOGURT, AND BUTTERMILK

All of the cultured, soured dairy products lose their smooth texture when frozen. They become grainy and sometimes separate out their water. Still, they can be used for cooking. Package as for milk or cottage cheese, storing the quantities you will use in recipes. Thaw in the refrigerator. Do not refreeze.

ICE CREAM AND SHERBET

Most commercial packaging is fine for freezer storage since ice cream should not be kept long—about 2 to 3 months maximum. Once you have dipped some out, cover the dipped-out portion with freezer wrap such as saran to keep it fresh.

Homemade ice cream, if you should be so fortunate to have some left, can be frozen. But not all recipes freeze well. The best-freezing ones contain gelatin, junket rennet, and a high percentage of cream. Package in air- and vapor-proof packaging.

RECIPES

CHEESE STRAWS

Munchy goodies that can be made when the time is right are great to have stored for snacks. This is my very favorite cheese straw recipe.

Temperature: 350°F
Cooking time: 18 to 20 minutes
Yield: 8 dozen 3-inch straws

1 pound sharp cheese, grated
¼ pound butter
1 egg
1 tablespoon cold water*

1¾ cups sifted all-purpose flour
½ teaspoon salt
¼ teaspoon cayenne
½ teaspoon paprika

1. Cream cheese and butter until soft, using low speed of electric mixer.
2. Add egg and water; beat well, using medium-high mixer speed.
3. Sift dry ingredients together; add in three additions; beat well after each addition, using low speed to combine ingredients, higher speed to mix.
4. Chill dough for 10 minutes. Preheat oven to 350°F.
5. Pack dough into cookie gun using saw-toothed disc. Make in long strips on ungreased cookie sheet. Or roll out about ⅛ to ¼ inch thick and cut into 3-inch strips, ½ inch wide, and twist with your fingers.
6. Bake 18 to 20 minutes in 350°F oven. Cool, then crack into 3-inch pieces, if you made in long strips.

FREEZING HINTS: Store in rigid freezer carton with layers of waxed paper between the layers of cheese straws. Seal and label. To serve, place on a favorite board, tray, or in a basket. They thaw very quickly and are ready for almost immediate enjoyment.

*Sometimes more water is needed.

NOTE: If desired, the straws can be sprinkled with grated Parmesan cheese.

MAXIMUM RECOMMENDED FREEZER STORAGE: 8 months

GREEK CHEESE PASTRIES

Even in today's global society, few are familiar with these delicate melt-in-your-mouth Greek pastries. They seem to suffer absolutely no loss in freezing.

Temperature: 350°F
Baking time: approximately 40 minutes
Yield: about 4 dozen

1 *pound cottage cheese,*
  small curd
1 *pound crumbled feta*
  *cheese**
2 *eggs*

¼ *cup chopped parsley*
  Pinch of salt
  *Strudel or filo pastry***
2 *sticks or 1 cup melted*
  butter

*Muenster cheese can be substituted if a milder flavor is preferred. Feta cheese is available from many delicatessens, specialty, or Italian grocery stores.
**Strudel pastry is often found in the freezer counter of specialty grocery stores.

1. Preheat oven to 350°F. Beat cheese, eggs, parsley, and salt together until well blended. .

2. Cut strudel pastry into 3-inch-wide strips—I save time by melting the butter on the cookie sheets (½ stick on each of four sheets) that I use for baking. Using a double-layer full-length strip of dough, dip quickly or brush with melted butter on both sides. Then place a teaspoonful of filling at one end of the dough. Fold one corner end over to the opposite side creating a triangular end, then fold back to other side continuing to form a triangle; repeat until you reach the end of the strip of dough. This creates a triangle-shaped pastry. Set each folded pastry to the side of the pan. If you didn't melt butter in the pan, generously butter the pan before placing the pastries on it.

3. Continue until all are formed, filling one cookie sheet then moving on to the next. Pierce the top of each with a toothpick. Bake until golden and flaky. Be prepared to make many, because they literally melt in your mouth and are proven favorites.

FREEZING HINTS: Package in rigid freezer cartons, with layers of foil or waxed paper between, seal, and label. Serve warmed on the foil or on a cookie sheet. Warm in a 300°F oven for 30 minutes if frozen, 15 minutes if thawed, or a minute or so in the microwave oven.

MAXIMUM RECOMMENDED FREEZER STORAGE: 3 to 6 months (I have at times kept these for one year and didn't notice any harm)

SWISS CHEESE FONDUE

Although the commercial versions can be quite tasty, I still think this recipe I got several years ago in Lucerne, Switzerland, is the best for fondue. There are a few tricks to remember: If the fondue begins to curdle, blend it in the electric blender. The baking soda adds a nice fluffy consistency, but timing and quantity are critical. Add only a bare pinch just before serving. This recipe can be doubled or tripled.

Temperature: low
Cooking time: 15 minutes
Yield: 1 to 2 servings

1 clove garlic
6–7 ounces Gruyerè or
    Emmenthal cheese, grated
    (Swiss cheese can be
    substituted)
1 tablespoon butter
¾ cup dry white wine

2 tablespoons kirsch (or
    cognac)
1 teaspoon cornstarch
    Dash of nutmeg
    Salt and pepper, if desired
⅛ teaspoon baking soda

1. Rub an earthenware casserole or fry-pan with garlic clove.

2. Add grated cheese, butter, and white wine. Cook over moderate heat, stirring constantly, until the cheese forms a thick mass. If it curdles, process in electric blender—then return to pan.

3. As soon as mixture starts melting stir in the kirsch with the cornstarch dissolved in it. Stir until consistency is smooth. Season. Add soda just before serving.

FREEZING HINT: If freezing freeze now, before adding soda. Place in freezer carton. To serve, warm and add soda when bubbly.

4. Fondue is best served in a pottery fondue warming dish. Many people prefer to serve it in a chafing dish. Fondue is traditionally served with crusty French bread or hard rolls to be torn apart or cubed in advance and pierced on the end of long fondue picks. The bread is then dunked in the fondue.

MAXIMUM RECOMMENDED FREEZER STORAGE: 2 months

QUICHE . . . ALL WAYS

For special light brunches, lunches, or suppers, I've always favored quiche. A good quiche in the freezer can transform a so-so light meal into sumptuous elegance—a nice way to send off weekend guests or please friends you bump into after a show. Serendipitous entertaining has always been fun for me—and I'm relieved of any advance anxiety by my frozen provisions.

Temperature: preheat to 425°F if unfrozen—450° if frozen; reduce heat to 325°F if unfrozen—350°F if frozen
Cooking time: 15 minutes, 30 minutes if unfrozen—15 minutes, 50 minutes if frozen (or until knife comes out clean when inserted in center)
Yield: one 9-inch quiche

1 unbaked 9-inch pie shell
 Pinch each of dry mustard
 and paprika
6 slices bacon, halved
6 thin slices Swiss cheese,
 halved
4 eggs

1½ cups light cream (or
 evaporated milk)
1 tablespoon flour
 Pinch of freshly grated
 nutmeg
 Pinch of cayenne pepper
 Few grinds of black pepper

104

1. Prepare (or use commercially frozen) one unbaked 9-inch pie shell. Fit into a 9-inch pie tin or 1½-inch-deep flan ring. Crimp edges. Place a piece of aluminum foil, shiny side down, in the pastry shell to form a lining, and fill with dried beans or rice, making certain the beans are distributed against the sides of the shell. This will keep the shell from puffing and shrinking during baking.

2. Bake in preheated oven at 400°F for 15 minutes on the lowest rack position. Remove from the oven; remove aluminum foil and rice or beans. (Keep rice or beans; they can be reused for this purpose.) Brush shell with beaten egg yolk and return to oven for 2 minutes to set the yolk. This will provide a seal for the crust and prevent its soaking up the filling and becoming soggy. Cool the shell slightly before adding the filling. Turn oven to 425°F if making quiche immediately and not planning to freeze.

3. Fry bacon until crisp and drain well. Overlap slices of cheese and bacon to cover bottom of crust creating a wagon wheel effect.

4. Using an electric blender, mixer, or wire whisk, blend remaining ingredients well to create a smooth texture. Pour over bacon and cheese.

FREEZING HINT: Place pan on a cookie sheet, freeze until solid, and package airtight; label.

5. To bake, preheat oven to 450°F if frozen, and 425°F if not, then place pie on middle rack and bake 15 minutes. Reduce heat to 350°F if frozen, and 325°F if not, and bake for 50 minutes if frozen and 30 minutes if not. Do not overbake. Insert a knife in center of quiche to test. If it comes out clean, allow pie to set a few minutes, cut, and serve.

How to Make "All Ways": Add 1½ cups chicken, crab, clams, lobster, shrimp, ham, spinach, or asparagus instead of the bacon or in addition to it. Thinly sliced tomato or onion are great toppers. Sometimes I substitute for the bacon, sometimes for the cheese, and sometimes for both—but then it seems to lose its quiche character and becomes more of a plain old custard. Dry sherry or other compatible wines and herbs can also be added.

MAXIMUM RECOMMENDED FREEZER STORAGE: 2 months

MANICOTTI

You can freeze this Italian specialty any number of ways: the sauce and the skins separately, the skins filled, or the whole casserole prepared ready for heating and serving. It has a flavor similar to lasagne and is a nice change. If you already have your own favorite spaghetti sauce substitute it if you like!

Temperature: high
Cooking time: 10 minutes each
Yield: 8 to 10 servings

> *Commercially made*
> *manicotti skins, or:*
> 2 *cups flour*
> 3 *eggs, beaten*
> 1 *tablespoon melted butter*
> 1 *tablespoon salt*
>
> 1 *cup warm water*
> 2 *pounds ricotta or*
>   *small-curd cottage cheese*
> 2 *teaspoons salt*
> ½ *cup Parmesan, ground*
> 1 *egg, beaten*

1. To prepare skins, mix first five ingredients together, adding warm water a little at a time, stirring while adding it.

2. Add more flour if necessary to yield a nice soft dough, kneading until well blended. Roll into a ball.

3. Cut ball in half and roll out until very thin and uniform. Bring a large pot full of water to a rolling boil.

4. Cut dough in 4x6-inch rectangles. Drop skins in carefully, cooking several skins at a time, being sure to cook each about 10 minutes.

5. Remove skins with a strainer and set aside. If desired, the skins can be prepared one day and then filled and cooked later. If so, dust each skin lightly with flour and separate with waxed paper. Refrigerate or freeze, depending on how soon you wish to serve.

6. Prepare filling by mixing together the cheese, egg, and salt. Prepare the sauce (see below).

7. Place a heaping tablespoon of cheese mixture on each skin and roll each up. Place a small quantity of sauce on bottom of two large greased casserole dishes. Then place alternate layers of manicotti and sauce. Bake 30 minutes in a 350°F oven or until cheese is melted and golden.

FREEZING HINT: Line casserole first with plastic or foil wrap, then add sauce and filled manicotti. Freeze until solid; remove from casserole and package in freezer wrap. Seal and label. To serve, thaw overnight or for a day in the refrigerator.

8. Serve manicotti with a side dish of extra sauce and a bowl of ground Parmesan for sprinkling on top.

MANICOTTI SAUCE

Temperature: simmer
Cooking time: 1 hour
Yield: enough for one recipe of
manicotti or 8 to 10 servings

1 *pound ground pork*	2 *8-ounce cans tomato sauce*
1 *pound ground beef*	1 *pint water (may use 1 cup*
6 *slices bacon, chopped*	*water and 1 cup red wine)*
2 *large onions, chopped*	1 *tablespoon salt*
2 *cloves garlic or ½ teaspoon*	1 *teaspoon basil, optional*
garlic powder	*Freshly ground black*
2 *# 2 cans whole tomatoes*	*pepper*
(Italian-style tomatoes are best)	1 *tablespoon parsley, dried*

1. Place the three meats in a large, deep pan and brown slowly using medium heat. Drain excess fat.

2. Chop onions. (Use blender, if one is available. To chop onions in a blender, add coarsely chopped onion, about one-half onion at a time, and turn to low speed. Remove. Saves tears!) Add onion to meat mixture.

3. Stir onion with the meat and cook until onion is soft.

4. Add spices, tomatoes, and water or wine. For best results, add 1 cup of water and stir in, then add the rest of the water or wine if you wish a more liquid consistency. Sometimes, more than a pint of water is needed if it simmers a long time or at a high heat.

5. Use sauce as stated in the preceding manicotti recipe.

FREEZING HINT: Sauce can be packaged in a rigid carton or jar; seal and label.

MAXIMUM RECOMMENDED FREEZER STORAGE: 3 months

8
Fruits

Fruits are almost certain to be one of your favorite frozen assets. Even with today's advanced technologies, fresh fruits out of season are either extremely "pricy" or unavailable. Many are not available commerically frozen—and if they are, usually the price is impractically high.

Fruit is actually fun to freeze too! It requires very little more preparation for freezing than it does for immediate serving. And there's really no comparison to canning, time and trouble-wise. Almost any fruit can be frozen. The variety and the ripeness determine the quality of the frozen fruit.

SELECTING AND PREPARING FRUITS

Select fruits of good eating varieties or newer hybrids that are especially recommended for freezing. Generally fruits that are attractively colored and have good flavor—neither overripe nor underripe—are best for freezing. Be certain fruits are well ripened. Many are improved by being spread out on papers in a clean, dark place overnight or until mellow ripe. Apricots, peaches, figs, and most berries are better after an overnight stay.

To make the decision on when to prepare fruit for freezing, you will have to use your judgment based on appearance and taste. Often, sorting out the riper fruit does a nice job of staggering your work and assures you of the best quality of frozen fruit.

Some fruits, such as pears, apples, and pineapple, require mellowing for several days. Again, the best way to know when they are ready for freezing is to judge them the way you would for eating out of hand.

Overripe and underripe fruits, such as you sometimes get when you have your own trees, need not be sacrificed. I like to mash or puree them for jams and jellies or perhaps fruit drinks, then freeze according to the fruit guide that follows later in this chapter.

When fruit is ready for freezing and you do not have the time to freeze it, refrigerate it.

When preparing fruit for freezing, always wash in ice water—a small amount at a time. You will minimize bruising and mashing and the fruit will not absorb as much water or leak as much juice. Carefully lower a few at a time into the ice water and drain on absorbent toweling. Always carefully clean, stem, and sort fruits. Berries of all types need particularly gentle rinsing to keep them from almost dissolving. Use a knife or huller on berries; never pinch them as this causes bruising. Pare off any overripe or underripe parts.

When crushing or mashing fruit, use the technique best suited to both the fruit and your own convenience. Soft fruits such as berries are best mashed or crushed with a wire potato masher, pastry blender, or two knives. Use an electric blender, food chopper, or food mill for firmer fruits such as peaches, plums, or the like. Make purees by either blending with an electric blender until pulverized or mashing through a colander or a strainer.

Always use utensils made of glass, stainless steel, aluminum, nickel, unchipped enamelware, earthenware, or good-quality tinware. Iron utensils, chipped enamelware, or poorly tinned utensils may give off-flavors. *Never* use galvanized cookware as the fruit juices may dissolve the zinc, creating a poison.

Checking this table will guide you in deciding how much sugar or syrup and how many containers and all the other materials you should have on hand for packaging. Another helpful guide for packaging smaller amounts is the following pound conversion chart:

Quantity Guide

	Amount of raw fruit to give 1 frozen pint	Number of pints from 1 peck	Number of pounds, fresh, in 1 peck
apples	1¼-1½ lb.	8-10	12 lb.
berries	1⅓-1½ pt.	......	....
cherries, sweet or sour	1¼-1½ lb.	9-11	14 lb.
cranberries	½ lb.	16	8 lb.
peaches	1-1½ lb.	8-12	12 lb.
pears	1-1¼ lb.	10-13	13 lb.
plums	1-1½ lb.	10-14	14 lb.
rhubarb	⅔-1 lb.	......	....
strawberries	⅔ qt.	......	....

Courtesy of New Jersey Extension Bulletin 390-A.

To know how much a bushel, or other popular container of fruit will yield, you may wish to consult the following chart:

Approximate yield of frozen fruits from fresh

FRUIT	FRESH, AS PURCHASED OR PICKED	FROZEN
Apples	1 bu. (48 lb.) 1 box (44 lb.) 1 ¼ to 1 ½ lb.	32 to 40 pt. 29 to 35 pt. 1 pt.
Apricots	1 bu. (48 lb.) 1 crate (22 lb.) ⅔ to ⁴/₅ lb.	60 to 72 pt. 28 to 33 pt. 1 pt.
Berries [1]	1 crate (24 qt.) 1⅓ to 1½ pt.	32 to 36 pt. 1 pt.
Cantaloups	1 dozen (28 lb.) 1 to 1¼ lb.	22 pt. 1 pt.
Cherries, sweet or sour	1 bu. (56 lb.) 1¼ to 1½ lb.	36 to 44 pt. 1 pt.
Cranberries	1 box (25 lb.) 1 peck (8 lb.) ½ lb.	50 pt. 16 pt. 1 pt.
Currants	2 qt. (3 lb.) ¾ lb.	4 pt. 1 pt.
Peaches	1 bu. (48 lb.) 1 lug box (20 lb.) 1 to 1½ lb.	32 to 48 pt. 13 to 20 pt. 1 pt.
Pears	1 bu. (50 lb.) 1 western box (46 lb.) 1 to 1¼ lb.	40 to 50 pt. 37 to 46 pt. 1 pt.
Pineapple	5 lb.	4 pt.
Plums and prunes	1 bu. (56 lb.) 1 crate (20 lb.) 1 to 1½ lb.	38 to 56 pt. 13 to 20 pt. 1 pt.
Raspberries	1 crate (24 pt.) 1 pt.	24 pt. 1 pt.
Rhubarb	15 lb. ⅔ to 1 lb.	15 to 22 pt. 1 pt.
Strawberries	1 crate (24 qt.) ⅔ qt.	38 pt. 1 pt.

[1] Includes blackberries, blueberries, boysenberries, dewberries, elderberries, gooseberries, huckleberries, loganberries, and youngberries.

Chart courtesy of USDA's Home and Garden Bulletin No. 10.

PACKAGING

Package in any air-, moisture-, and vapor-proof container. Either rigid plastic cartons or double waxed ones are favorites. However, some people prefer to use wide-mouthed glass jars as they feel food in glass freezes faster and gives a better-textured fruit for serving. Freezer-weight bags and heat-sealing bags are fine for individual or tray pack frozen fruits.

For pies—1 quart of fruit will yield filling for a 9-inch pie. There are a number of different ways you can freeze fruits for pies. Freeze the fruit with the sugar, seasonings, and thickener mixed, ready for adding to the pastry, unbaked or baked. Always double the amount of thickener when freezing, as freezing increases the juiciness of fruit. For time and space savings I like to prepare some of the filling alone, ready for adding to a crust. Baked pies keep about twice as long as unbaked.

For shortcakes, jam, or fruit toppings—either sugar-packed, crushed, or whole fruit may be prepared. Serve toppings with small ice crystals remaining in the fruit.

Orange or lemon peel may be frozen either grated or not. When time is short, you can just freeze the peelings for later grating—and I often find this system yields milder-flavored rind, too.

Prevent darkening of fruit. Fruits that darken after you cut or peel them, such as apples, peaches, apricots, and plums, need to be treated with some form of ascorbic acid (sometimes called citric acid, however ascorbic acid is technically the antioxidant) to prevent darkening. Either ascorbic acid or an ascorbic acid mixture is more effective than lemon juice. Ascorbic acid comes in crystalline, powdered, or tablet form. The tablets do not dissolve easily and are more expensive. All forms can be purchased at drugstores, some grocery stores, and locker plants. The powdered or crystalline ascorbic acid is available in 25- to 1,000-gram containers. One teaspoon weighs about 3 grams, which means there are approximately 8 teaspoons in a 25-gram container.

As a rule of thumb, add 2 teaspoons of ascorbic acid to each gallon of chilled syrup just before using the syrup to pack the fruit. Using too much can cause the fruit to be too sour.

If you wish to use ascorbic acid tablets, below is a table for converting the tablets to teaspoons. Tablets are usually sold in milligrams. Use the teaspoon equivalent, but crush the tablets first and dissolve in a small amount of water before adding to the chilled syrup.

Crystalline	Tablets
⅛ teaspoon	375 milligrams
¼ teaspoon	750 milligrams
½ teaspoon	1,500 milligrams
¾ teaspoon	2,250 milligrams
1 teaspoon	3,000 milligrams

Chart courtesy of USDA's Home and Garden Bulletin No. 10.

Ascorbic acid mixtures are popular for use in preventing darkening and are readily available in most groceries, variety stores, and drugstores. They usually cost less than the pure ascorbic acid but more is needed. They are made of ascorbic acid mixed with sugar, and just might be more expensive than the pure ascorbic acid. Follow the package instructions to know exactly how much to use.

Steaming is another method of preventing discoloration. The fruit is sliced or halved and steamed according to the time listed on the Fruit Freezing Guide below. I've used this mostly for pears and apples.

Pack fruit with sugar or syrup or plain, according to the fruit's tolerance and your desired use. Several fruits can be frozen any of five ways (see below). Others are more limited due to the fact that they oxidize or darken unless placed in an ascorbic acid mixture or are steamed or otherwise treated to prevent darkening. Due to the wide range of freezing possibilities and potential uses, you will want to be sure to label with as complete information as possible, listing the fruit, style of preparation, quantity, intended use, any peculiarities, and the date.

BASIC FRUIT PACKING METHODS

Syrup packs are generally preferred for desserts whenever perfectly shaped pieces and a sweet flavor are preferred. The syrup keeps the pieces from getting mashed. When using syrup, you have to plan ahead and chill it for the best-quality frozen fruit. I must admit I don't always have the opportunity to chill syrup in advance and have made it and cooled it by substituting cubed or crushed ice for part of the water. A great practice that saves planning is to always have a quart jar or more of the type of syrup needed for the fruit currently in season. I found this especially handy when I had an apricot tree in the backyard. With the chilled syrup on hand, whenever a few extra moments were available, I could prepare and package some apricots.

There are a number of concentrations of syrup. Due to a constant weight-control awareness, I always try to use the lightest sugar syrup tolerable for the fruit I'm freezing. Also, lighter syrups allow more fruit flavor to come through. The heavier syrups keep the fruit more perfectly formed while frozen—for fancy dessert serving. Also, they are sometimes needed for very sour fruits. In planning, allow about ¾ to 1 cup of syrup for each quart you're preparing.

SYRUP CONCENTRATIONS GUIDE

Percentage of Syrup	Amount of Sugar	Amount of Water	Yield of Syrup
20%	1 cup	4 cups	4¾ cups
30%	2 cups	4 cups	5 cups
35%	2 ½ cups	4 cups	5⅓ cups
40%	3 cups	4 cups	5½ cups
50%	4 ¾ cups	4 cups	6½ cups
60%	7 cups	4 cups	7¾ cups
65%	8 ¾ cups	4 cups	8⅔ cups

To prepare the syrup, completely dissolve the sugar in warm to hot water. Cool the syrup. When needed, add ascorbic acid or ascorbic acid mixture just before packaging.

Corn syrup can be substituted for part or all of the sugar. From 25% to 100% can be used for a blander syrup but most people substitute only part of the sugar.

CORN SYRUP GUIDE

	Amount of Sugar	Amount of Corn Syrup	Amount of Water	Yield of Syrup
Thin (20-30%)	1 cup	2 cups	6 cups	8 cups
Medium (40-50%)	2 cups	2 cups	5 cups	8 cups
Heavy (60-65%)	3 cups	2 cups	4 cups	8 cups

Dissolve the sugar first in cold water. Add corn syrup and stir until uniformly mixed. Add ascorbic acid according to type being used just before packaging fruit.

To use syrup, always place about ½ cup in the bottom of the container. Then add the fruit, adding more syrup as needed to keep the fruit covered with syrup. Top with crumpled piece of waxed paper, cellophane, or similar material to keep the fruit submerged and prevent oxidation or darkening of the fruit. Nondarkening fruits won't require the paper. Always allow adequate head space when using syrup to allow for expansion as it freezes. Allow head space as follows:

RECOMMENDED HEAD SPACE

Type of Pack	Container with Wide Top		Container with Narrow Top		Glass Container	
	Pint	Quart	Pint	Quart	Pint	Quart
Liquid Pack	½ inch	1 inch	¾ inch	1½ inches	1 inch	2 inches
Dry Pack	½ inch	½ inch	½ inch	½ inch	¾ inch	1½ inches

Sugar pack using dry sugar is often preferred for fruits that are juicy or very ripe. The choice of whether to use syrup or dry sugar is basically a personal preference—most fruits can be frozen either way. However, dry packing of fruit does not allow it to keep its shape as well as syrup. For toppings and later use in jams and the like, I prefer to use the dry sugar method. Contrary to some opinions, dry sugar works well on fruits that oxidize or darken. However, you must add ascorbic acid following package instructions and mix it into the sugar well. When ascorbic acid is used, wad a piece of waxed paper or cello wrap and place on top of the fruit before sealing to make sure the fruit does not darken.

The best way to mix the fruit and the dry sugar is to place the fruit in a large, flat pan such as an oblong baking pan. Add the sugar, following the proportions suggested in the Fruit Freezing Guide. A general rule of thumb is to allow 1 part sugar to 4 parts fruit, varied according to tartness of fruit and desired uses. Gently fold the fruit and sugar together until the sugar dissolves; then package.

An alternative method is to add the sugar in layers to the fruit, again following the suggested proportions. Add sugar after you have placed about an inch or so of fruit in the container and continue until the container is filled to within the recommended head space suggestion for dry pack.

Dietetic or low-calorie pack can be used to cut calories or eliminate sugar. Fruits can be packed either in water or with low or no-calorie sweeteners substituting for the sugar in the syrup. Saccharin is not a desirable substitute for freezing as a bitterness seems to develop.

I do not think the frozen fruit is as tasty or attractive when sugar is not used—but for low or no-sugar diets of any type, this method is fine. Use the label directions on the sweetener for quantitative substitutions for sugar when preparing the syrup. If a fruit darkens, add ascorbic acid mixture just as you would to the sugar syrup.

To pack in water, simply substitute plain water, adding ascorbic acid if needed. The advantage of plain water is that you can sweeten the fruit later as you wish when serving. Whether you artificially sweeten or not, pack as when using syrup, using the wadded paper or wrap on top of the fruit to prevent darkening. Also use the head space allowance just the same as when using syrup.

Dry pack is by far the easiest method. Berries of most any type freeze very well this way. Also, fruits that you wish to use for cooking, such as making jams, jellies, or pies, are great packed this way. Fruits that oxidize are usually not as satisfactory frozen this way because the ascorbic acid mixture seems to need the natural juice that occurs in the sugar pack or the syrup to coat the fruit for preventing darkening. When caught in a crunch, though, I have added ascorbic acid to fruits that darken and mixed it well with the fruit. The results were okay, but not as good as sugar or syrup pack. To package, just place the clean fruit in the carton, allowing the head space for dry pack.

Individual or tray pack is great for whole strawberries, blueberries, bing cherries, whole red raspberries, or any attractive fruit to be used in salads or as topping for special desserts. Prepare by freezing fruit in a single layer on a cookie sheet or tray. After solidly frozen, or in about 1 to 2 hours, package using the dry pack head space suggestion.

To place fruits in the freezer: When adding unfrozen fruit to the freezer, always place the packages close to the side walls of an upright freezer and against the walls or on a quick chill shelf in a chest freezer. Allow air circulation around packages. As soon as the foods are frozen, stack them, arranging the oldest dates continuously to the front.

SERVING

Most fruits have a better "just picked" flavor if served with slight ice crystals. Complete thawing tends to make fruits mushy due to their high water content. To thaw, you have several options and since fruit is rather insensitive to contamination, room thawing or any rapid thawing is fine. Fruit, in other words, is very different from meats, which are best thawed in the refrigerator or microwave oven. Thawing times are approximately as follows:

Refrigerator	about 8 hours/quart
On counter at room temperature of 70° to 75° F	about 4 hours/quart
In microwave oven (depends on fruit and manufacturer of oven)	average 2 to 4 minutes
In hot water	20 to 30 minutes
In front of electric fan	about 2 hours

Sugared fruits or those in syrup thaw faster than other packs. Fruits can be cooked from the frozen state; the cooking period will just have to be lengthened up to one-half longer.

Frozen fruits can be served plain and will be nearly like fresh.

REFREEZING

For best nutrition, do not refreeze. If there are any leftovers, they will keep better cooked if you're planning to keep them several days. Frozen fruits are juicier than fresh and will require about twice the amount of thickener when used in cooking. Or, part of the juice can be drained and used another way.

FRUIT FREEZING GUIDE

Apples. Wash, peel, and slice apples about ½ inch thick or thinner depending on end use.

Syrup Pack: Use 30% or 40% syrup, adding ascorbic acid according to type used. Fill freezer containers with about ½ cup syrup, adding apples and more syrup to cover fruit.

Sugar Pack: Slice apples into a lemon, salt, or ascorbic acid mixture, then steam or scald 1½ to 2 minutes; cool and drain. Add 1 cup sugar for each quart, stir to mix well. This is a good pack to use for pies.

Pack into rigid containers, allowing head space according to quantity and container use. Add crumpled piece of wrap to keep apples immersed and prevent darkening. Seal and label. Pack into rigid containers or plastic bags in boxes. Seal and label, noting type of pack.

Applesauce. Prepare applesauce as you would for immediate serving. A good proportion is to use ⅓ cup water per quart of apples. After cooking, strain and mash and add sugar to taste—usually ¼ to ¾ cup.

Pack into rigid containers, allowing recommended head space, seal and label, noting type of pack.

Baked Apples. Prepare as you would for table use, freeze on a tray or baking dish.

Pack same as above. For greatest versatility, freeze at least some of the apples individually, adding cooking juice. Seal and label, noting type of pack.

Apricots. Wash and sort as to size, keeping uniform sizes together. Halve and pit. Peel, if desired, or if skins are tough and you don't wish to peel, halves may be dipped for ½ minute in boiling water, cooled, and drained. Slice if desired.

Syrup Pack: Use 40% syrup, adding ascorbic acid according to type used. Fill freezer containers with about ½ cup syrup, adding apricots and more syrup to cover fruit.

Pack into rigid containers, allowing head space according to quantity and container used. Add crumpled piece of wrap to keep apricots immersed and prevent darkening. Seal and label, noting type of pack.

Sugar Pack: Add ascorbic acid in quantity based on type used to ½ cup sugar per quart of apricots. Place apricots in shallow pan, bowl, or dish. Stir well.

Pack into rigid containers, allowing adequate head space. Seal and label, noting type of pack.

An alternate method, if fruit is very ripe, is to mix ascorbic acid in ¼ cup cold water and sprinkle over fruit. Then sprinkle on sugar, mixing together in a flat, shallow dish or in container.

Crushed, Pureed: Add 1 cup sugar and ascorbic acid according to type used to each quart of chopped, mashed, or pureed fruit. Great for jam or toppings.

Pack into rigid containers, leaving adequate head space. Seal and label as to type of pack.

Avocados. Peel and mash pulp. Some also freeze them in halves or slices.

Unsweetened Pack: Add ascorbic acid according to type used and mix well.

Pack into rigid containers, leaving adequate head space. Seal and label, noting type of pack.

Sugar Pack: Mix 1 cup sugar with ascorbic acid to each quart of puree.

Pack into rigid containers, leaving adequate head space. Seal and label, noting type of pack.

Bananas. Peel and mash pulp.

Unsweetened Pack: Add ascorbic acid according to type used. Mix well.

Pack into rigid containers, leaving adequate head space. Seal and label, noting type of pack.

Sugar Pack: Add sugar according to desired end use—freezing quantity of bananas and sugar for recipe to be used—such as banana bread, cake, etc., or add 1 cup sugar to each quart, mixing well.

Pack into rigid containers, leaving adequate head space. Seal and label, noting type of pack.

Berries

Blackberries,
Boysenberries,
Dewberries,
Loganberries,
Nectarberries,
Raspberries,
Strawberries,
Youngberries. Wash gently, discarding both immature and overripe berries. Stem and remove any leaves. Drain well in a single layer.

Tray Pack: Freeze berries on a tray or cookie sheet until firmly frozen.

Pack in freezer-weight bags or rigid containers. Seal and label, noting type of pack.

Dry Pack: Pack berries into cartons or bags.

117

Pack berries into freezer-weight cartons or containers, leaving adequate head space. Label, noting type of pack.

Syrup Pack: Use 40%–50% chilled sugar syrup, adding about ½ cup to each carton before adding the berries. Add more syrup to cover.

Pack in rigid cartons or freezer-type glass jars, allowing adequate head space. Seal and label, noting type of pack.

Sugar Pack: Add ¾ cup sugar to each quart of berries and mix well in a flat, shallow pan or dish, mixing until the sugar is dissolved.

Pack same as above.

Puree: Crush berries, then add 1 cup sugar for each quart of berries and mix well or until dissolved.

Pack same as above.

Blueberries,
Elderberries,
and Huckleberries. Prepare for freezing as for other berries.

Dry Pack: Pack berries into cartons or bags.

Use freezer-weight bags or cartons and allow recommended head space. Seal and label, noting type of pack.

Syrup Pack: Use 40% chilled sugar syrup, adding about ½ cup to each carton before adding the berries. Add more syrup to cover.

Pack same as above.

Gooseberries. Pack using either method above, increasing the sugar syrup percentage to 50%.

Cantaloupe

(and other melons:
Honeydew,
Casaba, Persian,
and Watermelon). Cut in half, remove seeds, and scoop out melon balls or cut into cubes. Drain well.

Syrup Pack: Add 30% chilled sugar syrup, adding about ½ cup to the bottom of the carton. Add more to cover melon.

Place in rigid cartons, allowing recommended head space. Seal and label, noting type of pack.

Ginger Ale or Juice Pack: Either ginger ale or orange juice can be substituted for the sugar syrup.

Pack same as above.

Carambola. Wash, trim dark spiny edges, slice crosswise.

Syrup Pack: Use 40%–50% chilled sugar syrup, adding about ½ cup to the bottom of each carton. Add carambola slice and more syrup if needed.

118

Use rigid containers, allowing adequate head space. Seal and label, noting type of pack.

Sugar Pack: Add 1 cup sugar to each 5 cups fruit. Mix well.

Pack same as above.

Unsweetened Pack: Pack as is, without adding sugar.

Pack into bags in boxes or rigid containers. Seal and label, noting type of pack.

Carissa. Wash, peel if desired, cut in half lengthwise or leave whole.

Syrup Pack: 40–50% syrup, adding about ½ cup syrup to the bottom of each carton. Add carissa and more syrup as needed.

Pack same as above.

Cherries, sour. Stem, sort out soft, overripe, or discolored ones, and wash thoroughly. Drain and pit. Optional: to maintain high color, add ascorbic acid according to type being used.

Syrup Pack: Use 60–65% chilled sugar syrup, adding about ½ cup syrup to the bottom of each carton. Add cherries and more syrup, if needed.

Use rigid containers, allowing adequate head space. Add a piece of crumpled wrap to top of each if ascorbic acid is used. Seal and label type of pack.

Sugar Pack: Add 1½ cups sugar to each quart cherries and mix well.

Pack in rigid containers, leaving adequate head space, noting type of pack.

Crushed: Coarsely crush pitted cherries, then add 1 to 1½ cups sugar and mix until dissolved.

Pack into containers, leaving recommended head space. Seal and label, noting type of pack.

Puree: Boil crushed cherries only until the boiling point is reached. Sieve or blend. Then add ¾ cup sugar for each quart.

Pack same as above.

Juice: See general instructions for juices (page 122).

Cherries, sweet. Prepare the same as for sour cherries.

Syrup Pack: Use 40% chilled sugar syrup to which the recommended amount of ascorbic acid has been added.

Pack in rigid containers, leaving head space for liquid pack, crumpling piece of wrap to place on top to keep fruit submerged. Seal and label with type of pack.

Crushed: Coarsely crush pitted cherries. Then add ¾ cup sugar and ascorbic acid according to type being used and mix until dissolved.

Pack same as above.

119

Dry Pack: Leave stems on if desired.

Place in freezer-weight bags or rigid cartons. Seal and label, noting type of pack.

Coconut. Using fresh coconuts with milk, split, grate or grind the meat, and reserve coconut milk. Moisten grated meat with milk. Add ½ cup sugar to 4 cups moistened coconut meat.

Pack in freezer bags or containers allowing adequate head space. Seal and label, noting type of pack.

Crabapples. Prepare as for apples.

Cranberries. Wash, stem, and eliminate poor berries.

Dry Pack: Place berries into freezer-weight bags or cartons.

Allow recommended head space and seal and label.

Syrup Pack: Use 50% chilled sugar syrup, placing about ½ cup in bottom of container, add berries, and more syrup, if needed.

Place in rigid cartons, allowing recommended head space. Seal and label, noting type of pack.

Cooked Sauce: Prepare as for table use, adding 2 cups sugar per pound fruit or to taste.

Pack same as syrup pack.

Puree: Press cooked berries through sieve. Add more sugar to taste, if desired.

Pack same as syrup pack.

Currants. Wash and remove stems.

Dry Pack: Place currants in freezer-weight bags or cartons.

Allow recommended head space and seal and label.

Syrup Pack: Use 50% chilled sugar syrup, placing about ½ cup in bottom of container, add currants and more syrup, if needed.

Pack in rigid cartons, allowing recommended head space. Seal and label, noting type of pack.

Sugar Pack: Add ¾ cup sugar to each quart and stir until most of the sugar is dissolved.

Pack same as syrup pack.

Crushed: Crush currants and add 1⅛ cups sugar per quart. Mix until dissolved.

Pack same as syrup pack.

Figs. Handle gently. Sort and discard any bruised or very soft fruit. Be extra certain water is icy and wash. Use a sharp knife ot remove stem. Leave whole, halve, or slice. Peel or leave unpeeled.

Syrup Pack: Best for whole, halved, or sliced. Use 30–40% chilled sugar syrup, adding the recommended amount of ascorbic acid based on type used. Place about ½ cup syrup in bottom of rigid carton, add figs and more syrup, if needed.

Dry Pack: Pack into bags or cartons. For light-colored figs, add ascorbic acid according to type being used. Mix well until sugar dissolves.

Pack into rigid containers, allowing head space according to quantity and container used. Add crumpled piece of wrap to keep figs immersed and prevent darkening. Seal and label, noting type of pack.

Use freezer-weight bags or cartons, allowing adequate head space. Seal and label, noting type of pack. If using the ascorbic-acid-treated water, cartons must be used and a wadded piece of wrap should be inserted on top of fruit before sealing. Label with type of pack.

Crushed: Crush figs, add ⅔ cup sugar for each quart plus ascorbic acid according to type being used. Mix well until sugar dissolves.

Pack into rigid containers, leaving adequate head space. Seal and label, noting type of pack.

Grapefruit. Wash and peel, divide into sections, removing all seeds and membrane.

Syrup Pack: Use chilled 40% sugar syrup, adding about ½ cup to the bottom of the container, then the sections. Add more syrup, if needed.

Pack into rigid containers, leaving adequate head space. Seal and label, noting type of pack.

Dry Pack: Pack without syrup same as above.

Grapes. Wash and stem. Leave seedless grapes whole. Cut others in half and remove seeds.

Syrup Pack: Best for most uses other than juice or jelly. Use 40% chilled sugar syrup, adding about ½ cup syrup to the bottom of each carton. Add grapes and more syrup, if needed.

Pack into rigid containers, leaving adequate head space. Seal and label, noting type of pack.

Dry Pack: Pack into freezer cartons or bags. For short-term storage, grapes can be frozen in the bunch.

Use freezer-weight bags or cartons and allow recommended head space. Seal and label, noting type of pack.

Puree: Prepare by heating washed grapes to boiling. Drain juice and freeze separately. Cool the grapes and sieve. Add ½ cup sugar to each quart. Puree may develop a gritty texture because of tartrate crystals. Grittiness will disappear when heated.

Pack in rigid containers, leaving adequate head space. Seal and label, noting type of pack.

Guava. Wash, peel, and cut in half.

Cooked in Syrup: Cook until just tender in a syrup of 1 to 2 cups sugar to 4 cups water. Cool. Evenly divide fruit among containers, covering with syrup.

Pack into rigid containers, leaving adequate head space. Seal and label, noting type of pack.

Syrup Pack: Use 50–60% chilled sugar syrup and place about ½ cup in the bottom of each carton. Add halved guavas and top with more syrup, if needed.

Pack same as above.

Juices. Use good-quality fruit. Surface blemishes will not affect quality or flavor. Crush, grind, or chop fruits to gain high juice yield. Use cloth bag for pressing juice from soft fruits and to strain any juice. Two or more layers of cheesecloth can be used for straining firmer fruits, if desired. If juice is to be for jelly making, straining is best for clear, sparkling jellies. Some fruits yield higher quantity of juice when heated. For example, grapes and cherries will. As a rule of thumb *do not add sugar* to juice for jelly making (though it may be added just before serving) and *add sugar* for beverages. Sugar will be harder to dissolve when added to cold juice.

Most fruit can be made into juice, and most juices can be blended for exciting fruit drinks. Most juices you will make are concentrated and will need to be diluted to taste upon thawing for serving. Save freezer space by waiting to add water just before serving. Sugar, ascorbic acid, or any other seasoning should be added as listed for freezing the fruit under the directions in this table.

Pour juice into rigid cartons or bottles of most convenient size for intended use, allowing generous head space—at least ½ inch more than suggested for the fruit alone.

Kumquats. Wash; chill until firm. Use 60–70% chilled sugar syrup, adding about ½ cup to the bottom of the carton. Then add fruit and top with more syrup, if needed.

Pack into rigid containers, leaving adequate head space. Seal and label, noting type of pack.

Lemons, Limes. Wash, slice whole fruit, or freeze halves of whole or grated rind after juicing.

Sugar Syrup: For slices, use 20% chilled sugar syrup, placing about ½ cup in the bottom of a rigid carton, then slices and syrup to cover.

Pack into rigid containers, leaving adequate head space. Seal and label, noting type of pack.

Dry Pack: For rind halves or grated rind.

122

Package in the size container most frequently used. Pack grated rind in teaspoon or tablespoon packets for greatest convenience, as an example. Seal and label, noting type of pack.

Juice: Squeeze and freeze in ice cube trays.

Package in small plastic bags. Seal and label, noting type of pack.

Loquats. Peel and cut fruit in halves, removing blossom end and seeds.

Syrup Pack: Pack using 30% sugar syrup, adding ½ cup to bottom of carton. Add more if needed.

Pack into rigid containers, leaving adequate head space. Seal and label, noting type of pack.

Lychee. Wash, remove shells, and seed.

Syrup Pack: Use 40–50% syrup, adding ½ cup to bottom of carton. Pack with fruit and add more syrup if needed.

Pack into rigid containers, leaving adequate head space. Seal and label, noting type of pack.

Dry Pack: May freeze whole in shell.

Pack into cartons or bags. Seal and label, noting type of pack.

Mangoes. Wash. Peel, cut off and discard a slice from the stem end. Slice with a sharp knife, avoiding using the flesh near the seed as it is too stringy.

Syrup Pack: Use 20–35% chilled sugar syrup, adding ascorbic acid according to type being used. Place about ½ cup in the bottom of each carton. Add fruit, slicing directly into the syrup, adding more syrup if needed to cover the fruit.

Pack into rigid containers, allowing head space according to quantity and container used. Add crumpled piece of wrap to keep fruit immersed and prevent darkening. Seal and label, noting type of pack.

Sugar Pack: Place sliced mangoes in shallow pan or dish and sprinkle with ½ cup sugar to 5 to 6 cups fruit. Add ascorbic acid according to type being used. Mix well until sugar is dissolved, stirring as gently as possible.

Pack same as syrup pack.

Melons. See Cantaloupe.

Nectarines. Wash good-quality fruit, halve, and pit. Peeling is optional. Add fruit as soon as cut into syrup solution, working with one nectarine at a time. Fruit may be frozen in halves, quarters, or slices.

Syrup Pack: Use 40% chilled sugar syrup, and add ascorbic acid according to type being used. Add about ½ cup syrup to bottom

123

of carton and add fruit as soon as sliced or cut. Add syrup to cover, pressing fruit into syrup.

Pack into rigid containers, allowing head space according to quantity and container used. Add crumpled piece of wrap to keep fruit immersed and prevent darkening. Seal and label, noting type of pack.

Puree: Prepare same as peach puree (below).

Pack into rigid containers, leaving adequate head space. Seal and label, noting type of pack.

Oranges. See Grapefruit. Oranges are often cut in ¼-inch-thick slices, instead of sectioning.

Peaches. A favorite with most people and very versatile frozen. Best if packed with sugar and ascorbic acid. Select only good-quality, ripe peaches for freezing. Rinse and peel without dipping into boiling water for the best quality and most attractive frozen fruit. Either slices or halves are most popular.

Syrup Pack: Use 40% chilled sugar syrup and add ascorbic acid according to type used. Add about ½ cup syrup to bottom of each carton. Then slice or halve each peach as soon as peeled and add directly to the sugar syrup, making certain syrup continuously covers the fruit. Work with only one peach at a time. Press pieces of peach into syrup as they are added.

Pack into rigid containers, allowing head space according to quantity and container used. Add crumpled piece of wrap to keep fruit immersed and prevent darkening. Seal and label, noting type of pack.

Sugar Pack: Place sliced peaches in a large, shallow dish or bowl. Add ⅔ cup sugar for each quart peaches and ascorbic acid according to type being used. Mix until sugar is dissolved, working with only one quart fruit at a time to prevent darkening.

Pack same as syrup pack.

Puree: Good for using peaches that have good flesh, but are imperfect. Crush peaches coarsely or press through a sieve or blend in an electric blender. If desired, peaches can be cooked until tender and then sieved. To each 4 cups or quart of fruit, add 1 cup sugar and ascorbic acid according to type being used. Stir until well mixed and sugar is dissolved.

Pack into rigid containers, leaving adequate head space. Seal and label, noting type of pack.

Pears. Rinse pears, peel, cut in halves or quarters, and remove cores. If preferred, pears may be steamed for 1 to 2 minutes and placed in chilled syrup. Boiling in syrup assures better retention of shape.

Syrup Pack: Add pear pieces to 40% syrup and heat to boiling for 1 to 2 minutes. Remove from hot syrup. Pack immediately, using cold 40% sugar syrup treated with ascorbic acid according to type being used.

Pack into rigid containers, allowing head space according to quantity and container used. Add crumpled piece of wrap to keep fruit immersed and prevent darkening. Seal and label, noting type of pack.

Puree: Prepare according to directions for peach puree (above).

Pack into rigid containers, leaving adequate head space. Seal and label, noting type of pack.

Persimmons. Wash, peel, and firm fruit in ice water, then cut into sections. Be sure not to select persimmons that are too mushy.

Sugar Pack: Place pieces in large, shallow dish or pan and add ascorbic acid mixture according to type. Add ½ cup sugar to each quart of fruit. Mix until sugar is dissolved.

Pack into rigid containers, allowing head space according to quantity and container used. Add crumpled piece of wrap to keep fruit immersed and prevent darkening. Seal and label, noting type of pack.

Dry Pack: Sprinkle freshly cut fruit with ascorbic acid according to type being used. Mix evenly to coat, and pack.

Use freezer-weight bags or cartons, allowing recommended head space. Seal and label, noting type of pack.

Puree: Prepare according to directions for peach puree (above).

Pack into rigid containers, leaving adequate head space. Seal and label, noting type of pack.

Pineapple. Using ripe pineapple, peel, remove top, halve, and core. Slice, dice, crush, or cut into wedges or sticks.

Syrup Pack: Use 30% chilled sugar syrup and begin with about ½ cup in the bottom of each carton. Add fruit and more syrup to cover.

Pack into rigid containers, leaving adequate head space. Seal and label, noting type of pack.

Dry Pack: Pack fruit tightly into cartons.

Use freezer-weight bags or cartons and allow recommended head space. Seal and label, noting type of pack.

Plums (or prunes). Wash. Leave whole or cut into halves or quarters and remove pits.

Syrup Pack: Use 40–50% chilled sugar syrup and add ascorbic acid according to type being used. Add about ½ cup to the bottom of each carton. Add fruit and syrup to cover.

Pack into rigid containers, leaving adequate head space. Seal and label, noting type of pack.

Puree: Follow same instructions for peach puree (above).

Pack into rigid containers, leaving adequate head space. Seal and label, noting type of pack.

Pomegranates. Wash. Cut in half, place cut face down, and rap shell firmly with a knife handle. This will bring out the juice sacs.

Syrup Pack: Using 30% syrup, place ½ cup syrup in carton, add fruit and syrup to cover.

Use rigid cartons, leaving adequate head space. Seal and label.

Rhubarb. Rinse. Cut into 1- or 2-inch pieces. Heat in boiling water for 1 minute and immediately cool in ice water. This improves color and flavor.

Syrup Pack: Use either raw or parboiled rhubarb, and 40% chilled sugar syrup. Add about ½ cup syrup to the bottom of each carton. Add fruit and more syrup to cover.

Pack in rigid containers, leaving adequate head space. Seal and label, noting type of pack.

Puree: Boil rhubarb for 2 minutes using 1 cup water to each 1½ quarts fruit. Cool and sieve. Add ⅔ cup sugar to each quart fruit and mix well.

Pack same as above.

Strawberries. Follow instructions under Berries. Strawberries, packed in syrup or with sugar, may be sliced or crushed.

Watermelon. See Cantaloupe.

RECIPES

(See Fruit Salad Hints, poppy seed dressing p. 160.)

AMY'S APPLES

Our favorite baked apples! Make as many as you like. They're great baked in the microwave oven and served in a champagne glass!

Microwave baking time: 2½ to 3½
minutes each
Conventional baking time: 1 hour
at 375° F

Apples
Red hots
Marshmallows, optional

1. Core apples, cut into 8 sections, and place in glass for microwaving or muffin tin for conventional baking.
2. Place a heaping tablespoon of red hots in each cavity. Top with a marshmallow if desired.
3. If baking in a microwave oven, place in a champagne or other glass, cover with cellophane wrap, and cook 2½ to 3½ minutes. If baking conventionally, do not cover and bake 1 hour at 375° F.

FREEZING HINT: If freezing, cool and wrap each individually, using a plastic bag or other freezer wrap. Label.

MAXIMUM RECOMMENDED FREEZER STORAGE: 6 months

FLAMING APRICOTS

An easy-to-do, yet spectacular dessert!

Temperature: medium
Cooking time: 20 to 30 minutes
Yield: 4 to 6 servings

2 tablespoons butter
¼ cup light brown sugar
¼ cup light corn syrup
   Dash each of mace and
   nutmeg
12 frozen or fresh apricots

(can substitute peaches, strawberries, blueberries, or any other favorite fruit)
Pound cake
Vanilla ice cream
¾ cup rum

1. Using medium heat of surface unit and the blazer pan or any rather shallow pan (so flames will show when ignited) such as a frypan or casserole, melt the butter and add the sugar, syrup, mace, and nutmeg. Stir until bubbly.
2. Add fruit and cook until the fruit firms, yet is still rather soft. (Cooking fruit in sugar makes it get firmer—so, if soft fruit is desired, cook it in water, adding the sugar at the last, just before cooking or serving.)
3. Fruit can be cooked and covered for several hours before serving or it can be flamed immediately. Prepare the cake and ice cream for serving.
4. Heat rum until first bubble forms, then pour over hot fruit combination at the table—ignite and wait until flame dies to pour sauce over the cake and ice cream. Oh, be sure to stay and eat yours so you can hear all the compliments!

FREEZING HINTS: Frozen whole or halved apricots are great for this but other fruits are mighty tasty too! Follow freezing suggestions listed under Cherries Jubilee, following.

CHERRIES JUBILEE

Temperature: medium
Cooking time: 15 minutes
Yield: 4 to 6 servings

2 cups fresh or frozen cherries or 1 can (16 or 17 ounces) drained bing cherries

⅔ cup red jelly (can substitute juice from the cherries)

1 continuous orange rind, optional

3 ounces kirsch, cherry brandy, or cherry liqueur

3 ounces Cointreau (orange brandy)

5 ounces dry brandy
Ice cream
Pound cake

1. Combine cherries, jelly, orange rind, kirsch, Cointreau, and 3 ounces of the dry brandy. Allow to set for 2 hours for best flavor.
2. Heat the cherry mixture only until warm. Warm the brandy. Pour brandy over the warm fruit mixture and ignite.
3. Serve the sauce over cake squares topped with ice cream.

FREEZING HINT: Frozen whole bing cherries are great in this recipe. Use ones you merely rinsed off during the peak of the season and froze.

MAXIMUM RECOMMENDED FREEZER STORAGE: Try *not* to freeze already pre-pared Jubilee, as it loses all its "umph." Use leftover sauce on pancakes, fruit salad, etc.

FRUITED BUTTERSCOTCH CRISP

An all-time favorite at our house. Peaches have always been the most popular.

Temperature: 375° F
Baking time: 35 to 40 minutes
Microwave baking time: 12
minutes
Yield: Serves 6

1 cup brown sugar	⅛ teaspoon nutmeg
1 cup flour	½ cup shortening or butter
¼ teaspoon cinnamon	2 cups fresh or frozen fruit

1. Mix together dry ingredients and cut in shortening until like coarse meal.

2. Spread fruit in well-buttered baking dish. Sprinkle with crumb mixture.

3. Bake in moderate oven (375° F) until fruit is soft and crumbs are brown, about 35 to 40 minutes.

FREEZING HINT: Can be frozen after baking with fresh or frozen fruit. Seal well.

MAXIMUM RECOMMENDED FREEZER STORAGE: 4 months

9
Vegetables

Vegetables right from the garden—maybe your very own garden—year-round with freshly picked flavor are possible only when you freeze. Vegetables are easier and far safer to freeze than to preserve by any other method. Unfortunately they are not as easy to freeze as fruits.

Instead of sugar and ascorbic acid treatments, they require blanching to halt the maturation of the vegetable which is carried on by enzymic action. Enzymes within each vegetable cause it to ripen. They continue to be active even after the vegetables are picked, causing them to become overmature and lose their characteristic good, fresh flavors. The only action that can halt this process is heating and the heating process used to prepare foods for the freezer is known as blanching. To preserve the peak of flavor, accurate timing is required and the blanching process must be halted immediately at the end of the cooking period by chilling in ice water for an equal period.

Blanching, though somewhat time consuming, is much faster than canning, for which vegetables have to be either processed in a hot-water bath or in a pressure cooker. High, prolonged heat is necessary in canning because vegetables contain little or no acid and are susceptible to harmful bacteria and spoilage which can be poisonous, even lethal, to human beings. In freezing, processing is much quicker and easier and eliminates the worry of spoilage.

You might be wondering just what happens if you don't blanch. Without blanching, vegetables will continue to mature in the freezer and may develop off-flavors, discolor, or toughen so that they will no longer be appetizing after a few weeks of freezer storage.

A side benefit of blanching is that it heightens the color and makes the vegetables much easier to pack into freezing bags or cartons. Also, the nutritional losses are minimized. You can't avoid some minor nutritional loss because some of the water-soluble vitamins like B and C dissolve. Blanching does reduce the number of micro-organisms, too.

There are a few exceptions to blanching—bell peppers, whole tomatoes, herbs, and lettuce and similar salad vegetables when stored short-term for use in stews and cooked vegetable dishes.

SELECTING AND PREPARING
VEGETABLES

Only the freshest and best-quality vegetables should be frozen. Why go to the work of freezing less than fresh vegetables which will not be improved by the freezing process? They can never be a frozen asset; instead they create a liability in investments of time and money.

An old-fashioned rule of thumb about the timing for freezing vegetables is 3 hours from the garden to the freezer. Though an excellent guideline—unless you have your own garden or nearby vegetable market operated by a farmer with nearby gardens—following it is next to impossible. But the moral is still there!

After getting involved in many, many freezing fiascoes when I ambitiously overbought, I'd like to pass on a valuable piece of advice I learned long ago. Always underestimate what you can do in any given time and also underestimate your family's appetite. With the many, many scrumptious vegetables available during the growing season, it's almost more fun to freeze a wide variety of several vegetables than to go "whole hog" at the first of the season. You can easily take up too much space with early summer vegetables such as peas or green beans, leaving very limited space for corn, squash, and other favorites, let alone for fruits and other goodies.

After making a conservative estimate about the amount of freezer space you wish to devote to vegetables, determine just how much you'd like to devote to each vegetable within flexible limits. If for any reason your freezing plans are interrupted, refrigerate the vegetables until you have a chance to freeze them.

If you are ever in doubt as to whether a specific vegetable will freeze to your liking, freeze a package or two. Cook and serve it two weeks later. This, needless to say, can save untold grief. If the vegetable's availability is not that long, sample it after two to four days. Leaving the vegetable frozen for two weeks merely indicates how the quality will bear up when frozen longer.

When home gardening, think of yourself. Don't plant absolutely all of each vegetable at once. Stagger the plantings by about three weeks and you will have a much more pleasant garden-to-table or garden-to-freezer experience for each vegetable.

Prepare the vegetables for freezing by sorting out the best-quality ones in the amount you have time to freeze. Wash thoroughly in softened water, if at all possible, as it speeds and enhances the dirt removal. Packaged water softener can be added to the water, if desired. If the softener is perfumed or has any additives, the vegetables will require a second rinse. Podded vegetables such as peas, lima beans, and the like require only a rinsing if the pods are muddy.

Approximate yield of frozen vegetables from fresh

VEGETABLE	FRESH, AS PURCHASED OR PICKED	FROZEN
Asparagus	1 crate (12 2-lb. bunches) 1 to 1½ lb.	15 to 22 pt. 1 pt.
Beans, lima (in pods)	1 bu. (32 lb.) 2 to 2½ lb.	12 to 16 pt. 1 pt.
Beans, snap, green, and wax	1 bu. (30 lb.) ⅔ to 1 lb.	30 to 45 pt. 1 pt.
Beet greens	15 lb. 1 to 1½ lb.	10 to 15 pt. 1 pt.
Beets (without tops)	1 bu. (52 lb.) 1¼ to 1½ lb.	35 to 42 pt. 1 pt.
Broccoli	1 crate (25 lb.) 1 lb.	24 pt. 1 pt.
Brussels sprouts	4 quart boxes 1 lb.	6 pt. 1 pt.
Carrots (without tops)	1 bu. (50 lb.) 1¼ to 1½ lb.	32 to 40 pt. 1 pt.
Cauliflower	2 medium heads 1⅓ lb.	3 pt. 1 pt.
Chard	1 bu. (12 lb.) 1 to 1½ lb.	8 to 12 pt. 1 pt.
Collards	1 bu. (12 lb.) 1 to 1½ lb.	8 to 12 pt. 1 pt.
Corn, sweet (in husks)	1 bu. (35 lb.) 2 to 2½ lb.	14 to 17 pt. 1 pt.
Kale	1 bu. (18 lb.) 1 to 1½ lb.	12 to 18 pt. 1 pt.
Mustard greens	1 bu. (12 lb.) 1 to 1½ lb.	8 to 12 pt. 1 pt.
Peas	1 bu. (30 lb.) 2 to 2½ lb.	12 to 15 pt. 1 pt.
Peppers, sweet	⅔ lb. (3 peppers)	1 pt.
Pumpkin	3 lb.	2 pt.
Spinach	1 bu. (18 lb.) 1 to 1½ lb.	12 to 18 pt. 1 pt.
Squash, summer	1 bu. (40 lb.) 1 to 1¼ lb.	32 to 40 pt. 1 pt.
Squash, winter	3 lb.	2 pt.
Sweetpotatoes	⅔ lb.	1 pt.

Courtesy, USDA Home and Garden Bulletin Number 10.

Always change the water frequently and lift the vegetables out of the water. Don't just scoop out the whole bunch as soil settles to the bottom. Lifting them will keep the dirt from getting back on them.

Sort according to size, when freezing vegetables with varying sizes, such as ears of corn, green beans, or even peas. Larger vegetables require longer blanching than smaller ones and overblanching reduces the fresh flavor. Peel, trim, or cut into desired or recommended sizes as listed in the following Vegetable Freezing Guide.

A convenient way to gain frozen vegetable assets is to blanch and freeze extras when you cook fresh, in-season vegetables. Allow time for freezing when you see great-looking seasonal vegetables such as corn on the cob. This really almost takes the work out of freezing because it is done in small doses. Also, you'll never have any wasted vegetables. You'll be surprised how fast this system works to build a storehouse of frozen vegetables, hassle-free.

HOW TO BLANCH
AND CHILL VEGETABLES

Blanching can be done by either boiling in water or steaming. With home equipment and for time's sake, boiling is usually better. For vegetables you wish to leave as perfect as possible, such as asparagus or broccoli spears, you may wish to steam. Microwave blanching is another option not fully researched, but a great convenience. See page 134.

Always check a vegetable freezing chart and follow the times suggested precisely, making certain the time is adjusted according to the size of the vegetables. Altitudes over 5,000 feet require one more minute of blanching and chilling time. Remember that if a vegetable is not properly blanched, it loses quality in one to two months or less.

When blanching, work with a relatively small quantity at a time. To get optimum results in blanching, this rule—a gallon of boiling water per pound of vegetable—should definitely be followed.

Use an aluminum or enamelware or other good-quality blanching kettle. Never use a copper or iron utensil for blanching. Personally, my favorite blanching vessel is my electric deep-fat fryer, since it is already equipped with its own drain basket, making it very convenient for blanching. A pressure cooker or canning kettle can be adapted.

A blanching kettle must have a flat bottom, straight sides, a close-fitting cover, and preferably handles to make moving it convenient. The capacity should be at least 5 quarts. It must either come equipped with a strainer or a strainer must be purchased that will be spacious enough to hold the vegetables and still allow for easy lifting in and out of the kettle. Two strainers are most efficient. Ideally, the kettle will accommodate steaming, too. If not, flat screens can be purchased in varying sizes to fit across the kettle for steaming or a strainer with hooks or a cloth bag can be used.

To blanch, bring the water to a boil using one gallon for each pound of vegetable being prepared and up to two gallons for each pound of leafy vegetables. While the water is heating, prepare the vegetable a pound or two at a time as you would for table use. Place the prepared vegetable in the strainer and lower into boiling water. The goal is for the internal temperature of the vegetable to reach 180° F. Keeping the kettle covered during blanching keeps the heat higher. A boil must be maintained during the entire time. In timing blanching, start timing as soon as the vegetable hits the boiling water. By the way, you may use the same water for at least two or three times. Use your judgment to determine when to replace the water, based on the flavor and color characteristics of the vegetable you are freezing.

Steam scald by spreading a thin layer of the vegetable in a strainer or cloth held about two inches above the boiling water, keeping the kettle covered during the entire period. (Use a large, open kettle such as you would for blanching.) Time exactly.

Chilling is as important as blanching. Blanching stops the maturation process while chilling stops the cooking process, keeping the quality of the vegetable as high as possible. Approximately one pound of ice is required to chill one pound of vegetable. Keep the chilling water as chilly as possible. Plan ahead and freeze large cubes of ice in pans and bowls as they will melt much more slowly and be a lot more convenient to use. To preserve the most water-soluble nutrients, chill only until the vegetable is cool. For efficiency, use two strainers. This way the vegetable stays in the same strainer during blanching and chilling.

Next, **drain** the vegetable thoroughly. Extra water creates ice crystals which, if frozen slowly, can produce extralarge crystals and crush the cells of the vegetables, making for a less firm and less palatable vegetable.

HOW TO MICROWAVE BLANCH

An increasingly popular method of blanching is to use the microwave oven. Though more research is required, a rule of thumb is to place the cleaned and prepared vegetable in a covered casserole that is recommended for microwave oven use. The advantage of microwave blanching is that time is saved and it is more convenient. There are no large pots of boiling water.

To blanch, heat in the microwave oven for *one-fourth* the cooking period recommended in the oven user's guide for 2 cups of the vegetable being prepared, adding the amount of water suggested. Shake or stir the casserole in order to more evenly distribute the heat halfway through the blanching period if over 2 minutes or at the end of period if a short one. At the end of the blanching, check the appearance of the vegetable. It should be uniformly more brightly colored. If not, increase blanching time to *one-third* of the recommended microwave cooking time. Keep note of the time for future reference. Chill the vegetable in the casserole in ice water until cool, usually the same length of time as for cooking. Package.

Research is under way at various universities and manufacturers to determine if vegetables blanched in the packaging have acceptable quality. In my consultations with them I have felt a solution is needed for the problem of chilling. You might like to do some independent research of your own. Timing is the critical key. Perhaps in glass containers the chilling will work well. It's worth a try in the name of convenience! (See chart; page 219)

HOW TO PACKAGE

Vegetables are basically packaged two ways—dry or tray pack—although there are exceptions. For instance, broccoli and asparagus pack best if the heads and stems are alternated in a container, protecting their wholeness. A bag in a box is a workable exception as the box can be laid on its side. Commercial freezing bags and boxes are optional. You can save money by using freezer-weight bags inserted into other flat boxes from fruits, vegetables, margarine, freezer boxes, and the like. Any of the boxes can be used over and over again.

For your own convenience, always use either a piece of freezer tape or an adherent label of some sort so that you don't write on the carton. Writing on the carton can be quite a nuisance to remove or mark over. Do label packages clearly using a wax marking pencil or crayon listing the name of the vegetable and how it was prepared, the date, type of pack, and intended use, plus any other helpful information.

Head space is not very necessary as the air between the vegetables that seems unavoidable allows for the vegetables to expand. If rigid cartons such as glass or plastic are used, ½ inch head space is recommended. The only exception is when vegetables are packaged in liquid. Then allow one more inch.

Dry pack is probably most traditional. Well-drained vegetables are firmly packed in sealed bags inside boxes. The vegetable can be loosely placed in the bag, as in the case of a leafy vegetable, and shaken to compact it, or the bag can be firmly packed as the vegetables are added, as in the case of heavier vegetables such as green beans, corn, and carrots. As little air as possible should be allowed to get on the vegetable or to remain in the bags, meaning that time is of the essence in bagging vegetables. Air should always be forced out of the bags as they are packaged. This can be done by shaking or squeezing or both. After excluding as much air from the bag as possible, make a gooseneck, airtight twist on the bag and secure it with a band or twist.

Another method that's extra-convenient is to use heat-sealed heavy-weight plastic bags. The food can then be cooked right in the bag, which is especially good for microwave cooking. Rigid cartons can be used to mold either type of bag for storage neatness.

Tray pack vegetables are initially frozen until solid on a tray, then packaged. Because the vegetables are not stuck together, they are very flexible to use. You can take as much as you wish. Vegetables such as peas, beans, mixed vegetables, and corn are great packaged this way. To prepare them, place a single layer of vegetable on a large open tray. Place in freezer until just firm—about 1 hour. Some vegetables take a little longer. For convenience and greatest quality, after the first hour, check the vegetables every few minutes. Package in sealed bags or boxes, as above, allowing no head space.

Never overload the freezer. In each 24-hour period, never place more in the freezer than 3 pounds for each cubic foot. Place the packages in an upright freezer close to the side walls; in a chest freezer, place the packages on the bottom and close to the edges. Allow room for the air to circulate around each. After firmly frozen—about 24 hours—stack the packages, placing the most recent of each type closest to the back.

THAWING AND COOKING TIPS

The fantastically fresh flavor of frozen vegetables is assured when you have frozen them properly and then cooked them only until barely done. Overcooking is the poor flavor culprit in either process—providing the vegetables were at their peak when frozen, and they have not been freezer stored too long.

Cooking frozen vegetables is easy! Do not thaw the vegetables. Just cook from frozen except as noted below. The main secret is not to overcook as it destroys vitamins, nutrients, color, and flavor. When cooking, add the smallest possible quantity of water.

To cook, use about ¼ to ½ cup salted water for each pint of frozen vegetable. Bring the water to a boil, add the vegetables, cover, and reduce heat to low.

Little or no water is needed when cooking over especially slow heat, in heavy pans, in the oven in a sealed baking dish or foil, or when heated by microwave.

Lima beans and corn on the cob are exceptions. Lima beans require one cup of water. Corn on the cob needs to be thawed first at room temperature, then covered with water for cooking.

For cooking times, allow about one-half to two-thirds the cooking time required for fresh vegetables (see cooking chart page 138). Slow surface cooking, oven, and microwave cooking are exceptions. Your own judgment will be required to determine length of slow surface cooking, depending on the pan. For oven cooking, see tips on page 139. For microwave cooking times, consult the oven user's manual.

When cooking frozen vegetables, separate the vegetables with a fork after a few minutes of cooking time. Cover and cook until almost done, turning the heat off just before done. Add butter and preferred seasonings, and cover until ready to serve. (Covering keeps the air-volatile vitamin loss to a minimum.)

More about corn on the cob. For best results, partially thaw at room temperature, cover while cooking, and remove from water when hot. Do not hold in water or overcook as it produces sogginess. (See Oven Cooking Tips on page 139.)

Partially thawing greens of any type assures more even cooking without overcooking. Potatoes are another exception (see Oven Cooking Tips on page 139.)

Following is the timetable for conventional cooking of frozen vegetables:

Timetable for Cooking Frozen Vegetables in a Small Amount of Water*

Vegetable	Time to allow after water returns to boil† Minutes
Asparagus	5–10
Beans, lima:	
Large type	6–10
Baby type	15–20
Beans, snap, green, or wax:	
1-inch pieces	12–18
Julienne	5–10
Beans, soybeans, green	10–20
Beet greens	6–12
Broccoli	5–8
Brussels sprouts	4–9
Carrots	5–10
Cauliflower	5–8
Chard	8–10
Corn:	
Whole-kernel	3–5
On-the-cob	3–4
Kale	8–12
Kohlrabi	8–10
Mustard greens	8–15
Peas, green	5–10
Spinach	4–6
Squash, summer	10–12
Turnip greens	15–20
Turnips	8–12

*Use ½ cup of lightly salted water for each pint of vegetable with these exceptions: lima beans, one cup; corn-on-the-cob, water to cover.
†Time required at sea level; slightly longer time is required at higher altitudes.

Courtesy USDA Home and Garden Bulletin Number 10.

OVEN COOKING TIPS

Many vegetables heat beautifully in a covered dish in the oven. Whenever planning to use the oven for part of the meal, conserve energy (and money!) by using the oven for all parts of the meal. The same goes for broiler and surface cooking.

To oven heat, place vegetable in buttered, covered dish and season as desired; cover and bake, checking to see if the vegetables need separating after about 15 minutes. Cover and continue cooking for about 45 minutes for most vegetables. If no dish is available, frozen vegetable block can be sealed in foil.

Corn on the cob is really great heated in the oven. Partially thaw, brush with butter, place in shallow dish in 400°F oven for about 20 minutes, salt and serve.

Potatoes and French fried onions are best heated in the oven. To heat, place on a cookie sheet in a hot oven of 450°F for 15 to 20 minutes, stirring once or twice as they cook.

Baked potatoes can be reheated from frozen in the oven, or sliced or diced and fried, or thawed at room temperature and used in a combination dish such as potato salad. Mashed potatoes are best heated in a 325°F oven for 30 to 40 minutes.

REFREEZING

The beauty of frozen vegetables is that for any type of serving, you do not have to thaw any of the vegetables except corn on the cob. Therefore other than a power or freezer failure, refreezing partially thawed vegetables should not be much of a problem.

Basically the same general rules of thumb apply to vegetables as for other foods. If ice crystals remain, you can refreeze and should use the vegetables as soon as possible. Otherwise, if still cold to the touch and not frozen, you can cook and refreeze in a sealed package. You can always refreeze vegetables after cooking.

VEGETABLE FREEZING GUIDE

NOTES: *No head space* is required for vegetables unless a rigid container is used. Then ½ inch should be allowed. When packaging juice or in liquid, follow standard head space recommendations listed on page 113. In high altitudes over 5,000 feet, allow one more minute to each blanching and chilling period.

Artichokes. (whole, medium-sized). Cut off about 1 inch of tops, horny tips, and trim stems. Wash immediately after trimming in cold water. Pull away outer bracts until light yellow or white bracts are exposed. Blanch in 1 tablespoon ascorbic acid or ½ cup lemon juice to 2 quarts water, 10 minutes.

Pack in freezer-weight bags in boxes or rigid cartons using the dry or tray pack. Seal and label type of artichokes.

Artichoke hearts. Cut off top third of small artichokes, trim off stems. Blanch 3 to 5 minutes depending on size, using treated water as above.

Asparagus. Cut or break off tough end of each stalk. Wash thoroughly, leaving stalks whole or cut into 1-inch-long pieces. Sort as to size. Blanching—small: 1½ to 2 minutes; medium: 2 to 3 minutes. large: 3 to 4 minutes. Steaming is often preferred for asparagus and will require 3 minutes for small stalks and 4½ for medium and large stalks.

Pack into rigid cartons alternating tips and stems, or place bag in a box on its side and load, alternating tips and stems. Seal and label type of cut.

Avocados. See Fruit Freezing Guide (Chapter 8).

Beans, snap
either green or wax. Sort as to size, snip ends. Leave whole, cut into 2- to 3-inch lengths, or strip into French cut. Blanch 2 to 3 minutes.

Freeze on a tray, then package as soon as firmly frozen. Can be dry packed into freezer-weight bags and boxes or cartons. Seal and label for type of beans.

Beans, green Italian. Wash, snip off ends, break or cut into even lengths about 2 inches long.
Blanch 3½ minutes.
Package same as snap beans.

Beans, lima. Wash, shell, discard any irregular beans.
Blanch—small: 2 to 3 minutes; large: 3 to 4 minutes.
Package same as snap beans.

Beans, soy. Wash, blanch pods 5 minutes. Cool quickly and squeeze beans out of pods, discarding any poor-quality beans.
Freeze on a tray, then package as soon as firmly frozen. Seal and label for type of beans.

Beets. Trim off tops, leaving ½-inch stem. Wash, cook unpeeled until tender, allowing 25 to 30 minutes for small and 45 to 50 minutes for medium beets. (Beets over 3 inches in diameter are best not frozen.) Cool promptly in cold water; peel, slice, or cube.
Freeze on a tray, package as soon as firmly frozen. Or, can be dry packed into freezer-weight bags and boxes or cartons. Seal and label for type of beets.
Tiny beets, 1 to 1½ inches in diameter, can be blanched and left whole after peeling.
Pack same as other beets.

Beet greens. See Greens.

Broccoli. Wash; if insects are present in heads, soak heads-down in salt solution of ½ cup per gallon of cold water for ½ hour. Rinse. Cut stalks to fit intended containers and to a uniform size of approximately 1 to 1½ inches across. Blanch: 3 to 4 minutes. Steam: 5 minutes.
Pack into rigid cartons, alternating tips and stems; or place a bag in a box on its side and load alternating tips and stems. Seal and label.

Brussels sprouts. Using only good heads, wash, removing coarse outer leaves. Soak as above to bring out insects. Rinse, drain, and sort according to size. Blanching—small: 3 minutes; medium: 4 minutes; large: 5 minutes.
Pack in freezer-weight bags in boxes or rigid cartons, using the dry or tray pack. Seal and label.

Cabbage or Chinese cabbage. Wash, cut into medium or coarse shreds, wedges, or separate into leaves. Blanch: 1 to 1½ minutes. Steam: 2 to 3 minutes.

Freeze on a tray, then package as soon as firmly frozen. Can be dry packed into freezer-weight bags and boxes or cartons. Seal and label for type of cabbage.

Carrots. Remove tops, wash, scrape. Slice as desired or leave small ones whole. Blanching—whole: 5 minutes; lengthwise strips: 2 minutes; diced or sliced: 2 minutes.

Package same as cabbage.

Cauliflower. Wash and break into flowerets about 1 inch in diameter. Soak as for broccoli, rinse, drain, and quickly place in boiling water. Blanch 3 to 4 minutes.

Package same as cabbage.

Celery. Trim, discard blemished portions, wash, and cut into 1-inch lengths or dice. Blanch 3 minutes.

Package same as cabbage.

Celery root, Celeriac. Cut away leaves and root fibers and thoroughly scrub. Cook until almost tender—20 to 30 minutes. Cool. Peel and slice or dice.

Package same as cabbage.

Chard. See Greens.

Chayote. Wash, remove stem and blossom ends. Do not peel. Dice. Blanch 2 minutes.

Package same as cabbage.

Chiles. See Peppers, Green Chile.

Chives. See Herbs.

Collards. See Greens.

Corn, whole kernel. Matures rapidly and is at best quality for only about 48 hours, so work quickly with a small amount at a time. Husk, remove silks, trim ends. Then blanch and chill. When thoroughly chilled, cut kernels from the cob about ⅔ the depth of each kernel. Blanch—small, 5 minutes; medium, 8 minutes; large, 10 minutes.

Package same as cabbage. Seal and label type of pack.

Corn, on the cob. Prepare same as for whole kernel, except chill twice as long. Blanch—small, 7 minutes; medium, 9 minutes; large, 11 minutes.

Package each ear individually in plastic or foil and tightly seal in a large plastic bag. Label for size of ears.

Corn, cream-style. Prepare as for whole kernel corn. Cut corn at center of kernels and scrape cobs with dull side of knife to remove juice and heart of each kernel.

Freeze on a tray, then package as soon as firmly frozen. Can be packed into freezer-weight bags and boxes or cartons. Seal and label.

NOTE: If corn is cut off the cob without blanching, you must cook it before packaging, cooking 1 pint at a time in a 2-quart saucepan. Cook, stirring constantly, for 8 to 10 minutes. Chill in pan in ice water. Package as indicated for corn.

Cucumbers. End product is more "flabby" than when fresh. Fine for relish-type salads. Wash and thinly slice. Either generously salt both sides of each slice and drain on paper toweling and then freeze; or soak in cold salt water and place in vinegar, water, salt, and sugar solution such as for table use. Combine with onions, etc., to serve. No blanching required.

Pack in rigid containers, allowing 1 inch head space for the vinegar pack. Seal and label type of pack.

Dasheen (or Taro). Wash and peel. Dice or cut into strips. Blanch 2 to 3 minutes in 1 tablespoon ascorbic acid or ½ cup lemon juice to 2 quarts water.

Pack in freezer-weight bags in boxes or rigid cartons using the dry or tray pack. Seal and label type of pack.

Eggplant. Wash, peel, and slice into slices ⅓ inch thick. Preserve the natural color by soaking 5 minutes in 4 tablespoons salt to 1 gallon of water. Ascorbic acid mixture, used according to the package directions, can be substituted—using a 1 quart of water soak. Blanch 4 minutes.

Pack in freezer-weight bags in boxes or rigid cartons using the dry or tray pack. Seal and label type of pack.

Ginger root. Wash well and dry. No blanching necessary. To use, grate or slice while still frozen. Rewrap and return unused part to freezer.

Wrap each root in freezer wrap or plastic bag.

Grape leaves. Wash well. Blanch 1½ minutes.

Place in small freezer-weight plastic bags.

Greens
(beet, collards, kale,
kohlrabi,
mustard greens,
spinach, Swiss chard, any other leafy greens). Remove tough stems and old leaves. Then wash well, lifting them out of the water to avoid

143

getting soil. Cut in pieces if desired. Blanch 2 minutes except for collards, which require 3 minutes.

Place in small freezer-weight plastic bags.

Herbs (basil, chives, dill, marjoram, mint, parsley, rosemary, sage, thyme, tarragon). Wash, drain, then chop or shred off leaves. (For use in cooked dishes or salad dressings as thawed herbs are limp. Use 1½ times as much frozen herbs as dried.) No blanching necessary.

Place 1 tablespoon in plastic wrap packets and place all herbs in rigid carton. Seal, date, and label each.

Jicama. Wash, peel and slice as desired. No blanching necessary.

Pack in freezer-weight bags in boxes or rigid cartons using the dry or tray pack. Seal and label type of pack.

Kohlrabi. Wash, cut tops and roots off, and wash again. Peel and leave whole or slice into ¼-inch slices, or dice into ½-inch cubes. Blanch whole: 3 minutes; diced/sliced: 1 to 2 minutes.

Package same as for Jicama.

Lettuce, other salad greens. For short-term storage only—use only as an anti-waste measure when oversupplied or going away. Rinse, drain, and leave whole or coarsely chop. No blanching necessary.

Pack in small freezer-weight plastic bags. Seal and label.

Mixed vegetables. Process each vegetable as indicated and freeze using the tray pack method. Mix together desired vegetables as you package. Good for using up small quantities.

Freeze on a tray, then package as soon as firmly frozen. Pack into freezer-weight bags and boxes or cartons. Seal and label.

Mushrooms. Perhaps one of the most controversial of frozen vegetables, they seem to do well at least three or four different ways depending on your preferences and type of mushroom—also on the end use. *No-bother Style:* Dust off mushrooms, place on tray, and quick-freeze as directed for tray freezing. No blanching.

Package in freezer bags or cartons. Seal and label.

Traditional: Rinse mushrooms, drain. Sort according to size. Trim off ends of stems. If mushrooms are large, reserve whole for stuffing, slice, or quarter. Soak in a solution of ascorbic acid, using the amount recommended for the type being used to prevent darkening as for fruit. Soak 5 minutes. Then steam or blanch. (See chart below.) Many prefer steaming as they feel the mushrooms have more flavor steamed.

Freeze on a tray, then package as soon as firmly frozen. Can be dry packed into freezer-weight bags and boxes or cartons. Seal and label type of pack.

Timing Chart

	Blanching	Steaming
Sliced	3 min.	3½ min.
Quarters	3½ min.	4 min.
Whole	4 min.	5 min.

Sautéed: Sauté 1 pint of mushrooms at a time in a medium-hot frying pan in butter or margarine until almost done. Cool in pan, setting it in cold water. No blanching necessary.

Pack in freezer-weight bags in boxes or rigid cartons using the dry or tray pack. Seal and label type of pack.

Mustard greens. See Greens.

Okra. Wash, cut off stems, and blanch, slicing if desired after blanching. Blanch small pods: 2 minutes; large pods: 3 minutes.

Package same as mushrooms.

Fried, Southern style: If desired, dust in cornmeal or flour and sauté in butter, margarine, or drippings until almost done. Cool in pan in ice water.

Package same as mushrooms.

Onions. Peel, wash, chop, slice, or leave small ones whole. No blanching required. If French frying, fry as for table use, drain, and cool.

Freeze on a tray until firm. Then store in packets in frequently used amounts. Small whole onions can be placed in a bag or rigid carton. Place French fried onion rings in rigid containers with layers of waxed paper or wrap in between layers. Seal and label for type.

Parsley. See Herbs.

Parsnips. Use medium to small parsnips; remove tops, rinse, and peel. Then cut in ½-inch cubes or slices. Blanch 2 minutes.

Pack in freezer-weight bags in boxes or rigid cartons using the dry or tray pack. Seal and label type of pack.

Peas, blackeye or field. Shell peas, discarding hard ones. Blanch 2 minutes.

Package same as parsnips (above).

Peas, Chinese
pods or edible pod peas. Wash, remove blossom ends and strings. Leave whole. Blanch—small, 1½ to 2 minutes; medium, 2½ to 3 minutes.

Freeze on a tray, then package as soon as firmly frozen. Can be dry packed into freezer-weight bags in boxes or cartons. Seal and label type of pack.

Peas, green. Wash pods, shell a few at a time. Discard poorly formed ones. Blanch as you shell a quantity as air toughens peas. 1½ to 2 minutes.

Package same as peas above.

Peppers, sweet green. Wash, cut out stem and remove seeds. Leave whole for stuffing, halve, slice, or dice. No blanching required.

Pack in freezer-weight bags in boxes or rigid cartons using the dry or tray pack. Seal and label type of pack.

Peppers, green chile. The long, green chiles used for Mexican dishes are best parched under a broiler. No blanching necessary. Pierce the chiles once or twice with a sharp knife; then place on a foil-lined broiler pan and parch until skin is brown and blistered. Chill in ice until cool. Can peel before packaging if preferred—I don't!

Pack in frequently used quantities, such as 6 or 12 to a bag. Seal and label number chiles in each bag.

Peppers, hot. Small, hot peppers, either red, green, or yellow, can be packaged whole or chopped. No blanching necessary.

Pack in freezer-weight bags in boxes or rigid cartons using the dry or tray pack. Seal and label type of pack.

Pimiento. Pimiento peppers may be roasted in a 400°F oven for 3 to 4 minutes until peel is charred. Remove charred skin by rinsing pimientos in cold water, scraping with a knife when necessary. No blanching necessary.

Freeze on a tray, then package as soon as firmly frozen. Can be dry packed into freezer-weight bags in boxes or cartons. Seal and label type of pack.

Potatoes, white. Raw potatoes become mushy when frozen. The following styles of preparation are acceptable to most.
French fried (or shoestring): No blanching necessary. Cut potato strips rather small. Fry quickly to light brown.

Cool on absorbent paper. Package in rigid containers. Seal and label type of pack.

Hash-browned: Prepare as for table use, frying only to a light brown.

Cool. Package in rigid containers. Seal and label type of pack.

Mashed: Cook, then mash, adding milk and butter as usual. (Add beaten egg white for added fluffiness, if desired.)

Cool. Spoon into rigid freezer containers. Or make mounds and tray freeze, then package in cartons. Seal and label type of pack.

New: Use only very small potatoes. Boil in jackets. Peel.

Cool. Pack in freezer bag or container. Seal and label type of pack.

Stuffed, baked: Use good-quality baking potatoes. Bake as usual. Halve, scoop potato from shell, and mash. Add cream or milk, butter, and seasonings. Fold in beaten egg white. Refill shells, sprinkle with cheese, if desired.

Place in top-opening containers if tops are rounded, such as small foil pans with foil covers or in freezer bags or containers, if halves are put together. Seal and label type of pack.

Potatoes, sweet. Wash and cook until almost tender. No blanching necessary. Let stand at room temperature to cool. Peel, cut in halves, slice, or mash—sprinkling ascorbic acid mixture, dissolved, on the potatoes. (Use amount directed on mixture label to prevent darkening of fruit.) Or, lemon or orange juice may be used.

Pack in freezer-weight bags in boxes or rigid cartons using the dry or tray pack. Seal and label type of pack.

Pumpkin. Wash, cut into pieces, and remove seeds. Bake or steam until tender. No blanching necessary. Scoop pulp from skin and mash.

Pack same as sweet potatoes above. For convenience, package enough for intended use: pies, cakes, breads, etc. Seal and label.

Purees (great for baby food). Prepare and blanch vegetable according to instructions. This is especially good for irregularly shaped or trimmed, blemished vegetables. Strain or blend vegetables.

Freeze in small quantities or in ice cube trays according to desired end use. Package in plastic bags or cartons. Seal and label.

Rutabagas. Wash and remove tops. Peel and slice or dice into ¼-inch cubes. Blanch 3 minutes. Then mash after blanching, if desired, mashing or pressing through sieve or ricer.

Pack in freezer-weight bags in boxes or rigid cartons using the dry or tray pack. Seal and label type of pack.

Sauerkraut. Freshly made cured sauerkraut can be frozen. No blanching required.

Pack into rigid containers or bags leaving 1 inch head space. Seal, label type of pack.

Soybeans. See Beans, Soy

Squash, summer:
crookneck,
patty pan,
yellow,
zucchini Wash. Do not peel. (If preferred, skin can be removed.) Cut into slices ¼ to 1½ inches thick.

Blanch ¼-inch slices, 3 minutes; 1- to 1½-inch slices, 6 minutes.

Pack in freezer-weight bags in boxes or rigid cartons using the dry or tray pack. Seal and label type of squash.

Squash, winter:
acorn,
banana,
butternut,
Hubbard. Wash. Cut or break into pieces and remove seeds. Then prepare as for pumpkin. No blanching necessary.

Pack same as squash above.

Tomatoes. Many disagree on the merits of frozen fresh tomatoes. I have personally found them very satisfactory for use in cooked foods. Leave whole, quarter, or slice. No blanching necessary.

Freeze on a tray, then package as soon as firmly frozen. Can be dry packed into freezer-weight bags in boxes or cartons. Seal and label type of pack.

Stewed tomatoes: Prepare by cooking peeled, quartered tomatoes for 11 to 21 minutes or until tender. (Skins can be easily removed by quickly scalding for 2 minutes in boiling water.)

Pack in freezer-weight bags in boxes or rigid cartons, leaving ½ to 1 inch head space. Seal and label type of pack.

Tomato juice: Prepared by cooking tomato pieces until tender and then straining.

Pack into jars or preferred containers of right size for intended use. Allow 1 inch head space. Seal and label.

Tomato puree: Made from the solids remaining after straining the juice. Puree is excellent for cooking purposes.

Pack same as juice above.

Turnips. Prepare as for parsnips.

Water chestnuts. Unused portions of canned water chestnuts may be frozen. Fresh water chestnuts can also be frozen. Soak if dry, wash, and peel.

Pack quantity generally used into bags in boxes or cartons, seal and label.

RECIPES

Vegetable Side Dishes '

According to many research studies, in the everyday diets of most Americans side dishes are almost vanishing if salad is a course. When entertaining and for special occasions, side dishes of vegetables can be a delight of both taste and texture.

Fresh frozen vegetables cooked just to a touch—slightly underdone—are perfect. Another great way to prepare them is to place frozen vegetables in the oven when using the oven for the rest of the meal. This saves energy. Just place in a covered casserole, add seasonings, and at any moderate temperature between 300° and 400°F most leafy vegetables and common vegetables such as peas, corn, squash, and spinach cook in about 20 minutes whereas fibrous vegetables require about 30 minutes. Examples of fibrous vegetables are green beans, carrots, and broccoli. Always check a sample of the vegetable before serving.

This cooking method works great under the broiler or on a grill. Cook the seasoned vegetable wrapped in foil. Use approximately the same times . . . so you will want to start the vegetable before most meats.

Speaking of seasonings, try sampling the following selections—

On The Spicy Side

Just for fun, try seasoning your vegetables in various ways. For your convenience and enjoyment follow this seasoning chart.

- Asparagus: nutmeg, dry mustard, tarragon, caraway seed.
- Baked Beans, Pork and Beans: garlic powder, cloves, barbecue spice.
- Beets: celery seed, tarragon, cloves, nutmeg, allspice.
- Black-eyed Peas: sage, bay leaf, poultry seasoning, onion salt, garlic salt.
- Carrots: curry powder, ginger, mace, parsley flakes.
- Carrots and Peas: parsley flakes, dried dill, mint flakes.
- Corn: paprika, garlic powder, onion salt, onion powder.
- Green Beans: basil, garlic salt, dried dill, marjoram, savory.
- Hominy: chili powder, oregano, paprika.

149

- Kidney Beans: chili powder, dry mustard, instant minced onion.
- Lima Beans: onion salt, oregano, celery salt, chili powder.
- Mixed Vegetables: dry mustard, bay leaf, curry powder.
- Okra: basil, celery flakes, thyme, instant minced onion.
- Onions: chili powder, sage, caraway seed, poppy seed.
- Peas: savory, basil, onion flakes, parsley flakes.
- Potatoes: dill seed, paprika, garlic powder, rosemary.
- Sauerkraut: dried dill, celery seed, caraway seed, onion powder.
- Spinach, other greens: nutmeg, mace, dried dill, onion salt.
- Succotash: onion powder, thyme, majoram, parsley flakes.
- Sweet potatoes: allspice, cloves, cinnamon, nutmeg, cardamom seed.
- Tomatoes: thyme, oregano, basil, garlic powder, onion flakes.
- Wax Beans: instant minced onion, basil, rosemary, oregano.

Sauced Vegetables

Succulent vegetables are enhanced when served sauced. Try: Hollandaise, Mornay, Béarnaise, Béchamel, cheese, and mushroom sauces. For convenience, keep frozen sauces packaged in one-meal quantities.

Soufflés or custards made from frozen vegetables are super! Also vegetable combinations such as the following Stuffed Zucchini or Chinese Vegetables are excellent.

FRENCH PEAS

This dish is almost as good made with frozen leftover lettuce as with fresh.

Temperature: medium-high
Cooking time: 12 to 15 minutes
Yield: 4 to 6 servings

2 tablespoons butter	½ teaspoon salt
4–5 small white onions, halved	½ teaspoon sugar
1 quart frozen peas	Dash of freshly ground
1 teaspoon crushed tarragon	black pepper
1 teaspoon crushed basil	*½ small head of lettuce shredded

1. Heat butter in a heavy skillet, add onions, and stir and cook until onions are about half done (approximately 5 minutes).

2. Add peas, tarragon, basil, salt, sugar, and pepper. Stir and cook 5 to 7 minutes.

3. Add lettuce and cook until lettuce is wilted. Serve.

*Any type of lettuce or endive will work fine. Not-so-fresh lettuce in addition to the frozen works just as well as the very fresh.

FREEZING HINT: *Do not freeze leftovers;* instead save for including in tomorrow's salad.

STUFFED ZUCCHINI

Great with almost any meat or seafood dish. Especially appealing served with roasts or whole fish.

Temperature: any moderate
temperature being used for rest of
meal in 300-400° F oven
Baking time: 30 minutes or until
done
Yield: 6 servings

6 *small to medium-sized
    zucchini, fresh or frozen*
1 *cup frozen whole kernel
    corn (more for larger
    squash)*
2 *tablespoons chopped,
    frozen green pepper*
1 *tablespoon frozen chopped
    onion*
1 *teaspoon crushed thyme*

1 *teaspoon crushed tarragon*
½ *teaspoon salt
    Freshly ground black
    pepper*
¼ *cup Parmesan cheese,
    optional*
½ *cup cereal, cracker, or
    bread crumbs
    Butter salt
    Paprika*

1. If using fresh zucchini, parboil 5 minutes in salted water, then slice in half lengthwise. Scoop out center portion, using a teaspoon. Chop medium fine. (Frozen zucchini can be prepared this way before blanching.)

2. Lightly butter a baking pan. Place squash halves in pan, hollow side up. Evenly divide ingredients and add in order listed, layering on each. Add butter salt and paprika to taste.

3. Bake until done—about 30 minutes. Should be mushy—best if still slightly crisp.

Variations: Fresh tomato, ground meat of any type, or chile pepper may be substituted for the vegetables listed, or combined in any desired way.

FREEZING HINTS: This is a particularly flexible food to freeze. Can be frozen stuffed by preparing, then freezing on a baking sheet. When firm, package in individual wrap or bags, sealed and labeled. Or zucchini can be frozen intended for this use. Prepare as in step 1, packaging chopped pulp in a small bag enclosed with the halves. Leftover stuffed zucchini freeze fine too! Package individually.

MAXIMUM RECOMMENDED FREEZER STORAGE: 8 months

EGGPLANT GARLIC PATTIES

An all-time favorite in our house! We love them with almost any red meat, especially lamb and Syrian and Lebanese specialties. The batter or the cooked patties freeze beautifully.

Temperature: medium or 360°F in
electric skillet
Cooking time: 4 minutes each
Yield: 4 servings

1 *medium-sized eggplant*	½ *cup flour, cracker or bread*
Water	*crumbs, or less**
½ *teaspoon salt*	2 *tablespoons Parmesan*
¼ *teaspoon garlic powder*	*cheese, optional*
Freshly ground black	1 *egg, slightly beaten*
pepper	*Olive oil*

1. Rinse eggplant. Do not peel. Remove green top, then dice in small quantity of water.

2. Cook eggplant on high heat until steaming, then reduce heat to low to finish cooking. Cook until eggplant is soft.

3. Drain, reserving juice. Add ¼ cup liquid back to eggplant. Add salt, garlic powder, pepper, flour* or crumbs, cheese (if used), and egg. Mix ingredients together. If desired, freeze in rigid carton at this point. To cook, thaw several hours then proceed with recipe.

4. Heat skillet with enough olive oil to lightly cover surface until hot.

5. Spoon mixture into skillet, making several small patties. Fry until lightly browned, then turn each.

*Add flour gradually, using only enough to make a mixture the consistency of gravy.

CORN CUSTARD

From the deep South far into the Midwest, this is a favorite winter vegetable for special occasions.

Temperature: 325°F (can be
varied to suit temperature being
used for meat)
Baking time: 1 hour
Yield: 8 servings

3 eggs	½ teaspoon pepper
2½ cups frozen corn	2 cups milk, evaporated
¼ cup flour	milk, or light cream
¼ teaspoon baking powder	½ cup bread or cracker
1 tablespoon sugar	crumbs, optional
1 teaspoon salt	2 tablespoons soft butter

1. Using a wire whisk or an electric blender for a finer texture, beat the eggs, then add all the remaining ingredients except the crumbs and butter and beat well.
2. Pour into a buttered 1½-quart baking dish. If you wish, top with crumbs and dots of butter. Bake until an inserted knife in center comes out clean, and top is golden. Excellent to bake alongside beef, ham, or chicken. (Can be frozen for baking later, allow 1½ hours to cook from frozen state.)

Variations: Small oysters, minced onion, or green pepper can be added for variety in quantities to suit taste.

CHINESE MIXED VEGETABLES

Most Oriental- or Hawaiian-inspired meat, seafood, or egg main dishes will benefit by serving this vegetable combination alongside.

Temperature: medium-high
Cooking time: 12 to 15 minutes
Yield: 6 to 8 servings

2 tablespoons olive or peanut oil (can substitute part sesame oil)

2 cups celery cut diagonally in 1-inch pieces (can use frozen for slightly less texture)

1 teaspoon seasoned salt (or to suit taste)

1 teaspoon rubbed basil

Freshly ground black pepper

2 small cans water chestnuts, drained and halved

1 4-ounce can whole small mushrooms (or 1 cup fresh or frozen)

2 10-ounce packages frozen Italian green beans thawed on counter while preparing other vegetables*

1. Heat oil in large skillet until it is very hot. Add celery and all of the seasonings. Stir constantly while frying.

2. Cook until celery is about half cooked—still rather crisp. Then add the water chestnuts and mushrooms. Stir together.

3. When the mixture is heated through, add the partially thawed green beans. Stir until well mixed. Cover and turn off heat. Leave on unit or burner for a few minutes, then serve piping hot.

*Italian green beans are similar in taste and texture to snow peas and are generally much easier to get. Use snow peas if available or desired.

FREEZING HINTS: Do not freeze leftovers—use in salad or add to rice or chow mein, etc.

BURRITOS À LA BUTEL

Burritos are tremendous when made well—yet terribly disappointing when made poorly or served sauceless. This sauce is super and developed from my tasting it numerous times in a Juarez, Mexico, restaurant. The sauce freezes very well.

Yield: 6 burritos

6 white-flour tortillas
1 # 303 can pinto beans, drained
1 teaspoon bacon drippings
    Dash of garlic powder
    Dash of salt

2 green onions, finely chopped
½ cup grated Monterey Jack cheese
    Romaine lettuce or any bright green leafy lettuce, coarsely chopped

1. If tortillas are not freshly made, cover with aluminum foil and place on the dinner plates and warm in a 300°F oven.

2. Heat the beans in the drippings, mashing the beans to a pulp and seasoning to taste with the salt and garlic.

3. Spoon the hot bean mixture down the center of each warm tortilla. Top with chopped green onions and cheese. Roll and heat in the oven until the cheese melts. Nest chopped lettuce around the warm burritos. Serve with a generous supply of Burrito Sauce, recipe following.

NOTE: Chile con carne made from beef or pork can be inserted in the burritos if desired. Then the cheese and sauce are usually omitted.

BURRITO SAUCE

Yield: 1 pint

1 tablespoon butter, melted
1 medium onion, thinly sliced and separated into rings
4 to 6 green chiles parched, peeled, and chopped, or
6 to 8 banana peppers sliced into rings

2 medium tomatoes, chopped, or 1 8-ounce can tomato sauce
1 tablespoon flour
    Dash of garlic powder
½ teaspoon salt
1½ cups chicken stock (can be made with bouillon)

1. Melt butter in a frypan. Add the onion, chiles, and tomatoes and cook until the onion is transparent. Add the flour and stir. Cook until well blended.

2. Add the seasonings and the stock and cook until the sauce becomes smooth; allow to cook about 15 minutes to blend the flavors. Serve as a sauce with the burritos or use as a sauce over poached eggs atop tortillas to create Huevos Rancheros.

FREEZING HINTS: The tortillas, bean filling, and sauce freeze best individually. To freeze, package in rigid sealed cartons. If some filled burritos are left, they can be frozen individually wrapped if they have not been sauced. Label.

MAXIMUM RECOMMENDED FREEZER STORAGE: 3 months

SOUP

Soups warm the cockles of the heart and ready the appetite for more. Here are four extra-good ones!

FRENCH ONION SOUP

With this soup, "Homemade is better" couldn't be truer, although really good onion soup made the way it is on the banks of the Seine needs patient hours of barely bubbling. For very special eating, broil on a crusty cheesy topping.

Temperature: low
Cooking time: 4 to 6 hours
Yield: 10 servings

½ cup butter	¾ teaspoon celery salt
4 large onions, thinly sliced (about 10 cups)	¼ teaspoon salt
1½ teaspoons paprika	¼ teaspoon pepper
¼ cup flour	2½ quarts beef stock
¼ cup vegetable oil	1 cup dark beer, optional
	½ cup red, dry wine

1. Melt butter in large, heavy stewing kettle, then sauté onions, and add paprika.
2. Make roux (thickening for sauce) by browning flour in oil in separate skillet, stirring continuously for best results.
3. Add roux, celery salt, salt, pepper, and beef stock to onions.
4. Simmer on low heat for 4 to 6 hours.

To serve, add the beer and wine and let soup simmer while preparing the cheesy crusts for the tops of each—the one great way to eat it. Serve with a glass of red wine.

FREEZING HINTS: Package in freezer cartons, being certain to portion out some single servings for a marvelous lunch or light supper alone.

MAXIMUM RECOMMENDED FREEZER STORAGE: 3 months

CHEESE TOPPING

10 *1-inch-thick slices French bread*
    Olive oil
    Garlic powder
10 *slices Swiss cheese*
 1 *cup (about) Parmesan cheese, grated*

1. Using the lowest setting on your toaster, toast, drying out the bread slices and creating a golden color. If your toaster will not accommodate the thick bread, toast in 325°F oven for 15 minutes on a side.

2. As soon as toasted, brush with olive oil and sprinkle lightly with garlic powder. Set aside, or you can freeze them to shortcut the preparation time.

3. Ladle soup into deep crockery bowls with a lip. Place bread on top and cover with slice of cheese and sprinkle with Parmesan. Broil 5 to 10 minutes. When cheese is melted and golden, serve immediately.

CREAM OF CELERY SOUP

Cooking time: 45 minutes
Yield: 4 servings

1½ *cups diced celery*	1 *teaspoon salt*
½ *cup water*	½ *teaspoon monosodium*
1 *tablespoon butter or*	*glutamate, optional*
margarine	¼ *teaspoon pepper*
3 *tablespoons chopped onion*	1 *tablespoon parsley flakes*
2 *tablespoons flour*	2½ *cups skimmed milk*

1. Add celery to boiling water in a saucepan and cook for 5 to 10 minutes or until tender. Drain and set aside.

2. Melt butter or margarine in a 4-quart saucepan, add onion and cook

until onion is clear. Blend in flour, salt, monosodium glutamate, pepper, and parsley flakes. Heat until mixture bubbles. Remove from heat.

3. Gradually add 1 cup of milk and stir constantly until mixture thickens. Cook 2 to 3 minutes longer. Add celery and remaining milk. Bring to boiling, stirring constantly, and reduce heat to simmer for 10 minutes.

FREEZING HINT: Freeze in sealed cartons, packaging some single servings. Label.

MAXIMUM RECOMMENDED FREEZER STORAGE: 3 months

WATERCRESS AND POTATO SOUP

Cooking time: 40 minutes
Yield: 4 servings

4 cups chicken broth	1 tablespoon instant minced onion
2 medium potatoes, cut into cubes	½ teaspoon salt
1 cup coarsely chopped watercress (can substitute lettuce or spinach)	⅛ teaspoon pepper
	1 cup skimmed milk
	Cracked pepper (optional)

1. Place chicken broth in medium saucepan; add potatoes, watercress, and onion.

2. Cover; bring to a boil on high heat, switch to low, and continue cooking until potatoes are tender (about 20 minutes).

3. Pour vegetables and some of broth into blender jar. Blend at high speed until smooth.

4. Return mixture to saucepan with remaining broth. Add salt, pepper, and milk. Ladle into soup bowls; sprinkle with cracked pepper.

FREEZING HINT: Place in sealed cartons, storing some single servings. Label.

MAXIMUM RECOMMENDED FREEZER STORAGE: 3 months

BLACK BEAN SOUP

Great served before Puerto Rican or Cuban meals.

Temperature: simmer
Cooking time: 2 hours or until
tender

2 cups black beans
6 cups cold water
¼ pound cooked ham, diced
4 cloves garlic, crushed
2 teaspoons salt
4 tablespoons dehydrated
    onion flakes
2 whole cloves
½ teaspoon cumin

1 teaspoon ground red chile
    or to taste
1 lime, juiced
¼ cup rum
4 green onions, finely
    chopped
½ cup grated Monterey Jack
    cheese
Fresh lime wedges, optional

1. Soak beans in water to cover overnight.
2. Drain and add 6 cups water and all ingredients except rum, green onions, and cheese. Cover and simmer for 2 hours.

FREEZING HINTS: Ladle into freezing containers. To thaw, place in refrigerator or on counter for about 4 hours. Heat until simmering and serve as suggested.

To serve, add rum and ladle soup into bowls; top with chopped green onions and grated cheese. Serve fresh lime wedges on the side if more lime is desired.

MAXIMUM RECOMMENDED FREEZER STORAGE: 4 months

Special Salad Secrets

Salads made of unlikely freezables such as gelatin and cucumbers can be frozen. The usual tossed green types do not freeze, but leftover frozen cooked vegetables can be marinated in dressing for adding to green salads. (That's a great way to use leftover vegetables too.)

There are many, many other types of salads. For example, marinated fruits or vegetables are absolutely delightful and very gourmet. They can serve as a garnish as well as a salad.

In this short section, I'd like to share with you my two favorite dressings—poppy seed for fruit and vinaigrette for vegetables. The crispy texture of partially thawed frozen vegetables that have been frozen in vinaigrette is great!

POPPY SEED FRUIT SALAD DRESSING

This dressing has been a favorite ever since my college freshman foods course when I had the delightful assignment of making a similar version for a fresh orange and onion salad—I thought "ugh" when given the assignment, but I soon loved it! Serve over any variety of various shapes, colors, and textures of fruit, partially thawed or fresh.

Yield: 1½ cups

1 cup oil	1 teaspoon mustard
⅓ cup vinegar	1 teaspoon celery seed
¾ cup honey	1 small green onion
1 teaspoon salt	1 tablespoon poppy seeds

1. Place all ingredients in blender bowl in order listed and blend on high speed until onion is pureed.
2. Store in refrigerator in a covered container.

FREEZING HINT: For long-term keeping, freeze in convenient one-meal quantities in jars or cartons. Seal and label.

MAXIMUM RECOMMENDED FREEZER STORAGE: 6 months

SAUCE VINAIGRETTE

Yield: enough for 4 to 6 servings

6 tablespoons olive oil or vegetable oil	Several grinds of the pepper mill
2 tablespoons wine vinegar	1 teaspoon prepared mustard, optional
½ teaspoon salt	Several dashes of paprika

1. Using a whisk or fork blend all ingredients to a froth. Pour over desired vegetable, garnishing with capers, pimiento, or other desired garnish.

Optional additives: garlic, herbs, or chopped fresh onion.

FREEZING HINTS: Make a large quantity and freeze in amounts perfect for your family, plus a few single-serving quantities. Package in jars or cartons. Seal and label.

MAXIMUM RECOMMENDED FREEZER STORAGE: 6 months

10
Grains, Cereals, and Nuts

Who ever heard of freezing grains or cereals? I often grew impatient looking through stacks of freezer publications through the years to find out just what happens when you freeze them. Finally, I decided to experiment myself and have been delighted I did. I have long had sources of different flours and grain products because my brother is a miller and my dad a farmer. I also snatch up regional specialties during frequent travels.

Grains and cereals under normal storage conditions can become stale and off-flavored or even worse—buggy. Freezing proved to be an ideal answer for maintaining flours and keep them bug free—and I could use the flours or grains without thawing. Chips and crackers keep well frozen too.

Whenever I'm short on freezer space, I just take out the grain products until the space shortage is over, then return them with no harm done. If you are not a lucky, big freezer owner and are perpetually plagued with freezer space shortages, you can freeze grains for two to three days. Even this short storage period will kill any bugs and their larvae and keeps the grains and cereals fresher.

Recent research shows that freezing vastly improves not only the freshness and flavor of grains, legumes, and cereals, but preserves their nutritive values—a very important finding since the world's population inevitably becomes more dependent on them and other meat substitutes as the effects of the world food shortage becomes more pronounced. Grain will be increasingly important as a protein source. One pound of grain will produce approximately enough protein for four persons for one day, depending on the type of grain and other variables. However, to produce one pound of beef, 17 pounds of grain are required—quite an astonishing fact! This obviously means 16 pounds of grain are squandered for every pound of beef we eat.

A USDA study conducted at the University of Maryland reported in July 1974 that the percentage of retained nutrition when grains, cereals, and legumes are frozen varies. Dry grains such as rice have a higher general vitamin content when frozen. Their protein content is not impaired by either room temperature storage or freezing. Moist grains such as corn and wheat retain a much greater general nutritive content when frozen. Oily grains such as soybeans lose 60% of their general nutritive values

162

stored at room temperatures. This is especially significant since soybeans are the basis for many meat substitutes such as bacon, ham, etc. Freezing prevents this loss.

And if you are serious about natural foods, buy whole grains and freeze them in freezer-proof bags or containers. Whenever you wish to make your favorite whole grain breads, grind the grain yourself just before using. A blender or home use grinder is great for grinding grains such as wheat, corn, and oats. The flavor and sense of accomplishment are well worth the effort.

You've probably already tucked nuts in your freezer because they're relatively expensive and used in small quantities. However, techniques for freezing nuts seem to be few, especially in print. I find I can keep nuts on hand in all forms—chopped, ground, whole—even toasted, spiced, or in the shell. Freezing prevents rancidity as well as infestation.

Coconut freezes too, both the prepared varieties and fresh meat or milk. The fresh coconut is most convenient if the milk is frozen separately and the flesh ground or grated and frozen.

PACKAGING

Freezing grains, cereals, and nuts is easy. All you have to do is package in airtight freezer-type packaging. I generally prefer to leave the flour, grain, etc., in the commercial package and place within a freezer-type plastic bag and seal. This is a very convenient way to preserve the label, and saves making an extra one.

All that is needed is a date, made by writing with a wax pencil on a piece of freezer tape or on the package before wrapping. Moisture- and vapor-proof freezer containers also are very good. Remember that salted or seasoned products keep about one-half or one-third less long and should be labeled accordingly.

RECIPES

GRANOLA

Save lots of cash and add much more flavor to Granola by making it yourself. Alter the ingredients to your own taste and what you have on hand. Excellent as a snack, topping, or cereal with milk.

Temperature: 300°F
Baking time: 1 hour
Yield: about 4 quarts

5 cups old-fashioned
   oatmeal (about 1 box)
1 cup coconut, any type
1 cup wheat germ
1 cup powdered milk
1 cup soya grits

¼ cup sesame seeds
1 cup nuts
1 cup raw honey
1 cup salad oil
   Assorted dried fruit to taste

1. Mix first seven ingredients together.

2. Add oil and honey; mix until all ingredients are coated. May need more honey.

3. Spread on cookie sheets and toast 1 hour each in 300°F oven, stirring occasionally.

4. Remove from oven and add white or dark raisins, any chopped, dried fruits, such as dates, prunes, apricots, candied fruits, or orange or lemon peel, that you desire.

5. This is good as finger food or cereal for breakfast with milk. The Swiss call it *familie.* It's good over ice cream, puddings, or pie fillings.

FREEZING HINT: Freeze in convenient-sized containers.

MAXIMUM RECOMMENDED FREEZER STORAGE: 3 months

NUTS AND BOLTS

Ever buy some cereal that you thought you'd like and didn't? If it is not sugared, you are in luck, as this tasty snack is perfect for using up tad ends of cereals or those that just don't tickle your taste buds. To live up to the title, try to include some Cheerios and some long rod-like cereal or pretzels. You can save up cereal dabs in the freezer until you have enough to make this—a real time and money saver!

Temperature: 250°F (180°F in
electric portable appliance)
Baking time: 45 minutes
Yield: about 8 cups

2 cups cereal of any type,
   such as mini shredded
   wheat, flakes, or a mixture
   of several
2 cups Cheerios
2 cups pretzel rods or
   "rod-like" cereal
2 cups mixed nuts (peanuts

   and almonds are especially nice)
1 stick butter or margarine, melted
1 tablespoon Worcestershire sauce
   Few dashes of hot red
   pepper sauce
1 teaspoon seasoned salt
   Few drops of garlic juice or
   ¼ teaspoon garlic powder

1. Mix all cereals and nuts together on a shallow baking pan or in an electric skillet or deep fat fryer.

2. Drizzle on butter or margarine. Dash on seasonings. Stir well until all ingredients are evenly coated.

3. Bake, using 250°F oven or 180°F in an electric portable appliance, stirring very gently after 15 minutes. Remove from heat when cereals become golden—may take less time than 45 minutes.

FREEZING HINTS: Freeze in desired serving quantities. Needs very little thawing. Warms to room temperature in about an hour. May be warmed on cookie tray for about 15 minutes in a warm (300°F) oven if desired.

MAXIMUM RECOMMENDED FREEZER STORAGE: 3 months

GRIT SOUFFLÉ

A super soufflé with a Southern twist—great for midnight buffets or brunches—especially well suited for entertaining as it holds well at warm temperatures for buffet serving.

Temperature: 300°F
Baking time: 45 minutes
Yield: 12 to 16 servings

2 cups 3-minute grits	*Few drops of Tabasco*
2 quarts boiling water	*sauce*
1 teaspoon salt	1 *stick butter*
1 stick garlic cheese, thinly	2 *eggs, beaten*
sliced	⅓ *cup melted butter, optional*
1 tablespoon sherry	⅓ *cup grated Parmesan*
2 teaspoons Worcestershire sauce	*cheese, optional*

1. Cook grits in boiling salted water (may use ½ milk) until done, but not dry.

2. Add the garlic cheese, sherry, Worcestershire sauce, Tabasco, butter, and eggs and mix well.

3. Pour into well-buttered 9 x 13-inch or other large casserole. Refrigerate overnight, bake immediately or freeze.

FREEZING HINTS: When planning to freeze for a length of time, keep from tying up your baking dish by lining it with two pieces of foil crisscrossed, buttering it, and adding grits ingredients. Freeze until firm, then remove from casserole; package and label. To serve, pop frozen ingredients into the casserole and bake for 1½ hours if frozen or 45 minutes if thawed or until hot. This is not temperature sensitive and heat can be varied to suit other foods in oven.

WILD RICE PILAF

Especially great for festive occasions and winter holidays or dinner parties. I'm very fond of serving this with fowl.

Temperature: 350°F
Baking time: 1½ hours
Yield: 5 to 6 servings

½ cup butter
½ pound mushrooms or
  4-ounce can mushroom
  stems and pieces
1 clove garlic
1 tablespoon minced green
  pepper

1 cup raw wild rice
½ cup slivered almonds
1 teaspoon salt, few grinds of
  black pepper
3 cups chicken broth

1. Sauté all of the ingredients but the chicken broth in the melted butter.
2. Place in large, shallow baking dish. Add broth. Stir until mixed.
3. Seal well with foil or lid. Bake for 1½ hours at 350°F.

FREEZING HINTS: Bake for 1 hour and freeze well sealed. To serve, heat for 1 hour at 350°F or until hot. Leftovers can also be frozen, but will be a mushier consistency when served.

BARLEY PILAF

An unexpected delight—not many people cook with barley and therefore don't know what they're missing. Serve this tasty pilaf with hearty meat dishes such as beef stroganoff.

Temperature: 350°F—can be
adjusted to any desired
temperature
Baking time: 1 hour total
Yield: 6 to 8 servings

3 tablespoons butter	1 teaspoon salt or more
1 cup sliced mushrooms	½ teaspoon freshly ground
1 medium onion, chopped	black pepper
1 clove garlic, minced	2 cups meat broth or stock
½ green pepper, chopped	½ pimiento pepper, diced, or
1 cup barley	1 (2-ounce) jar chopped pimiento

1. Heat butter in casserole and sauté mushrooms, onions, garlic, and green pepper until golden on first side. Turn and add barley and brown lightly.

2. Add the broth and seasonings, except for the pimiento. Bake in a 350°F oven for 30 minutes. If serving immediately, bake until liquid is absorbed and barley is tender; garnish with pimiento, olives, or nuts.

FREEZING HINTS: Freeze in rigid containers of desired capacity. Seal and label. To serve, thaw in refrigerator 8 to 10 hours, then place in buttered baking dish and bake for 30 minutes (at any moderate temperature) if thawed. Taste to adjust seasoning, If frozen, bake for 1 hour or until hot. Garnish with chopped pimiento, olives, or nuts.

MAXIMUM RECOMMENDED FREEZER STORAGE: 4 months

GREEN CHILE CHEESE 'N' RICE BAKE

This delicious low-cost, no-meat main or side dish has never failed to become a favorite with anyone I've served it to.

Temperature: 350°F
Baking time: 30 minutes
Yield: 8 servings

8 ounces Monterey Jack cheese, sliced	4 cups cooked rice, slightly underdone
1 pint of sour cream	Salt and pepper to taste
1 4-ounce can chopped green chile	½ cup grated Cheddar cheese

1. Cut the Jack cheese into ½-inch strips. Mix the sour cream and green chile together.

2. In a buttered 2-quart casserole, alternate layers of rice, cheese strips, and cream-chile mixture. If freezing, don't bake (see below). Bake at 350°F for 30 minutes.

3. After 15 minutes of baking time, sprinkle the top of the casserole with the grated Cheddar. Bake and serve hot.

FREEZING HINTS: Place two pieces of foil criss-crossed and overlapping the sides of the casserole. Butter or spray with nonstick coating and add ingredients as suggested. Freeze until firm—or about 24 hours. Remove from casserole and package airtight; label. Do not bake before freezing. Casserole will thaw in about 4 hours at room temperature or overnight in the refrigerator. To serve, peel off foil and pop casserole into baking dish. Bake thawed casserole as directed or bake frozen, increasing the time by one-third to one-half.

MAXIMUM RECOMMENDED FREEZER STORAGE: 2 months

SUGAR-GLAZED WALNUTS

Crunchy and great tasting, each of these special nut treats is handy to have ready in the freezer for parties.

Temperature: 350°F
Baking time: 5 to 6 minutes, until
crisp and golden
Yield: 1 pound

1 cup light brown sugar
1 teaspoon cinnamon

1 pound walnut halves or
   large pieces (1 quart)
½ cup butter (¼ pound)

1. Toss together sugar, cinnamon, and walnuts in large bowl. Place on cookie sheet.
2. Cut butter in 8 pieces and arrange over top.
3. Place in oven and cook 5 to 6 minutes or until butter is melted.
4. Immediately after cooking, pour nuts onto strip of foil and toss to coat all nuts with sugar mixture. Serve warm or cold.

FREEZING HINT: Place in desired container, seal, and label.

MAXIMUM RECOMMENDED FREEZER STORAGE: 6 months

TOASTED BUTTER PECANS

Temperature: 350°F
Baking time: 10 to 15 minutes
Yield: 1 pound

1 pound pecan halves (about
   4 cups)

1 tablespoon seasoned salt
¼ cup butter (½ stick)

1. Put pecan halves on cookie sheet. Sprinkle with seasoned salt. Cut butter into 4 pieces and arrange evenly over top.

2. Place in oven and cook 10 to 15 minutes. Mix to evenly distribute butter. Serve warm or cold.

FREEZING HINT: Place in desired container, seal, and label.

MAXIMUM RECOMMENDED FREEZER STORAGE: 3 months

3-WAY CANDIED WALNUTS

Yield: each cup of walnuts gives
about 40 pieces

Honey Candied:

1½ cups sugar	½ cup water
¼ teaspoon salt	½ teaspoon vanilla
¼ cup honey	3 cups walnut halves

1. Boil together in small saucepan sugar, salt, honey, and water to soft ball stage.

2. Remove from heat, add vanilla and walnuts. Stir until creamy; turn out on waxed paper. Separate walnuts and cool.

MAXIMUM RECOMMENDED FREEZER STORAGE: 3 months

Sherried:

1½ cups sugar	1 teaspoon grated orange
¼ teaspoon salt	rind
½ cup sherry	2½ cups walnut halves

1. Boil together sugar, salt, and sherry to soft ball stage.

2. Remove from heat and add orange rind. Stir in walnuts and continue stirring until syrup is cloudy and walnuts are well coated.

Separate walnuts on waxed paper and cool.

MAXIMUM RECOMMENDED FREEZER STORAGE: 2 months

Minted:

1 cup sugar	1 tablespoon light corn syrup
¼ teaspoon salt	½ teaspoon mint extract
⅓ cup water	2 cups walnut halves

1. Boil together, stirring often, sugar, salt, water, and corn syrup to soft ball stage.

2. Remove from heat and add mint extract. Stir in walnuts and stir until syrup is cloudy and nuts are well coated. Separate nuts on waxed paper and allow to cool.

FREEZING HINT: Place in desired container, seal, and label.

MAXIMUM RECOMMENDED FREEZER STORAGE: 2 months

11
Breads

Nothing is homier than the aroma of baking bread. Bread has often been called the staff of life, yet so much store bread is like baked fluff that the calories and the place of honor hardly seem merited. You can change that. Bake and freeze bread instead of buying tasteless bread.

Crusty, golden breads made from a variety of fresh, good-quality ingredients are hard to beat. You may shudder at the thought of bread baking, but many people of all ages have found the therapy of punching and pulling bread to be great for relief of aggression—and what fantastically flavorful results!

You don't have to be a baker, though. If you are fortunate enough to live near a good-quality bakery—or better yet, a baker's surplus store of delicacy breads—you will find a joy in getting good bargains and freezing them for use at will.

I always bring back as many loaves as I can reasonably accommodate in my freezer when in an area with exceptional bread, such as San Francisco with its sourdough bread.

Bread is a marvel! It is about the only food that actually improves with freezing. The condensing of moisture during the freezing process actually yields fresher-tasting bread than the same bread served without freezing. A word of caution—do be practical about the amount of bread you buy. The potential savings possible for freezing a cubic foot of bread bought at a good price could hardly measure up to the savings for, say, a cubic foot of steak bought on special. Of course, you'll want to dovetail your freezer storage planning with the seasons and allow much more space before summer for fruits and vegetables, before buying a beef, or just before the holidays.

Baked or partially baked breads and quick breads are really the best ways to freeze bread, I think. Actually, baked is the surest bet and requires the least special experimentation. For freezing, half-baked works well only for rolls. Loaves will not bake in the center, yielding poor flavor and quality.

To half-bake, prepare as usual. When ready to bake, use a baking temperature 100°F lower than the temperature called for in the recipe and bake for one-half the baking period. Check the rolls: they should have ris-

171

en, but not browned. If they pop back when touched, they are done sufficiently. Cool, package, and label.

Unbaked or raw dough never seems to be much of a convenience to me! The only two apparent advantages are that the marvelous aroma can be enjoyed later as the bread bakes and that sometimes circumstances just bear down and you have to freeze the dough when you run out of time for baking. Often more yeast is needed to freeze raw dough, but research has never revealed any guidelines (meaning you will have to experiment). Try adding a little more yeast first, then increase if the bread doesn't rise and have the texture you like.

Always pat the dough after the first rising into thin disks or oblongs for freezing. This speeds up thawing, which, by the way, is the major inconvenience. The thawing time is often about the same as the time required to prepare the bread to the same point. However, it will rise as it thaws. When thawed, punch it back and let it rise again before shaping it.

Batters for muffins, waffles, and pancakes fall in the same category of convenience to me, requiring about the same time to thaw as to make. The only reason for freezing batters is to keep from throwing them out when time simply won't allow for baking. Waffles are much more convenient frozen after baking as they are great toasted. Muffins are much easier to pop ready-baked right into a hot oven than to mess around thawing batter. Not everyone agrees with me on this point—some recommend freezing batter. If you decide to freeze muffin batter, freeze it in the muffin liners in a muffin pan until firm; then remove the liners from the pan, bag them, and seal with freezer wrap.

PACKAGING

To prepare baked or half-baked breads, cool the baked bread and package airtight in good-quality freezer-weight packaging; seal well and label. Foil is extra handy as packages of frozen bread can be popped right into the oven for thawing, heating, and serving. However, if you are a lucky microwave oven owner, plastic bags will be handier.

To freeze unbaked or raw dough, place the disks or oblongs on lightly oiled cookie sheets and freeze solidly—this takes about 24 hours. Then package in airtight freezer wrap such as plastic or foil. Seal and label.

TO SERVE

Frozen breads taste freshest served warm.

Foil-wrapped frozen loaves of bread can be warmed in a regular gas or electric oven, microwave oven (if foil is removed), bread warmer, or electric skillet. Use a moderate temperature—350°F to 400°F in a regular oven, 100°F less in a bread warmer or electric skillet—for about 15 minutes, depending on the size of the loaf. Larger loaves take longer. When the crust is hot to the touch, loosen the foil and allow the outside crust to crisp for about 15 more minutes. The timing is variable depending on the type of bread. Denser breads made with whole grains are slower to thaw and the size and shape of the loaf are factors. Flat, hearth-type breads thaw more quickly. Or, you may wish to thaw the bread in the microwave oven. Here, you'd best follow the manufacturer's instructions since there are a wide variety of defrost settings and some ovens do not have them at all. Just a few minutes is all that will be required. Remove the wrapping for the final seconds or minutes of warming for crisper crusts.

Another option is to take the bread out of the freezer and set it on the counter. Always leave the packaging in place while thawing. On the counter, the average loaf will be thawed in about 2 hours, and muffins or rolls in about 1 hour. Sliced bread and waffles for toasting do not need to be thawed. Just toast frozen.

To serve half-baked rolls, heat in hot oven using baking temperature that the recipe indicates and bake 10 or more minutes until golden and piping hot.

To use raw doughs—which I don't recommend for freezing in the first place—long thawing times will be required before baking.

RECIPES

The following breads are each extra-special favorites that do beautifully when frozen. Package them in a plastic bag or other freezer wrap. Seal and label. Separate freezer instructions are *not* noted for each as the same packaging and freezing techniques explained above apply to all.

Basic Yeast Breads

GOOD WHITE BREAD

A dependable, versatile recipe with a wide range of variations.

Temperature: 375° F
Baking time: 45 minutes
Yield: two 9x5-inch loaves

1 package active dry yeast	2 teaspoons salt
¼ cup warm water	2 tablespoons sugar
2 cups milk	6½ cups all-purpose flour
2 tablespoons melted margarine	

1. Sprinkle yeast over warm water and stir until dissolved.

2. Combine milk, melted margarine, salt, and sugar and stir until well blended.

3. Add 3 cups of flour, 1 cup at a time. Stir in fourth cup of flour and beat until dough is smooth and elastic. Mix in fifth cup of flour to make a stiff dough.

4. Measure sixth cup of flour and sprinkle about half the amount on bread board. Turn out dough and knead, keeping a coating of flour on dough.

5. Continue kneading and adding flour until dough no longer sticks. Dough should be smooth and satiny.

6. Put dough in greased bowl, grease top lightly, cover with waxed or cello paper, and let rise until almost doubled.

7. Punch dough down and squeeze out air bubbles with hands. Shape into a smooth oval and divide into equal portions to make two loaves.

8. Shape loaves and place in two 9x5-inch greased pans, seam side down. Cover and let rise in warm place until almost doubled.

9. Preheat oven to 375°F during last 10 minutes of rising and bake for 45 minutes.

MAXIMUM RECOMMENDED FREEZER STORAGE: 4 months for white bread; 3 months for variations

VARIATIONS

DARK BREAD

1. Follow Good White Bread recipe except:

2. Use ½ cup wheat germ, ½ cup buckwheat flour, 1 cup rye, and 4 cups whole wheat flour.

3. Omit sugar and use ½ cup dark molasses with 1½ cups milk instead of 2 cups milk.

HERB BREAD

1. Follow Good White Bread recipe except:

2. In step 4, knead in one of the following herbs:

2 tablespoons dill weed	3 teaspoons oregano
2 tablespoons savory	3 teaspoons thyme
3 teaspoons basil	5 teaspoons marjoram

PUMPERNICKEL BREAD

1. Follow Good White Bread recipe except:
2. Use 1 cup whole bran cereal, 2 cups rye flour, and 3 cups whole wheat flour instead of all-purpose flour.
3. Add 1 tablespoon caraway seed.

SOY GRAHAM BREAD

1. Follow Good White Bread recipe except:
2. Use 1 cup soy flour, 2 cups graham flour, and 3 cups all-purpose flour.

OLD WORLD RYE BREAD

Beautifully dark and flavorful—adds the right accent to European menus!

Temperature: 375° F
Baking time: 35 to 40 minutes
Yield: two 1¼-pound loaves

2 cups rye flour	1 cup warm water
¼ cup cocoa	1 tablespoon salt
3¼ cups all-purpose flour	2 tablespoons caraway seed
2 packages active dry yeast	(optional)
½ cup warm water	1 tablespoon melted
½ cup molasses	shortening or oil

1. Measure rye flour and combine with cocoa. Measure all-purpose flour.
2. Soften yeast in ½ cup warm water.
3. Combine molasses, 1 cup warm water, salt, and caraway seed.
4. Beat in shortening, rye flour mixture, yeast mixture, and 1 cup all-purpose flour.
5. Add enough flour to make soft dough.
6. Turn onto lightly floured board. Knead thoroughly, adding flour until dough becomes smooth, elastic, and no longer sticky.

175

7. Place in lightly greased bowl. Grease top of dough and cover.

8. Let rise in warm place until doubled.

9. Shape into two loaves, either oblong or round. Put oblong in loaf pan and round on cookie sheet.

10. Let rise until doubled. Preheat oven to 375°F during last 10 minutes of rising.

11. Bake for 35 to 40 minutes.

MAXIMUM RECOMMENDED FREEZER STORAGE: 2 months

FRENCH BREAD OR ROLLS

A true Continental bread using no fat and only a bit of sugar. There are many theories as to whether sugar, shortening, or ascorbic acid should be used and in what quantities for the best French bread. I've always liked this one. It's best served freshly baked or warmed from the freezer.

Temperature: 425°F
Baking time: 30 to 35 minutes for loaves; 20 to 25 minutes for rolls
Yield: two 9x5-inch loaves or 24 hard rolls

2 *cups warm water*	2 *teaspoons salt*
1 *package active dry yeast*	5¾ *cups sifted all-purpose flour*
1 *tablespoon sugar*	1 *egg white*

1. Measure water into warmed bowl and sprinkle yeast over top. Stir until dissolved.

2. Add sugar, salt, and 3 cups flour and beat until smooth and shiny. Stir in 2½ cups flour.

3. Sprinkle remaining ¼ cup flour on bread board or pastry cloth. Turn dough out on flour and knead until satiny smooth.

4. Shape into smooth ball and press top of ball into lightly greased bowl, then turn dough over. Cover and let rise until doubled.

5. Punch down and divide into halves. Shape each half into a ball, cover, and let rest for 5 minutes.

6. Rub a little shortening onto palms of hands. Roll each ball of dough on floured bread board to form a long, slender loaf about 3 inches in diameter. Start rolling at the center and gently work hands toward ends of loaf. Do this several times to make well-shaped loaves. Space loaves about 4 inches apart on greased baking sheet.

7. Using a sharp knife, slash the top of the loaf about ¾ inch deep and

176

about 1½ inches apart. For rolls, use kitchen shears and make 2 slashes at right angles to each other about ¾ inch deep.

8. Cover and let rise until a little more than doubled. Preheat oven to 425°F during last 10 minutes of rising.

9. Bake loaves for 30 to 35 minutes, rolls 20 to 25 minutes or until done. Remove from oven, brush with egg white, and return to oven for 2 minutes. Remove from baking sheet and cool on rack.

MAXIMUM RECOMMENDED FREEZER STORAGE: 4 months

MOLASSES OATMEAL BREAD

Yummy toasted or served very warm oozing with butter.

Temperature: 400°F
Baking time: 45 minutes
Yield: two 9x5-inch loaves

2 *packages active dry yeast*	½ *cup dark molasses*
½ *cup warm water*	1 *tablespoon plus 1 teaspoon salt*
1½ *cups boiling water*	2 *eggs*
1 *cup quick oatmeal*	5½ *cups sifted all-purpose*
⅓ *cup shortening*	*flour*

1. Soften yeast in warm water and set aside.
2. Combine 1½ cups water, oatmeal, shortening, molasses, and salt.
3. Cool to warm; add softened yeast and mix well. Stir in eggs.
4. Add flour and mix until dough is blended.
5. Place in greased bowl and turn once to grease surface.
6. Cover and place in refrigerator for 2 hours.
7. Shape into two loaves on floured surface and place in greased 9×5-inch loaf pans; cover.
8. Let rise in warm place until doubled. Preheat oven to 400°F during last 10 minutes of rising.
9. Bake for 45 minutes or until golden done.

MAXIMUM RECOMMENDED FREEZER STORAGE: 3 months

DILLY CASSEROLE BREAD

Fun for buffets, patio parties, and informal lunches or suppers.

Temperature: 350°F
Baking time: 70 to 90 minutes
Yield: 1½- to 2-quart casserole

1 package active dry yeast
¼ cup warm water
1 cup creamed cottage
  cheese, heated to warm
2 tablespoons sugar
1 tablespoon instant minced
  onion

1 tablespoon butter
2 teaspoons dill seed
1 teaspoon salt
¼ teaspoon soda
1 egg
2¼–2½ cups all-purpose flour

1. Soften yeast in water.

2. Combine remaining ingredients with softened yeast in large mixing bowl.

3. Form stiff dough by adding flour gradually at medium speed, beating well after each addition. Add enough flour to make stiff dough. Cover and let rise in warm place until light and doubled.

4. Stir down dough and turn into well-greased 1½–2 quart casserole. Let rise in warm place until light.

5. Preheat oven to 350°F during last 10 minutes of rising. Bake for 40 to 50 minutes or until golden brown.

6. Brush with soft butter and sprinkle with salt.

MAXIMUM RECOMMENDED FREEZER STORAGE: 2 months

POPPY SEED-SWIRLED EGG BREAD

Especially good toasted or thinly sliced for serving with coffee or tea.

Temperature: 375°F
Baking time: 20 to 25 minutes
Yield: two 9x5-inch loaves

¼ cup warm milk
½ cup poppy seeds
1 tablespoon melted butter
½ cup almonds, ground
2 teaspoons grated lemon
  peel
2 packages active dry yeast
¼ cup warm water

1 cup milk
⅓ cup melted butter
¼ cup sugar
2 teaspoons salt
5½ cups all-purpose flour,
  approximately
1 teaspoon vanilla
4 eggs

1. Prepare filling by combining ¼ cup milk and poppy seeds. Let stand for 1 hour. Stir in 1 tablespoon melted butter, almonds, and lemon peel.

2. Soften yeast in warm water. Combine 1 cup milk, ⅓ cup melted butter, sugar, and salt in a large bowl.

3. Add 2 cups flour to milk mixture and beat well. Stir in softened yeast and vanilla.

4. Beat in eggs, one at a time. Stir in enough flour to make a moderately stiff dough.

5. Turn onto floured board and knead until smooth and satiny. Cover and let rise in greased bowl until doubled.

6. Punch down, divide into two equal portions, and let rise 10 minutes. Roll out each half of dough into a 6x18-inch rectangle. Spread with half of filling. Roll into a tight loaf.

7. Place loaves, seam side down, in greased 9x5-inch loaf pans. Let rise until doubled.

8. Preheat oven to 375°F during last 10 minutes of rising.

9. Bake for 20 to 25 minutes or until well browned. Brush top with butter.

MAXIMUM RECOMMENDED FREEZER STORAGE: 2 months

POTATO BREAD WITH SOUR CREAM AND CHIVES

A hearty bread, good with steaks and broiled meats.

Temperature: 400°F
Baking time: 30 to 40 minutes
Yield: 9x5-inch loaves

6–6½ cups sifted all-purpose flour	1 10½-ounce can condensed cream of potato soup
2 packages active dry yeast	
1½ cups milk	½ cup sour cream
2 tablespoons sugar	¼ cup snipped chives
2 teaspoons salt	1 teaspoon crushed tarragon
2 tablespoons butter	1–1½ cups flour

1. In large mixer bowl, combine 2½ cups of flour and yeast.

2. In saucepan, heat together milk, sugar, salt, and butter until warm, stirring constantly. Add to dry ingredients in mixer bowl.

3. Add soup, sour cream, chives, and tarragon. Beat 1 minute on low speed and 3 minutes on high speed, scraping sides of bowl constantly.

4. By hand, stir in enough of remaining flour to make a moderately stiff dough.

5. Turn out on floured surface. Knead until smooth, kneading in about 1 to 1½ cups flour.

6. Place in greased bowl, turning once to grease surface. Cover and let rise until doubled.

7. Punch down, cover, and let rest 10 minutes. Punch down, divide dough in half, and shape into loaves.

8. Place in two greased 9x5-inch loaf pans and let rise until almost doubled.

9. Preheat oven to 400°F during last 10 minutes of rising.

10. Bake for 30 to 40 minutes.

MAXIMUM RECOMMENDED FREEZER STORAGE: 2 months

DOUBLE QUICK ROLLS

These are light and airy—they use a mixer and need no kneading.

Temperature: 400°F
Baking time: 20 to 30 minutes
Yield: 12 large rolls

1 package active dry yeast	1 teaspoon salt
1 cup warm water	1 egg
2 tablespoons sugar	2 tablespoons soft shortening
2¼ cups all-purpose flour	

1. Dissolve yeast in warm water in large mixer bowl.

2. Stir in sugar, half of flour, and salt. Beat until smooth, using medium speed of mixer.

3. Add egg and shortening. Beat in remaining flour until smooth.

4. Scrape down sides of bowl; cover and let rise in warm place about 30 minutes.

5. Stir down batter and spoon into 12 large greased muffin cups, filling half full.

6. Let rise in warm place until dough reaches top of muffin cups.

7. Preheat oven to 400°F during last 10 minutes of rising.

8. Bake for 20 to 30 minutes.

Variation: Brush with slightly beaten egg white, then sprinkle with poppy or sesame seeds just before baking.

MAXIMUM RECOMMENDED FREEZER STORAGE: 4 months

Sourdough Breads

Sourdough breads have a unique yeasty-chewy quality that is very appealing. Have fun experimenting with these recipes, but remember that metal utensils cannot be used.

SOURDOUGH STARTER

2 packages active dry yeast
2 teaspoons sugar

2 cups warm water*
4 cups all-purpose flour

1. Sprinkle yeast into a crock or a wide-mouth jar with a cover. (Never use a metal container.) Add sugar and water and mix until smooth.
2. Sift flour twice. Add all at once and beat to a smooth batter.
3. Keep in a warm place 24 to 30 hours. It should be sour and ready to use.
4. Always refresh starter immediately after removing all but one cupful. Add 1 cup water, at room temperature, and 1 cup of sifted flour, and stir until mixture is well blended. (It is not necessary to stir until smooth; the yeast will smooth the batter as it rises.)
5. Let stand at room temperature about 3 hours and place in the refrigerator. (It will keep several days, but seems better if used at least once a week.)
6. To increase the starter, after 2 days divide the batter equally and to each half add 1 cup of warm water and 1 cup of flour. When the batter has soured for at least 8 hours, combine the batters to have a larger amount. (When adding water and flour, never add more than 1 cup of each at a time.)
7. Proceed as directed for sourdough recipe.

*Can substitute 1 cup evaporated milk and 1 cup water, heated to warm. (Often hot tap water will make a warm mixture which is satisfactory.)

SOURDOUGH BISCUITS

You will never taste any lighter, fluffier biscuits!

Temperature: 375°F
Baking time: 30 to 35 minutes
Yield: fourteen 2-inch biscuits

½ cup starter
1 cup milk
2½ cups all-purpose flour
¾ teaspoon salt
1 tablespoon sugar

1 teaspoon baking powder
½ teaspoon soda (more if
    batter is still sour)
¼ cup each of oil and melted
    margarine

1. Mix starter, milk, and 1 cup flour in a large glass bowl or crock. Cover and let rise at least 5 hours.

181

2. Turn out onto 1 cup of flour on board. Combine salt, sugar, baking powder, and soda with remaining ½ cup flour and sift over top of dough.

3. Mix with hands, kneading lightly, to biscuit consistency.

4. Roll to ½-inch thickness, cut and dip in warm oil and margarine mixture. Place biscuits, touching, on a greased baking sheet. Set in warm place and let rise at least ½ hour. Preheat oven to 375°F during last 10 minutes of rising.

5. Bake 30 to 35 minutes or until golden brown.

MAXIMUM RECOMMENDED FREEZING STORAGE: 4 months

SOURDOUGH PAN BREAD

An old settler's favorite, 'twas probably stirred, raised, and baked in the old blue granite pan.

Temperature: 400°F
Baking time: 45 minutes
Yield: two 9x5-inch loaves

1 cup starter	2 tablespoons sugar
2½ cups water	1 tablespoon salt
5 cups all-purpose flour	1½ teaspoons soda
3 tablespoons melted shortening	2½ cups all-purpose flour
	¼ cup melted butter

1. Mix 1 cup starter, water, and 5 cups flour in large bowl. Cover and leave 18 to 24 hours at room temperature.

2. Combine melted shortening, sugar, salt, and soda. Add to first mixture and stir vigorously until blended.

3. Turn out dough onto 2½ cups flour n a board. Knead until satiny, adding more flour if needed.

4. Divide dough in half. Shape into two loaves and place each in a buttered 9x5-inch loaf pan. Let rise until nearly doubled. Preheat oven to 400°F during last 10 minutes of rising.

5. Brush loaves with melted butter and bake for 45 minutes or until golden done.

VARIATIONS:

Oatmeal Pan Bread: Use 1 cup oats for 1 cup flour called for in recipe.
Cornmeal Pan Bread: Use 1 cup cornmeal for 1 cup flour called for in recipe.

MAXIMUM RECOMMENDED FREEZER STORAGE: 4 months

SOURDOUGH WAFFLES

A wilderness adaptation. Pancakes can also be made using this recipe. To make them, do not whip whites—instead, add the whole eggs and reduce oil to 2 tablespoons.

Yield: four 4-section waffles

½ cup starter
2 cups scalded milk or 1 cup water and 1 cup evaporated milk

2 cups all-purpose flour

1. Combine these ingredients in a glass or pottery bowl or pitcher and mix, then allow to set out overnight.

Next morning add:

2 eggs, separated
2 tablespoons sugar
½ teaspoon salt

1 teaspoon soda
4 tablespoons salad oil, melted butter, or drippings

1. Preheat the waffle iron following manufacturer's instructions.
2. Beat the egg whites until stiff but not dry. Combine the rest of the ingredients with all but ½ cup of the mixture, using no metal utensils. At least ½ cup should be reserved in a glass jar for future use.
3. Fold in the beaten egg whites. Bake on hot griddle until each is golden. Serve with maple syrup, another favorite syrup, or fruit jam.

MAXIMUM RECOMMENDED FREEZER STORAGE: 2 months

HUSH PUPPIES

An old Tennessee recipe—it's especially fun to take all the dry ingredients premeasured and mix together along on your fishing and camping trips to fry with the fresh-caught fish.

Temperature: 350°F
Frying time: 3 to 5 minutes
Yield: 6 to 8 servings

2 cups white cornmeal
1 tablespoon flour

½ teaspoon soda
1 teaspoon baking powder

2 teaspoons sugar	1 cup buttermilk
1½ teaspoons salt	1 egg, beaten
1 small onion, finely chopped	

1. Mix all dry ingredients together.
2. Add chopped onion, buttermilk, and egg. Mix well.
3. Use 2 teaspoons of same size to shape and drop dough into deep fat (350°F). (One inch fat will do—especially when camping.)
4. Hush puppies will turn a golden brown and float to the top when done.

MAXIMUM RECOMMENDED FREEZER STORAGE: 1 month

PIZZA DOUGH

For a thin, crisp crust, this recipe is a real winner!

Temperature: 400°F
Yield: four 9-inch pizzas

1 package active dry yeast	¼ teaspoon salt
1 cup warm water	4 cups sifted all-purpose
2 tablespoons shortening	flour

1. Dissolve yeast in warm water.
2. Add shortening, salt, and flour. Mix and knead until smooth.
3. Place in a greased bowl. Grease top and cover. Let rise in warm place until doubled.
4. Divide dough into 4 equal portions. Roll each portion into a 9-inch circle and pinch edges of circle up to form a rim.
5. Spread with desired filling. Freeze filled or unfilled.

MAXIMUM RECOMMENDED FREEZER STORAGE: 3 months

REFRIGERATOR SWEET YEAST DOUGH

Good for planning ahead for any anticipated demand for sweet breads.

2 packages active dry yeast	1¾ cups milk, scalded
¼ cup warm water	½ teaspoon salt
¼ cup sugar	4 eggs, slightly beaten
1½ cups melted butter	8 cups all-purpose flour

184

1. Sprinkle yeast into warm water and stir until dissolved.
2. Add sugar and ½ cup melted butter to milk.
3. Add softened yeast and salt. Beat in eggs.
4. Measure flour into a large bowl and add milk mixture. Mix until mixture forms a ball.
5. Knead dough on a floured board until dough is smooth and elastic. Let rest 5 minutes.
6. Roll dough into a rectangle 12×36 inches and ½ inch thick.
7. Spread one-third of the remaining butter over center third of the dough. Fold the right third of the dough over the buttered section and spread one-third of the remaining butter on that surface. Fold the left third over the buttered section.
8. Turn dough a quarter turn and roll into a rectangle ½ inch thick.
9. Spread the center third of the rectangle with the remaining one-third butter. Bring ends of rectangle to meet in center, fold in half, and bring edges together.
10. Place dough in a greased bowl, cover and let rise in warm place until almost doubled.
11. Punch dough down, wrap in airtight wrap and chill at least three hours or overnight.
12. Shape as directed for Cinnamon Rolls or Cinnamon Nut Raisin Loaf.

CINNAMON NUT RAISIN LOAF

Termperature: 375°F
Baking time: 30 to 35 minutes
Yield: four 9x5-inch loaves

1 recipe *Refrigerator Sweet Yeast Dough (above)*	1 *cup brown sugar*
½ *cup melted butter*	2 *tablespoons cinnamon*
2 *cups raisins*	*Melted butter*
1 *cup finely chopped nuts*	*Powdered sugar*

1. Divide dough into 4 equal parts. Work with one part of dough at a time, keeping remainder refrigerated.
2. Roll dough into a rectangle 8×16 inches and ¼ inch thick.
3. Brush 2 tablespoons of the melted butter over surface and sprinkle evenly with ½ cups raisins and ¼ cup chopped nuts.
4. Combine brown sugar and cinnamon and sprinkle ¼ of mixture over dough.
5. Beginning at narrow end, roll up tightly and seal ends and bottom.

6. Place in greased loaf pan, cover, and let rise until dough is within ½ inch of top of pan.

7. Preheat oven to 375°F during last 10 minutes of rising.

8. Bake for 30 to 35 minutes or until well browned. Brush with melted butter while hot and sprinkle with powdered sugar. (You may wish to add more powdered sugar before serving if freezing.)

9. Repeat steps to make a total of four loaves.

MAXIMUM RECOMMENDED FREEZER STORAGE: 2 months

APRICOT NUT STRUDEL

An easy-to-make pastry with a rich, marvelous flavor.

Temperature: 375°F
Baking time: 45 minutes
Yield: 8 dozen ¼-inch slices

1 cup soft margarine
1 8-ounce package soft
 cream cheese
2¼ cups all-purpose flour
2 cups apricot preserves*

1 15-ounce package white
 raisins, chopped
2 cups chopped pecans
1 4-ounce package flaked
 coconut

1. Cream margarine and cheese together. Blend in flour until mixture forms a ball. Chill for 3 hours or overnight.

2. Divide dough into 4 parts. Roll each part on floured surface into a 14x16-inch rectangle.

3. Spread preserves on dough, being careful not to tear dough. Sprinkle with raisins, nuts, and coconut. Roll as for jelly roll and turn ends under. Preheat over during last 10 minutes of preparation.

4. Place on ungreased baking sheet and bake 45 minues or until golden brown.

5. Freeze when cool or place in refrigertor several hours before slicing. Serve warm or at room temperature.

*Can substitute any other favorite preserves such as strawberry, blueberry, cherry, etc.

MAXIMUM RECOMMENDED FREEZER STORAGE: 2 months

STOLLEN

The best of all stollens—well worth the extra effort. For years I've been making a recipe every other year for serving on Christmas morning with pink champagne!

Temperature: 325°F
Baking time: 1 hour
Yield: 2 large loaves

¾ cup butter
½ cup sugar
1 teaspoon salt
½ teaspoon nutmeg
½ teaspoon mace
Grated rind of 1 lemon
Grated rind of ½ orange
2 eggs
¼ cup dark rum, brandy, or sherry
1 cup milk
1 package active dry yeast
¼ cup warm water

6 cups all-purpose flour, approximately
1 cup raisins
1 cup currants
¼ pound each candied orange peel, lemon peel, and citron
1 slice candied pineapple
1 cup toasted almonds
½ pound candied whole cherries
¼ cup melted butter
Powdered sugar

1. Cream butter, add sugar gradually and cream until fluffy. Blend in salt, nutmeg, mace, lemon rind, and orange rind.

2. Add eggs, one at a time, beating well after each addition. Add liquor and milk.

3. Soften yeast in water and stir into mixture. Add flour until dough is easy to handle. Turn out on a lightly floured board and place the mixing bowl upside down over dough and allow to stand 10 minutes. Uncover dough and knead until satin smooth.

4. Do not work more than ½ cup into dough wil kneading because too much flour makes the bread coarse.

5. Mix together all fruit except cherries, then dredge with ¼ cup flour, making sure each piece is covered.

6. When dough is smooth, add the fruit and almonds, a small amount at a time, until the fruit is spread throughout the dough. Continue until all is used.

7. Poke holes in the dough with forefinger and place a cherry in each hole. This prevents mashing the cherries.

8. Divide the dough in half ad place in large well-greased bowls; brush generously with melted butter and set in warm place to rise. Since the dough in heavy with fruit, it will require about 8 hours to rise.

9. To form, turn out on a lightly floured board, punch down and divide in half. To make typical stollen-shaped loaf, first pat dough into oblong shape, then fold in half lengthwise.

10. Place loaves on a greased baking sheet; brush with butter and let rise until doubled.

11. Preheat over to 325°F during last 10 minutes of rising.

12. Bake for 1 hour. While baking, brush several times with melted butter. When baked, dust generously with powdered sugar. (Serve warm, adding more sugar just before serving.)

MAXIMUM RECOMMENDED FREEZER STORAGE: 2 months (I've often kept them for one year.)

PUMPKIN BREAD

Pumpkin pie flavor baked right into a moist bread.

Temperature: 375°F
Baking time: 75 minutes for large
loaves; 45 minutes for small loaves
Yield: two 9x5-inch loaves or 3
small loaves

3 cups sugar	2 teaspoons soda
1 cup minus 2 tablespoons salad oil	1 teaspoon nutmeg
4 eggs, well beaten	1 teaspon cinnamon
3½ cups all-purpose flour	2 cups cooked pumpkin
1½ teaspoons salt	Chopped nuts (optional)

1. Combine sugar, oil, and well-beaten eggs in a large bowl of mixer. Beat until completely mixed.

2. Preheat over to 375°F.

3. Combine dry ingredients and add to egg mixture, stirring well after each addition. Gently fold in pumpkin and nuts.

4. Pour batter in prepared bread pans and bake for about 75 minutes for large loaves and 45 minutes for small loaves. Cool before removing from pans.

MAXIMUM RECOMMENDED FREEZER STORAGE: 2 months

Waffles

Here are two very special waffle recipes. They are guaranteed nutritious, using whole grains, and if you like, the granola waffles can be made from your own granola. For greatest serving convenience, individually wrap waffles for freezing in cello or plastic wrap and place in freezer-weight bags or containers. The easiest way to serve frozen waffles is to pop them into the toaster. Always serve crispy and hot with warm syrups or toppings.

ALL-WHEAT AND APPLE WAFFLES WITH CIDER SYRUP

Yield: four 4-section waffles

2 eggs, separated
1 tablespoon honey or sorghum
1¼ cups milk
½ stick butter or margarine, melted
2 medium peeled apples, coarsely chopped or grated

¾ cup whole wheat flour
¾ cup all-purpose flour
2 tablespoons wheat germ or bran flakes
½ teaspoon salt
1 teaspoon cinnamon
½ teaspoon nutmeg

1. Prepare the syrup below, if desired. Preheat waffle iron as manufacturer directs. Whip egg whites until stiff and set aside. Handiest to use the mixer and small bowl—it's not necessary to rinse the beaters.
2. Combine the egg yolks, honey, milk, and butter in the big bowl of the mixer and mix until blended, using a medium speed. Add the apples and dry ingredients and mix on low speed to combine, then switch to medium to create a smooth batter.
3. Using the lowest speed, fold in the beaten egg whites. Add about ¾ cup batter to the waffle iron at a time and bake. Serve with Cider Syrup.

CIDER SYRUP

1 cup dark brown sugar
1 cup apple cider
1 tablesppon butter or

margarine
¼ teaspoon each of nutmeg and cinnamon

1. Combine in a saucepan or syrup server and heat together until slight-

ly thickened—about the same length of time the waffles require to prepare.

MAXIMUM RECOMMENDED FREEZER STORAGE: 2 months

GREAT GRANOLA WAFFLES

Yield: eight 4-section waffles

2 eggs	cereal or 1 cup whole
2 cups milk	wheat flour
1 stick butter or margarine,	1¾ cups all-purpose flour
melted	1 teaspoon salt
2 tablespoons honey	1 tablespoon grated orange
¾ cup granola	peel
1 cup wheat or bran flake	3 teaspoons baking powder

1. Prepare the orange blossom syrup below, if desired. Preheat the waffle iron as manufacturer directs. Using the large bowl of the electric mixer, combine the eggs, milk, butter, and honey. Mix until foamy.

2. Add the rest of the ingredients and mix first wth the lowest speed, then switch to medium and mix until well blended. Add about ¾ cup batter to the waffle iron at a time and bake. Serve with Orange Blossom Syrup.

ORANGE BLOSSOM SYRUP

1 cup honey	1 tablespoon butter
⅓ cup orange juice	1 teaspoon grated orange peel

1. Combine all ingredients in a medium-sized saucepan. Using very low heat, stir and cook until waffles are baked.

MAXIMUM RECOMMENDED FREEZER STORAGE: 1 month

12
Desserts

Generally, pastries of all descriptions are great frozen and you'll be happy to have a variety of frozen desserts ready to serve in the freezer.

Do plan ahead, thinking through what your eating plans will be before launching a full-blast baking binge! Many delicacies are good only when eaten within two weeks—such as meringue pies—or within two months—such as rich frozen desserts like Bavarian creams, bombes, fruit sponges, and mousses.

However, I would like to make one point absolutely clear: desserts won't spoil or become bad if they're stored longer than the recommended storage time. They do start losing their peak flavor, texture, and highest eating quality. So try to plan to eat everything within the recommended storage time. But don't fret, or worse yet, don't throw things out if you don't make it. The key is to prepare the number, kind, and type of desserts based on your family's eating preference and plans. For example, don't overdo desserts when diets are in order.

Great efficiencies can be realized and you can really have fun launching baking binges or preparing quantities of pies, cookies, and layers and layers of cakes. When you get right down to it, the mess of baking really takes the most time—getting ready, getting set, and the cleaning up. This is the rationale I've discovered through the years and it has really paid off in delicious productivity. Also, for me baking is very relaxing. To stay relaxed, don't take on baking binges when time is limited or your mood isn't with it—you'll find it more like work then.

PIES AND PASTRY

Nearly everyone loves pie—or nearly everyone I know loves a good pie—yet they are so messy and time consuming to do one at a time.

Freezing pies probably has more techniques, tips, and do's and don'ts than perhaps any of the other food categories. To bake or not to bake is often the question on pies. Pastry automatically turns out better when frozen raw. It's easier to make too, because you don't have to wait for the

191

dough to chill before rolling it. You just make it and roll it immediately. Now this is only for unbaked pastry. If you're baking before freezing, you still need to chill pastry before rolling for very flaky crusts.

The pros and cons of baking pies before freezing are:

Baked pies can be kept twice as long as unbaked. This is a persuasive reason for baking some of the pies and leaving some unbaked when preparing great numbers of pies from a seasonal fruit. Another approach is to freeze just a reasonable, usable quantity unbaked and freeze the rest of the fruit ready for filling pies later.

Unbaked pies have got more going for them. In addition to being quicker (no chilling of the crust before rolling), they're easier to freeze and to make. Also, the quality of the pastry is super—really better than if baked before freezing. The fresh-baked flavor and aroma offers another delicious benefit.

Pie pointers: For the fillings, use fresh or partially thawed frozen fruit treated with ascorbic acid, lemon juice, or steam, as recommended in the Fruit Freezing Guide in Chapter 9 for each individual fruit. Use spices—especially cloves—somewhat sparingly. Cloves tend to become bitter. Tapioca or flour is butter than cornstarch for thickening—use more when freezing unbaked pies as fruit when frozen before cooking is juicier and requires more thickening. Prepare the crusts just as you would for immediate baking. You can roll the crust without chilling first. Don't cut slits in the top crust. Brush the bottom crust with melted butter or margarine or egg white to keep fruit from soaking in. Never place a warm or hot filling in the pie; always be sure filling is cool or cold.

Pies other than fruit pies can be frozen. Pumpkins pies are best frozen unbaked but pecan pies should be baked first. Custard pies do not freeze well. Cream-type pie fillings are debatable—the filling becomes grainy and watery unless a modified food starch is substituted for the usual thickening agent such as flour, cornstarch, or tapioca.

Meringues can be frozen for a very short time—up to two weeks. However, even in two weeks the meringue sometimes shrinks from the crust and becomes tough. Chiffon pies can be kept a short time, up to two months, when put in baked pie shells.

Pastry itself can be frozen either in flat rounds or made into pie or tart shells.

Packaging Pies and Pastry

Baked pies: As soon as baked and cooled, top pie with another inverted pie plate or paper plate and package in freezer wrap. Another less satisfactory method is to freeze the baked pie for about 1 hour then package.

When doing this, you run a greater risk of the crust crumbling. Seal and label.

Unbaked pies: When preparing the pies, do not cut any perforations in the top crust. Freeze until firm, then package in foil, a large freezer-proof plastic bag, or any other freezer-proof packaging. Seal and label.

Specialty pies: Freeze until firm, then package as above. If the filling is high and delicate, as in a meringue or chiffon pie, either place an inverted pie plate or paper plate on top before packaging or place packaged pie in a rigid carton. Overwrap with freezer wrap if not a sealing carton, then label.

Pastry and tart shells: Freeze either baked or unbaked. Unbaked pastry offers more versatility in that it can be rolled any desired way after thawing. Baked crusts can be packaged as soon as baked and cooled in airtight freezer-weight packaging. Unbaked can be frozen in flat rounds or formed into edged crusts in pie plates. For either, freeze first, then separate with paper and package two or more together. The availability of pie plates will determine which way to freeze the pastry. However, some people remove the plates after quick freezing and package in layers separated with packaging. To bake, they place in pie plates.

To Serve Pies

Baked pies: Thaw in 325°F oven until warm—about 25 to 30 minutes. Or, thaw at room temperature, leaving wrapped in packaging. Allow 6 to 8 hours to thaw thoroughly. Or quick-thaw in a microwave oven following manufacturer's instructions.

Unbaked pies: If possible, place in a Pyrex baking dish to be able to see browning. Bake frozen in preheated 400°F oven for about 1 hour or until golden. Peek at the pie after about 45 minutes to be certain it is not browning too rapidly. An alternate method is to start the pie baking in a preheated 425°F oven for 15 minutes, reducing the heat to 350°F for 30 minutes or until done. (Use 25°F hotter oven for metal pans.)

For best results, always place fruit pies or any two-crusted pies on the lowest oven shelf position to assure the bottom crust browning before the filling boils. If baking in a non-self-cleaning oven, bake the pie on a cookie sheet to keep any boil-over from dirtying the oven. Actually, baking on a cookie sheet is always a good idea, even in a self-cleaning oven, as it prevents a mess and saves energy.

Chiffon, baked pumpkin, or pecan pies: Should be thawed in the refrigerator. Unbaked pumpkin pies should be baked frozen in a preheated 425°F oven for 15 minutes, then for about 30 minutes in a 350°F oven or until filling is done. A knife inserted in pie should come out clean.

CAKES

Cakes freeze very well. Sometimes it's special to save part of a memorable cake from a birthday, wedding, or special holiday. When you eat it, it's like a party all over again!

Cake pointers: When in a cake-baking mood, you may want to double or triple favorite recipes and keep them frozen for instant celebration cakes. We enjoy the festivity of a special cake created in honor of any out-of-the ordinary occurrence, like losing a tooth or being elected cheerleader.

There are a few special cautions: First of all, I feel freezing the *batter* is really not much of a frozen asset. Thawing takes several hours—up to 8 if in a loaf pan or large-volume container. The batter is best frozen in a greased and floured baking pan, which is a real nuisance and space consumer. When baking, the batter should be completely thawed unless you want to have a deformed, peaked cake—or want to spend forever baking it. (If in a hurry, you can thaw in a slow oven before turning to a hotter heat to finish baking—a risky procedure.) Also, baking powder seems to be affected by freezing in a raw batter and high-volume cakes are harder to achieve.

Select rich cakes for freezing baked. Almost any butter cake, especially of the one-bowl variety, freezes beautifully. Pound cake and fruit cake are great. Fruit cakes seem to improve! The longer they are stored, the more mellow they seem to become. Even though the recommended storage time is only one year, I have kept fruit cakes frozen and served them every Christmas for up to five years. We are fond of several different kinds and enjoy keeping a variety on hand. We seem to eat very little of any one kind at once. And it is fun to remember that one was from when we lived in New York City, or Albuquerque, or when Amy got her big dolly for Christmas.

When baking cakes for freezing, do not use synthetic vanilla as it becomes strong and rather unpleasant, whereas pure vanilla freezes well. For spice cakes, use less spice—especially cloves, as it becomes stronger when frozen.

Cream or custard fillings or frostings made with cooked egg white should not be frozen. They get spongy and almost disappear when thawed—a very disappointing experience! The best types of frosting for freezing are the confectioner's sugar, fruity, or other cooked types that do not call for an egg white or custard base.

In general, frozen cake tends to become drier after the second day. Keep this in mind when you're packaging and thawing cakes.

Packaging Cakes

Unfrosted cakes are most easily frozen individually. They freeze best when frozen first on a cookie sheet, cutting board, or other flat surface until firm—about 1 hour—and then are wrapped airtight in recommended freezer wrap. A favorite of mine is a large plastic bag, but other freezer wraps can be used. Seal and label.

Frosted cakes are definitely best when frozen first until firm and then wrapped. I prefer to freeze them on foil-covered cardboard so as not to tie up any of my plates or platters.

When the frosting is firm (allow at least 2 hours for the buttery types) package airtight in a plastic freezer-weight bag or other good-quality freezer wrap. Seal and label. Cupcakes or portions of cake can be frozen individually for single servings. Freeze first, then package, seal, and label. *Raw batter* should be frozen first, then packaged, sealed, and labeled.

To Serve Cake

To serve unfrosted cakes, thaw at room temperature in the packaging for about 1 hour. Or unwrap and pop into a slow oven—about 300°F for 10 minutes. Or quick-defrost in a microwave oven following the manufacturer's instructions. Frosted cakes must be unwrapped before thawing so that the packaging does not damage the frosting as it thaws. To prevent the frosting from sweating as it thaws—particularly if it is chocolate or some other deep color—cover loosely with plastic wrap or with a cake safe lid that does not touch the frosting.

Raw batter should be thawed thoroughly for best results before baking. The thawing time is dependent on the size of the cake and will usually take several hours.

COOKIES

Cookies can be frozen baked or unbaked depending on your whim and the time available either at the moment of mixing or later when you wish to serve them. Of course, baked cookies are quicker to serve, requiring only momentary thawing. But the aroma and fun of freshly baked cookies, when you don't have to spend the time mixing, is a real treat. Also, dough or batter is easier to freeze than crispy, crumbly cookies. Perhaps you'll want to have some of both constantly on hand. Recipes that are rich and high in fat freeze best.

Packaging Cookies

Unbaked cookies of the refrigerator or rolled varieties are best frozen in a roll ready for slicing and baking.

These may be baked without thawing. Drop and bar types of cookies stored in a rigid, wide-mouth container are ready for dipping or pouring out into the baking pan. Or, drop cookies can be frozen already portioned. Freeze firm, then package. Baked cookies need to be protected from crushing while frozen. To do so, separate with layers of wrap or cardboard, depending on how delicate the cookies are. Cardboard is sturdier and prevents most crushing. Very delicate cookies such as meringues and lacies should be packaged only a few layers deep to provide maximum protection. Package in a firm container. I have always liked to use tin boxes or the very heavy freezer-weight plastic containers. Occasionally I have used cardboard boxes overwrapped with freezer-weight packaging. Always be certain to seal well, then label.

To Serve Cookies

Baked cookies thaw almost immediately and can be served right out of the freezer, except for the chewy bar types, which take a little longer.

Unbaked doughs of the sliced or already portioned drop cookies can be baked frozen. Dough in a container will take longer to thaw. The type of carton and size will determine the thawing time. Thaw at room temperature.

MISCELLANEOUS SWEETS

Meringues freeze beautifully, but must be used within two weeks because they become crumbly and seem to almost disintegrate soon after that. To package, place in a rigid carton, separating the layers of meringues with double layers of paper or light cardboard.

Cream puffs can be frozen either raw, baked, plain, or filled. To freeze, place on a cookie sheet and freeze until firm, then package in a rigid container. Raw dough must be left on the cookie sheet.

Frozen desserts such as ices, mousses, sherbets, or Bavarian creams made with a cooked base, gelatin, or marshmallow are successfully frozen. Ones made with a basis of egg white are not good frozen. Freeze gelatin-based desserts before they set. Whipping, or adding cream or cheese yields best results. For convenience you may wish to freeze them in individual freezer-proof serving dishes. When firmly frozen, package in freezer wrap, seal, and label.

Fruit desserts such as baked apples are very versatile when individually packaged in plastic bags or cartons, then grouped into a larger carton. Seal and label.

RECIPES

PIES

FRENCH PASTRY

My all-time favorite pastry—you can hardly fail to produce a beautiful flaky-crusted pie with this recipe.

Yield: three 9-inch crusts

3 cups all-purpose flour
(sifted)
1¾ cups shortening
(lard is preferred)*

1 egg
1 tablespoon vinegar (dark)
2 teaspoons salt
5 tablespoons water

*Lard yields a flakier crust.

1. Blend flour and shortening until mixture resembles coarse meal.
2. Beat egg, vinegar, salt, and water with a fork. Add to flour and shortening.
3. Blend together well, then roll out on lightly floured board and use as desired.

FREEZING HINTS: Freeze baked or unbaked. This very tender crust turns out beautifully without chilling—even when baking immediately. You can freeze filled or as flat pastry.

MAXIMUM RECOMMENDED FREEZER STORAGE: 6 to 8 months when baked, 2 to 4 months unbaked, 6 months when frozen as pastry only

PINK ADOBE FRENCH APPLE PIE

A super-special rendition of French apple pie from the famous Pink Adobe restaurant in Santa Fe, New Mexico. Once you've tried it, you will be hooked! Rosalea sells as many as she can make frozen in addition to serving so many slices nightly in her charming little adobe restaurant that she almost always runs out. A hint is to order the pie as you come in—or if you're real determined, you may order it when you make your reservation.

Temperature: 450°F for 10 minutes, 350°F for another 30 minutes

1 recipe pastry for
  double-crusted 9-inch pie
1 pound sliced apples
2 tablespoons lemon juice
½ teaspoon cinnamon
½ teaspoon nutmeg
½ cup white sugar

¼ cup seedless raisins
1 cup brown sugar
2 tablespoons flour
¼ stick butter
½ cup shelled pecans
¼ cup milk (ample)

1. Put the apples in the pastry-lined pie tin and sprinkle with the lemon juice, nutmeg, and cinnamon.

2. Spread evenly with the white sugar and raisins.

3. Mix the brown sugar, flour, and butter in a bowl. When well blended, spread over the contents of the pie tin and sprinkle with pecans.

4. Add most of the milk, lightly sprinkling over apple mixture. Cover with the pastry top and freeze until firm. If not freezing cut a pattern in the top crust and brush it with milk, then sugar and a light sprinkling of cinnamon. Bake as directed in a preheated 450°F oven.

FREEZING HINTS: After firmly frozen, package airtight, seal, and label. To serve, warm pie about 30 minutes in a 325°F oven if baked. If unbaked, preheat oven, cut a pattern in top crust, then proceed as above.

MAXIMUM RECOMMENDED FREEZER STORAGE: 4 months

Always serve with sauce as follows:

RUM OR BRANDY HARD SAUCE

½ cup butter
1½ cups powdered sugar

1 tablespoon boiling water
1 teaspoon rum or brandy

1. Cream the butter until light; beat in the sugar and add 1 tablespoon boiling water, then beat in the liquor and serve with the pie, which should always be served warm on warm plates so that this sauce oozes down into the rich pie. It's marvelous!

ORANGE LACED RHUBARB PIE

Ever since trying this ages-old recipe from England, I cannot bear the thought of making rhubarb pie any other way; the same goes for strawberries. Gooseberries, too, are great fixed this way, using only about ½ cup

more sugar depending on your taste and the way the berries were frozen or if they are fresh.

Temperature: 375°F
Baking time: 50 to 60 minutes
Yield: one 9-inch pie

1 recipe pastry for
  double-crusted 9-inch pie
¾ cup light brown sugar
2 tablespoons flour
2 pints frozen rhubarb
  (or 3½ to 4 cups fresh)

1 small orange, thinly sliced
  with seeds and outside
  membrane removed
3 tablespoons butter
  Several generous grates of
  fresh nutmeg or about ¼ teaspoon

1. Line 9-inch pie plate with pastry. Mix sugar and flour together.
2. Add ⅓ flour-sugar mixture to bottom of pie on top of pastry. Add ⅓ of the fruit, placing a layer of rhubarb on top of the flour-sugar mixture and topping with the orange slices. Repeat twice more.
3. Dot with butter and grate nutmeg over top. Arrange lattice crust over top of pie and freeze.

FREEZING HINTS: Freeze first, then package in freezer wrap, seal, and label pie.

4. When ready to bake, brush the top crust with milk, then sprinkle on sugar. Bake in a preheated 375°F oven.

MAXIMUM RECOMMENDED FREEZER STORAGE: 6 to 8 months baked, 2 to 4 months unbaked

BLUEBERRY PIE

My own concoction made from Maine's bounty.

Temperature: 450°F for 10
minutes, 350°F for 40 minutes or
until done
Yield: one 9-inch pie

1 recipe French pastry
  (above)
2 pints fresh or frozen
  blueberries
3 tablespoons cornstarch

1 tablespoon flour
⅓ cup brown sugar
½ cup white sugar
1 teaspoon grated orange
  rind

199

2 tablespoons fresh orange juice
2 tablespoons Cointreau
½ teaspoon salt

½ teaspoon nutmeg
½ teaspoon cinnamon
½ teaspoon ground coriander

1. Prepare pastry and line bottom of pie pan.
2. Mix together remaining ingredients. Pour into pastry-lined pan.
3. Top with second crust. Freeze. Or, if baking immediately, brush crust with milk and sprinkle with sugar.
4. Bake in preheated 450°F oven for 10 minutes, then reduce heat to 350°F and bake 40 more minutes or until done.

FREEZING HINTS: Freeze until firm, then package, seal, and label. To bake, pierce crust in preferred pattern, brush with milk, sprinkle with sugar, and bake as in step 4.

MAXIMUM RECOMMENDED FREEZER STORAGE: 6 to 8 months baked, 2 to 4 months unbaked

GOURMET PUMPKIN PIE

A great pumpkin chiffon.

Temperature: 450°F for 10 minutes, 325°F for 50 minutes
Yield: two 9-inch pies

3 eggs, separated
2 cups pumpkin puree
½ cup sugar
¼ cup molasses
1 teaspoon salt

¾ teaspoon cinnamon
¾ teaspoon nutmeg
2 cups heavy cream
3 ounces orange-flavored liqueur
2 9-inch pie shells

1. Preheat oven to 450°F. Beat the egg whites until they hold a definite shape. In a large bowl, beat the three egg yolks slightly and using the low speed of the electric mixer, stir in the pumpkin, sugar, molasses, salt, cinnamon, and nutmeg.
2. Stir in the cream thoroughly. Fold in the egg whites and the liqueur.
3. Pour the mixture into two prepared pie shells and bake on the lowest shelf position of the oven at 450°F for 10 minutes. Reduce the temperature to 325°F and continue baking for 50 minutes, or until the pies are firm in the center.

FREEZING HINT: Freeze until firm, then package, seal, and label.

MAXIMUM RECOMMENDED FREEZER STORAGE: 2 months

KAHLÚA PIE

Just like an after-dinner drink—only better—it is both a cordial and a dessert!

Yield: one 10-inch pie

1 8½-ounce package
   chocolate wafer cookies
   (not cream filled), about 36
6 tablespoons melted butter
   or margarine
2 tablespoons sugar
1 teaspoon instant coffee
½ cup water

1 10-ounce package large
   marshmallows, about 38
½ cup Kahlúa
1 cup whipping cream,
   whipped
½ square (½ ounce)
   unsweetened chocolate

1. Reserve 12 chocolate wafers to stand up around edge of pie. Crush the remainder of wafers to make about 1½ cups crumbs. Mix chocolate cookie crumbs, butter, and sugar and press lightly onto bottom of 10-inch pie plate.

2. Stand reserved 12 wafers around edge of plate to form scalloped top. With fingers, press cookie crumbs to form solid crust.

3. Stir together instant coffee and water. Add marshmallows and cook until melted.

4. Place pan in large pan or sink of ice water (or chill in refrigerator if time permits) stirring occasionally, until thickened.

5. Stir Kahlúa into marshmallow mixture. Fold in whipped cream. Pile into prepared crust. Refrigerate several hours or overnight, or freeze.

FREEZING HINTS: Prepare pie, do not garnish. Place in freezer until firm; then package, seal, and label.

6. To serve, shave chocolate with vegetable peeler, and use to garnish top of pie.

MAXIMUM RECOMMENDED FREEZER STORAGE: 2 months

FRUIT SUNDAE PIE

For quick, dressy pies with an unending variety of flavors—make these ahead or while dinner is cooking.

Yield: one 9-inch pie

1 crumb, coconut, or pastry
   crust, any desired flavor

1 quart vanilla, lemon, or
   compatible flavor of ice cream

1 pint frozen fruit in heavy
  syrup, such as
  strawberries, raspberries,
  peaches, apricots, or
  blueberries

2 tablespoons liqueur *or fruit
  puree, optional (favorites
  are Grand Marnier,
  fruit-flavored or dry
  brandy)*

1. Layer ice cream with partially thawed fruit.
2. Drizzle liqueur between layers of ice cream and fruit. Freeze until firm.

FREEZING HINT: Package in freezer wrap, seal, and label.

3. To serve, it is not necessary to thaw. You may want to garnish with fresh fruit, flowers, nuts, or cookie crumbs.

MAXIMUM RECOMMENDED FREEZER STORAGE: 1 month

CAKES

RED VELVET CAKE

The story goes that a few years ago a woman was so impressed with the deep red cake she was eating she asked the waiter for the recipe, which he promptly presented on a silver platter with a bill for $100.00. Perhaps this is only folklore, but Red Velvet cake is indeed special and very attractive—great for Valentine's Day or any other occasion when red seems right.

Temperature: 375°F
Baking time: 25 minutes
Yield: two 8-inch layers

2 *cups sifted all-purpose flour*
½ *teaspoon salt*
2 *tablespoons cocoa*
1 *teaspoon baking soda*
½ *cup shortening*
1½ *cups sugar*

2 *eggs*
1 *teaspoon vanilla*
1 *cup buttermilk*
2 *ounces red food coloring (2
  large or 4 small bottles)*
1 *teaspoon vinegar*

1. Preheat oven to 375° F. Grease and line with waxed paper two round 8-inch layer cake pans.
2. Measure dry ingredients, then sift together.
3. Cream shortening and sugar together using medium speed of mixer. Add eggs one at a time and beat until fluffy after adding each. Add vanilla and blend.

202

4. Combine liquid ingredients—buttermilk, **vinegar**, and food coloring. Then add dry ingredients in four additions alternately with the liquid ingredients, beginning and ending with the dry ingredients.

5. Bake in a preheated oven for 25 minutes at 375°F. When done, cool on a wire rack for 10 minutes before turning out of pan. Frost with white frosting, using either one of the following.

FREEZING HINTS: Freezes well either frosted or not. Because this cake is so lavish and beautiful looking when freshly frosted, I usually frost just before serving. Freeze before packaging, sealing, and labeling.

MAXIMUM RECOMMENDED FREEZER STORAGE: 4 months

CREAMY FROSTING

Both of the following recipes are great for freezing and can be varied with flavorings and colorings for other cakes.

Yield: Enough to frost between
layers and the top of one 8- or
9-inch layer cake

5 tablespoons flour	1 cup sugar
1 cup milk	¼ teaspoon salt
1 cup butter	1 teaspoon vanilla

1. Cook flour and milk until thick, stirring constantly using medium heat. Remove from heat.

2. Cover pan and let stand until cool.

3. Cream butter until fluffy using medium-high speed of electric mixer. Add sugar, salt, and vanilla; cream until light.

4. Add cooked mixture gradually using high speed of electric mixer. Mix until it resembles whipped cream.

5. Split each layer in half, if desired, and frost between layers and on top.

DECORATOR FROSTING

Yield: Enough to frost the top and
sides of an 8- or 9-inch layer cake

1 1-pound box powdered sugar	¼ teaspoon salt
¾ cup white hydrogenated shortening	1 teaspoon vanilla

1. Using low speed of electric mixer, combine ingredients. Then switch to high and beat until fluffy.

2. Split each layer in half and frost between the layers and on top.

OATMEAL CAKE

A good use of leftover oatmeal—this yummy, moist cake is a great traveler for picnics and campouts, and it freezes beautifully.

Temperature: 350°F
Baking time: 35 minutes
Yield: one 9 x 13-inch cake

1¼ cups boiling water	1 teaspoon cinnamon
1 cup quick cooking oatmeal	½ teaspoon nutmeg
½ cup hydrogenated shortening	½ teaspoon salt
1 cup dark brown sugar	1¾ cups sifted all-purpose flour
1 cup white sugar	1 teaspoon baking soda
2 eggs	3 tablespoons water

1. Boil water, stir in oatmeal, and set aside for 20 minutes. Or you can use leftover oatmeal.

2. Preheat oven to 350°F. Grease and flour the bottom of the cake pan.

3. Combine all of the remaining ingredients with the cooled oatmeal mixture in the large electric mixer bowl and beat at medium speed of electric mixer for 3 minutes or until well blended.

4. Pour batter into pan, smoothing it out to the corners of the pan. Prepare the Broiler Frosting while the cake is baking.

5. When cake is done, top with Broiler Frosting.

FREEZING HINTS: For fresh-baked flavor, cool the cake and do not frost. Freeze until firm and package airtight, seal, and label. To serve, thaw the cake on the counter for about 1 hour wrapped. Loosen the wrap somewhat and heat in a 325°F oven until hot—about 15 minutes or more. Add warm frosting and broil on.

MAXIMUM RECOMMENDED FREEZING TIME: 4 months

BROILER FROSTING

Yield: enough frosting for one
9x13-inch cake

6 tablespoons butter	1 cup flaked coconut
½ cup dark brown sugar	½ cup chopped pecans

204

1 teaspoon vanilla
½ cup chocolate milk

(evaporated milk can be substituted)

1. Cream the butter and brown sugar until well blended.
2. Add the rest of the ingredients and thoroughly mix. Spread on the hot cake, then place under broiler until frosting is bubbly.

DEVIL'S FOOD CAKE

Who wouldn't take the devil's dare when it comes to eating this fragrant, flavorful fudge-topped cake? I've never found a recipe as all-round good as this one and it freezes beautifully!

Temperature: 350°F
Baking time: 35 minutes or until
cake springs back when pressed
Yield: two 9-inch layers or one
9x13-inch loaf cake

6 tablespoons cocoa	2 cups sugar
1 cup boiling water	3 eggs
1 teaspoon soda	½ cup buttermilk or sour milk
1 teaspoon vanilla	2 cups cake flour
½ cup shortening	½ teaspoon salt

1. Preheat oven to 350°F. Mix cocoa and water into a smooth paste. Add soda and vanilla and set aside while preparing the cake batter.
2. Cream the shortening and sugar, using medium speed of the mixer. Add the eggs one at a time and beat vigorously with medium-high speed of the mixer until smooth after adding each.
3. Sift the cake flour; measure and sift with the salt and add alternately with the buttermilk using low mixer speed. Beat on medium speed until smooth and well mixed, then add the cocoa mixture and mix well, bake in 350°F oven. When cooled, top with the following fudge frosting.

FUDGE FROSTING

Yield: enough for one 2-layer cake

2 cups sugar	3 tablespoons cocoa
1 cup brown sugar	3 tablespoons corn syrup
1½ cups cream	Nuts, if desired

1. Mix the sugars and cocoa together; add the syrup and cream. Stir until it boils over medium heat. Omit stirring until a soft ball forms. Then remove from heat.

2. Beat vigorously, adding more cream as needed to make a creamy fudge. Frost cake and sprinkle with nuts if desired while still warm.

FREEZING HINTS: I definitely prefer to prepare the inseparable fudge frosting for this cake after it has thawed and is ready for serving. The fudge freezes well but sometimes can crack and chip off or become blotched, ruining the appearance of this great confection. To freeze, freeze the layers or loaf cake, then package, seal, and label.

MAXIMUM RECOMMENDED FREEZER STORAGE: 4 months

JAM CAKE

An old-fashioned Tennessee recipe almost always prepared for the holidays. Jam cake's rich spiciness makes it an excellent accompaniment for coffee, milk, or egg nog.

Temperature: 375°F
Baking time: 35 to 40 minutes
Yield: three 9-inch layers

½ cup butter	nutmeg, allspice,
2 cups sugar	cinnamon
6 eggs, separated	2 teaspoons soda
2 cups blackberry jam	4 cups flour
2 teaspoons each of cloves,	1 cup sour milk

NOTE: You may wish to decrease the spices if you do not care for highly spiced foods.

1. Preheat oven to 375°F and grease and line three 9-inch or four 8-inch round cake pans with waxed paper. Cream butter and sugar.
2. Beat yolks well and add to sugar and butter. Add jam and spices.
3. Sift soda with flour and add alternately with milk.
4. Fold in well-beaten egg whites.
5. Bake for 35 to 40 minutes.

Jam Cake is best topped with the following filling:
2 cups sugar   ½ cup butter   2 cups sweet milk
1. Cook mixture on medium heat until it begins to thicken.
2. Spoon hot filling on each layer before adding the next one.

FREEZING HINTS: Can be frozen either frosted or not. Since the cake is traditionally a holiday specialty, and if you're making it for the holidays, you may wish to frost it and put it on the special plate you're planning to serve it from. The more preplanning you do like this, the more you'll be able to enjoy the holidays. Freeze until firm; then package airtight, seal, and label.

MAXIMUM RECOMMENDED FREEZER STORAGE: 2 months

LEMON PUDDING–POUND CAKE

Combine the tart, tangy flavor of lemon from a pudding mix with a cake mix and you have a streamlined version of Grandmother's favorite.

Temperature: 375°F for 25
minutes, 325°F for 35 minutes
Yield: one 10-inch cake

1 package 2-layer-size
  yellow cake mix
1 3¾-ounce package or
  3⅝-ounce package instant
  lemon pudding

4 eggs
10 ounces lemon-lime soda
  such as 7-Up
¾ cup salad oil

Glaze:
2 cups sifted confectioners'
  sugar

⅓ cup lemon juice

1. Beat eggs until thick and lemon-colored.
2. Add cake mix, pudding (dry), lemon-lime soda, and salad oil; beat at medium speed for 10 minutes.
3. Pour into ungreased 10-inch tube pan with removable bottom.
4. Bake at 375°F about 25 minutes and turn down to 325°F for last 35 minutes. Remove hot cake, on pan bottom, from pan.
5. Using a fork, prick holes in top of cake; drizzle glaze over top and spread on sides of cake.
6. For Glaze: Combine lemon juice and confectioners' sugar and heat until sugar melts. Drizzle over warm cake.

FREEZING HINTS: A great freezer—keeps very well since it's so moist. Frost while warm; then freeze, package, seal, and label.

MAXIMUM RECOMMENDED FREEZER STORAGE: 6 months

JANE'S COFFEE CAKE

One of my very favorite flavored cake-like coffee cakes.

Temperature: 350°F
Baking time: 40 to 50 minutes
(longer for a bundt pan)
Yield: 12 to 16 servings

¾ cup butter or margarine
1¼ cups sugar
1 teaspoon vanilla
3 eggs
1 cup sour cream
2¼ cups flour
½ teaspoon baking powder

1 teaspoon salt
1 cup walnuts
1 teaspoon cinnamon
2 tablespoons sugar
⅓ cup orange juice
2 tablespoons brown sugar

1. Heat oven to 350°F. Grease a 9-inch tube or bundt pan. Blend butter and sugar until fluffy, using medium speed of a mixer. Beat until mixture is light. Add vanilla and eggs one at a time, beating after each addition until batter is fluffy. Blend in sour cream, using lowest speed.

2. Sift flour, baking powder, baking soda, and salt. Add to creamed mixture and beat until half blended, using low speed (don't overbeat).

3. Spoon half of batter into prepared pan. Mix nuts and cinnamon and 2 tablespoons sugar. Sprinkle half of mixture over batter. Top with remaining batter. Sprinkle with remaining nut mixture.

4. Cut through batter. Bake 40 to 50 minutes or until inserted toothpick comes out clean. Combine juice and brown sugar; cook until sugar is melted. Brush over top and sides of warm cake.

Variations: Instead of the orange juice, mix ¾ cup powdered sugar, 1 tablespoon butter, and a little lemon juice and enough milk to make a thin frosting, then dribble it over the cake when done and cooled. When I use this topping I also add ½ tablespoon grated lemon rind to batter.

MAXIMUM RECOMMENDED FREEZER STORAGE: 3 months

BESSIE LEE'S FAVORITE FRUITCAKE

Bessie Lee has long been one of my very favorite home economics teachers. She headed the home economics education department at the U.S. Indian School in Albuquerque, New Mexico, and taught for years—a fascinating lady with a quick wit and lots and lots of great homemaking ideas . . . and recipes. This was her traditional Christmas fruitcake of which she made vast amounts for presents.

Temperature: 300°F
Baking time: about 1 hour
Steaming time: 1 hour or more
Yield: 16 to 17 pounds

5½ pounds chopped, mixed
    candied fruit
1 pound chopped, pitted
    dates
2 pounds pecan halves
1 pound black walnuts
    (optional: another pound
    of pecans may be used)
1 pound flour
1 pound butter

1 pound sugar
1 dozen eggs
1 teaspoon nutmeg
1 teaspoon allspice
2 teaspoons cinnamon
1 cup sherry wine or pickled
    peach juice
½ pint plum jelly or any
    light-colored jelly
Apricot brandy, as desired

1. Place all the fruit, dates, and nuts in a large bowl. Add all the flour and mix well.

2. Cream the butter and sugar until very fluffy using medium-high speed of the electric mixer. (Make sure you use a very large mixing bowl.)

3. Separate the eggs. Beat the yolks until fluffy and lemon colored and add to the creamed mixture. Beat the whites until soft peaks form and set aside.

4. Add the spices, wine, and jelly to the butter and sugar mixture and mix until very well blended.

5. Fold in the beaten egg whites. Add the fruit-nut mixture and stir until well mixed.

6. Butter the cake pans and line the bottoms with waxed paper. Any size pans may be used. Fill about ⅔ full.

7. Place foil over the top of the cake pans and steam cakes for 1 hour for the 1-pound size (a small loaf pan or coffee can, for example). If large pans are used, allow about ½ hour for each additional pound (for example, you would steam a 3-pound cake for 2 hours).*

8. After steaming, remove foil and bake in a 300°F oven until an inserted toothpick comes out clean. (One-pound cakes require about 1 hour of baking time.)

9. When done, cool 10 minutes on a wire rack, then remove from baking pans. Sprinkle or brush with apricot brandy—the amount you use will depend on your personal taste. Wrap or seal in airtight wrap until Christmas.

*To steam the cakes, use a large roaster or canner and place about ½ to ¾ inch water in bottom of pan. Place a metal trivet such as a wire cooling rack in the bottom and arrange cakes on it, making sure the bottoms of the cakes are not touching the water. Place the lid on the pan. Use medium heat on the surface unit or place in the oven at about 350°F, making sure you adjust the temperature to maintain about a medium boil. Add water as needed.

NOTES: This recipe works equally well quartered or halved if you wish to make less cake. For the best flavor, prepare the fruitcake about one month before Christmas. Any leftover fruitcake can be sealed tightly and frozen for a year or more. In fact, this is the recipe I once kept frozen for five years.

I always package the cakes I plan to give as gifts in doubled layers of cellophane—one layer of freezer quality layered with one bright color such as red or green. The ribbon or decorative touch should be added after removing from the freezer.

MAXIMUM RECOMMENDED FREEZER STORAGE: at least 1 year

CHEESECAKE TORTE

Cheesecake lovers are sure to rally 'round this one.

Temperature: 350°F
Baking time: 1 hour
Yield: one 9-inch cake

Crust:

2 cups zwieback crumbs	½ cup (1 stick) butter or
1 cup sugar	margarine, melted
1 teaspoon cinnamon	

1. Place 7 or 8 zwieback into an electric blender container. Cover and process using low speed until crumbed. (The longer the process time, the finer the crumbs will be.) Empty into mixing bowl and repeat until 2 cups of crumbs are obtained. If no blender is available, use a rolling pin to crush the zwieback. Combine crumbs with sugar, cinnamon, and butter.
2. Set aside ¾ cup. Press remaining crumb mixture on sides and bottom of buttered 9-inch springform pan.
3. Chill while making filling.

Filling:

4 cups small-curd cottage cheese	3 tablespoons lemon juice
	1 cup whipping cream
6 eggs	1 teaspoon vanilla
1½ cups sugar	½ cup flour
⅛ teaspoon salt	½ cup chopped pistachio
2 teaspoons lemon rind pieces	nuts

1. Preheat oven to 350°F. Divide all ingredients in half, except pistachio nuts, and add to blender. Blend, using medium speed, until mix-

210

ture is quite smooth and creamy. After blending half the ingredients, pour the mixture into large bowl for mixer.

2. Blend second half of ingredients, add to first mixture in mixing bowl, and mix together until well blended.

3. Pour into prepared springform pan. Combine reserved crumb mixture and nuts; sprinkle over top.

4. Bake in preheated oven at 350°F for 1 hour. Open door and let cool in oven. Remove from pan. Chill or freeze before serving.

FREEZING HINTS: Freezing the baked cheesecake works well as the cake is best served chilled.

MAXIMUM RECOMMENDED FREEZER STORAGE: 4 months

CREAM PUFFS

Cream puffs, eclairs, or profiteroles have always been regarded as a superachievement and a real party dessert. And they aren't that hard to make with this never-fail recipe. They're marvelous frozen, ready for filling with any of a range of fillings, sauced or not. Make them in various sizes for either desserts or hors d'oeuvres.

Temperature: 400°F for 30
minutes, 350°F for 5 minutes
Yield: 6 large or 32 small
bite-sized

½ cup milk or water	Pinch of sugar
¼ cup butter	2 eggs
½ cup sifted flour	Few drops of cream, milk,
Pinch of salt	or egg yolk, optional

1. Heat milk and butter together on medium heat. When slow simmer begins, add flour, salt, and sugar. Preheat oven to 400°F.

2. Cook and stir until batter leaves the sides of the pan and forms a ball. Remove from heat and stir in eggs one at a time, beating well after each.

3. Using two large spoons for the large puffs, two small spoons for the smaller ones, spoon out highly rounded heaps of batter and place about 2 inches apart on ungreased baking sheet. For golden brown crusts, brush with cream, milk, or beaten egg yolk.

You may freeze the puffs on baking sheet at this point for a period up to two weeks for very fresh-tasting puffs. Package, seal, and label when firmly frozen.

4. Or, you may wish to at least chill for 30 minutes in your refrigerator as an extra assurance for hollow puffs.

5. Bake for 30 minutes in preheated 400°F oven, then reduce heat to 350°F and bake for 5 more minutes. Do not open oven door during entire baking period. At end of baking, remove one of the puffs and leave out for a few minutes. If it does not shrink or fall down, they are done. If making the tiny-sized puffs, shorten the first portion of the baking to 20 minutes and bake for 10 minutes following at 350°F.

6. To serve, slit along base of each puff with a sharp knife to open for filling. If large ones, fill with whipped cream (liqueur flavored if desired), ice cream, or custard. For no-work custard filling, use a canned pie filling. Frost or serve sauced with desired fruit or chocolate sauce. If serving the tiny puffs as a dessert, stack in groups of three to five on each plate or in a tall pyramid on a platter. Serve glazed or sauced. For hors d'oeuvres, stuff with any meat salad such as chicken, ham, tuna, or cheese. Pickles, olives, nuts, or other desired condiments make for tasty fillings, too.

FREEZING HINTS: Freeze either after spooning for a short storage period, or freeze after baking if you wish to freeze for longer periods and with less bulk. For baked puffs, cool, then freeze on cookie sheet until firm. If desired, puffs can be filled then with whipped cream or ice cream filling (do not freeze custard-base fillings). When puffs are firm, package unfilled ones in bag, foil, or rigid carton. Filled ones should be packaged in rigid carton or in box and overwrapped. Seal, package, and label.

MAXIMUM RECOMMENDED FREEZER STORAGE: 2 months

MERINGUES

Fun to have on hand for short-term storage, meringues are a great way to use lots of egg whites and a simple, low-calorie way to serve pudding or frozen or fresh fruits. And they are so elegant and no fuss at serving time!

Temperature: 300°F
Baking time: 1½ hours
Yield: 10 individual servings

6 egg whites	1 teaspoon vanilla
¼ teaspoon salt	2 cups sugar
1 teaspoon vinegar	

1. Preheat oven to 300°F.
2. Add salt, vinegar, and vanilla to egg whites; beat until mixture forms peaks, using high speed of electric mixer.

3. Add sugar gradually; continue beating until very stiff.

4. Spoon 10 large mounds on cookie sheet covered with plain ungreased paper.

5. Hollow out cups with bowl of spoon.

6. Bake in slow oven (300°F) 1½ hours.

7. Remove from paper immediately and cool.

8. Fill with pudding, fruit, or ice cream for serving.

FREEZING HINTS: When cool, package in airtight rigid cartons and seal and label. Since they are so fragile, be certain to handle carefully and separate the layers of meringues with double layers of paper. Use a carton that cannot be bent or allow any damage to the meringues. Tin cans or containers are extra good.

MAXIMUM RECOMMENDED FREEZER STORAGE: 2 weeks

13
Microwave Cooking Magic

Freezers and microwave ovens make a perfect marriage! Both appliances spell convenience and together they are unbeatable at providing the ultimate in cooking flexibility. On just a moment's notice frozen foods can be thawed, cooked, and served thanks to the super-speed of microwave cooking. However, microwave thawing and cooking are only as convenient as the packaging.

PACKAGING

To really maximize the benefits of the two appliances, you should keep in mind your microwave oven when packaging foods for the freezer. Remember, no metals should be used in packaging foods for microwave unless the range manufacturer approves it. Check the user's manual to see if foil trays such as are used for commercially prepared TV dinners and casseroles are approved for use in your oven. Foil and metals of any type, including china or pottery with metallic coatings or finishes, reflect the microwaves, preventing the foods from cooking uniformly.

Since the rate of speed in microwave cooking depends on the amounts of fat and water contained in the food, the different foods in a TV dinner cook at varying rates. For best results, package each food separately rather than in dinner form and the quality will be much better.

Packaging materials that are suited to freezing for microwave cooking include glass, china, and pottery of any nonmetallic type. (If the container is metallic, it will get hotter than the food and slow the cooking of the food. To check, place a glass measuring cup of water and the dish in the oven at the same time. After a minute, if the dish is hotter than the water, do not use that dish.) Heatproof plastic, paper, wood, straw, and seashells are also suitable for microwave cooking.

The most convenient and time-saving method of packaging foods intended for microwave cooking is in the container or wrap you will cook in. You don't have to tie up your favorite serving dishes, though. You can layer criss-cross pieces of cello, plastic, or foil wrap on a plate, platter, or

214

in a casserole, then add the food. Freeze until firm, usually a matter of a few hours. Pull the food out of the dish still under wrap. Package airtight for freezing. To heat, unwrap outer package, peel off underwrap, and place the food in the dish it was frozen in; heat and serve in just moments.

Some paper plates are especially treated for freezer-to-microwave cooking and are so labeled. An easy technique is to place the food in a paper bowl or on a plate and cover with another, sealing with freezer tape, egg white, flour and water, or other nontoxic glue or paste.

Microwave ovens vary greatly as to features, and may be either 2450 MHz or 915 MHz (MHz is the frequency). The 915 MHz models are generally housed in a conventional oven and are coupled with conventional bake and broil units offering the flexibility of microwave, conventional cooking, or a combination of the two which can make a difference in freezer packaging. You should refer to the manufacturer's use and care book for specific instructions and help in freezer-microwave cooking.

FROZEN FOOD COOKING
TECHNIQUES FOR MICROWAVE

Methods for handling food for microwave cooking are pretty much the same regardless of the kind of food.

To thaw frozen food, the first consideration is whether your microwave oven has a defrost or low power cycle or control. If your oven has one, use it for defrosting, as the low power or cycling heat will assure the freshest-tasting frozen food as quickly as possible. If your range does *not* have this cycle, you can thaw foods best by cooking them in short intervals, letting them rest a few seconds or minutes, turning the foods and cooking a bit again until they reach the desired texture. Always consult the manufacturer's instructions for any specific recommendations.

Covering is desirable when thawing, heating, or cooking as it controls the moisture content, evenness of cooking, and helps prevent spattering.

Cover foods you are defrosting with a solid nonmetallic lid, plastic, or cello wrap. This will help to keep the steam within the dish and aid in thawing. Solid lids such as glass or plastic or even a plate distribute steam most evenly. This is especially good when thawing liquids and casseroles. Leave the lid on the container or dish after removing from the oven so that the built-up steam can circulate.

Plastic or cello wrap serves about the same purpose as a lid and can be used as a substitute.

Waxed paper will not form a good seal. It is good if you wish to keep the heat in, but not for keeping all the steam as with thawing meats, fruits, breads, and pastries.

Paper towels are best for thawing and cooking high fat content foods, such as bacon, or foods in which you want the moisture to evaporate, such as crusty hard rolls, doughnuts, and the like.

For crisp tops on foods that spatter, such as casseroles, thaw with a lid, plastic wrap, or plate; approximately one-half way through the thawing/ cooking, remove and place paper toweling on top to aid crisping. A little experimentation will yield the best techniques for your own taste.

Turning and stirring are necessary to thaw and cook food evenly in a microwave oven. The best technique for a casserole is to thaw it on the defrost setting if available, or a few minutes of resting. Every few minutes, stir it and give the dish a quarter turn. With layered foods, such as lasagna, be sure to turn the casserole a quarter turn at least once or twice. This assures even thawing and cooking.

Small quantities of food are better to work with than large ones because smaller loads will absorb the energy more evenly, producing better results. When thawing, defrost one package at a time rather than two at once.

In general, most foods require about one and one-half to two times as long to heat to serving temperature if starting with frozen food and cooking with microwaves. If uncertain about the thawing and cooking times for a food not listed here, find the food most nearly like it and use those times. The manufacturer's book that came with your range also should be a help.

Moist foods heat faster than dry ones. Fats and sugars in foods increase their speed of heating too.

Tips on Appetizers and Snacks

Finger foods of all types are favorites for microwave cooking and they take virtually no time at all. Parties are special when you have the microwave oven conveniently placed so that guests can cook their own snacks such as meatballs or shrimp as desired. When serving appetizers, prepare them before working on the main course and dessert. Set aside. Then when you want to serve them, pop the appetizers in the oven. Remove any food that is in the oven, checking the time. When appetizers are done, return the food and finish cooking.

Cheese is best served at room temperature or bubbly hot. Thawing or heating cheese is very easy. Microwave heating is speedy, just 30 seconds for small wedges or cubes and up to a few minutes for larger chunks. (Go easy—it's hard to quickly chill runny cheese.) Turn cheeses a quarter turn halfway through the thawing period.

Frozen dips heat beautifully for quick serving. Place in a serving dish and thaw, using heat for just a few seconds. Allow standing time. Hot dips can be thawed and heated all in one quick process. For the average 1½-

to 2-cup quantity allow 3 to 5 minutes for thawing, twice that for heating. Watch carefully, stirring and turning every 2 minutes, keeping covered when not stirring.

Meatballs, individual shrimp, mini lobster tails, or other bite-sized items will heat in just over a minute. Set on 30 seconds, turn the paper towel or saucer you are heating them on a quarter turn, and heat for another 30 seconds or so.

Frozen nuts, chips, or dry snacks of almost any type will heat and crisp in the microwave. For each half-cup, allow 30 seconds. If not as warm as you'd like, heat longer—but it's always best to look before it's too late!

Tips on Meats and Seafoods

When beginning to prepare a meal, start thawing and cooking the meat first. Exceptions would be long-cooking vegetables or breads that should be served hot and are coupled with a quick-cooking main dish such as seafood. Plan your menu when using the microwave so that if there is a long-cooking meat, the vegetables and bread can be cooked quickly. Most meats improve with a short standing period during which the juices have a chance to be reabsorbed, giving more flavor and tenderness. The short standing period is good for the meat and allows time to cook other foods.

For seafood and roasts, undercook to allow for cooking during the standing period. For lobsters or large servings of seafood, undercook by a minute or two, then cook the vegetable; then everything will come out together, piping hot and delicious. Allow up to 20 minutes' standing time for roasts of 6 pounds or more that you want to serve well done. For beef roasts that you wish to serve rare to medium rare, undercook by 5 to 10 minutes. Serve immediately after the short standing time.

Whenever char grilling, grill extra meats for freezing and quick serving from your microwave oven.

Seafoods such as clams and oysters, for serving raw or cooked, can be easily shucked if given a minute or so in the microwave oven to soften the muscle. Experiment to determine timing. For a start, try 1 minute.

Tips on Main Dish Casseroles

Combination casseroles cook beautifully in a microwave oven. Usually you will want to thaw and cook in one continuous process. Allow about one-third to one-half more time for cooking frozen main dishes. Since a family-sized recipe serving four to six requires about 15 minutes to cook in the microwave oven, allow another 7 minutes or more for defrosting. The user's manual and your experimentation will determine the exact times for your favorites.

217

If you wish a crispy topping, replace the lid with a paper towel about 5 minutes before serving. Remember to turn the dish every 5 minutes or according to the manufacturer's instructions. Stir casseroles unless they are layered or molded as in lasagna or meatloaf. Allow the casserole to rest a few minutes between cooking periods and turn a quarter turn once or twice to equalize the cooking and prevent overcooking.

Tips on Vegetables

For the sake of convenience and saving time, blanch the fresh vegetables you wish to freeze following the microwave blanching chart on page 219.

When you're in a hurry, dribs and drabs of fresh vegetables from the garden can be blanched quickly by placing freshly rinsed vegetables in a covered dish and "microwaving" for 2 to 3 minutes, stirring halfway through the period. Chill an equal amount of time and package.

Never thaw vegetables. Cook them frozen, except corn on the cob which heats faster after 1 to 2 hours' countertop thawing. Other exceptions are frozen French fries and hash browns. Thawing in a microwave oven before broiling or frying produces a taste more like freshly made fries and they're less soggy, too.

When serving vegetables add various seasonings, toppers, and sauces. See some of my favorites on pages 149–50.

Tips on Fruits

Frozen fruits thaw beautifully in the microwave oven. See the manufacturer's recommended timing. Jams and jellies are unbelievably good, freshly made in 4 minutes in the microwave.

To speed up freezing fruit, prepare the sugar syrup you use for freezing fruits right in a heatproof quart measuring cup—and you will have the speed of microwave heating, plus the convenience of being able to pour right from the measure. Other pitchers work just as well as long as they can withstand high heat.

Tips on Bread, Butter, and Jam

Bread of all descriptions heats very quickly in the microwave oven. And day-old bread tastes fresher than fresh! To heat to serving temperature, place the bread in airtight packaging (open the end if you wish a very moist bread), removing wrap after one minute of warming. If a crusty outside is desired, place bread in paper toweling or bag before heating.

218

Waxed paper is a compromise for nut breads and other quick breads, preventing the sogginess of plastic bag heating and the crispiness of heating in paper. Check your microwave range manufacturer's instructions for specific time recommendations. This table provides a guide:

MICROWAVE VEGETABLE BLANCHING CHART

Vegetable	Amount	Casserole Size	Amount of Water	Time in Minutes
Asparagus	1 lb. cut into 1- to 2-in. pieces	2-qt.	¼ cup	2½ to 3½
Beans, Green or Wax	1 lb.	1½-qt.	½ cup	3½ to 5½
Broccoli (1-in. cuts)	1 bunch 1¼–1½ lbs.	2-qt.	½ cup	3 to 5
Carrots	1 lb., sliced	1½-qt.	¼ cup	3½ to 5½
Cauliflower	1 head, cut into flowerets	2-qt.	½ cup	3 to 5
Corn on the Cob*				
Onions	4 medium, quartered	1-qt.	½ cup	2½ to 4
Parsnips	1 lb., cubed	1½-qt.	¼ cup	2 to 3½
Peas	2 lbs., shelled	1-qt.	¼ cup	3 to 4½
Spinach	1 lb., washed	2-qt.	None	2 to 3
Squash, Summer Yellow, Zucchini	1 lb., sliced or cubed	1½-qt.	¼ cup	2½ to 4
Turnips	1 lb., cubed	1½-qt.	¼ cup	2½ to 4

* SPECIAL DIRECTIONS FOR CORN ON THE COB: For most even blanching, cut corn off the cob before blanching. Cook corn cut from 4 ears at a time. Place cut corn in 1-qt. casserole. Add ¼ cup water. Cover. Cook 4 to 5 minutes, stirring after 2 minutes. Cool by setting casserole in ice water.

Chart, courtesy of General Electric Company

BREAD THAWING TIMES IN MICROWAVE OVEN

Type	Thawing Time in Regular Microwave Oven	Thawing Time with a Defrost Feature
Loaf of Bread Also Nut Bread	1½ minutes	1½ to 2 minutes
Rolls (4 to 6 servings) Doughnuts and Muffins	¼ to ½ minute	¾ to 1¼ minutes
Coffee Cakes	2½ minutes	3 minutes
Single Slice or Roll	10 to 15 seconds	15 seconds

Butter and margarine are soft for spreading if slightly warmed in the microwave oven. If you are a frequent traveler or if you are cooking for only one or two people, keep butter or margarine frozen—then defrost for one-half minute per stick. Place wrapped stick of butter or margarine on dish suitable for microwave oven use and warm to spreading consistency. One tablespoon will melt in 10 seconds.

Freezer jam is spreadable in 1½ to 2 minutes of warming in the microwave oven. Even better, make fresh jam in just minutes from frozen fruit.

Tips on Desserts

Most microwave-freezer desserts, including pies, cakes, cookies, and cobblers, can be cooked ahead or while the main course is being cleared from the table.

Personal favorites are crisps and frozen fruits, such as peaches, apricots, rhubarb, strawberries, apples, and blueberries. For crisps, use a standard topping of brown sugar, butter, flour, oatmeal, or other cereal. You can cook them quickly while you clear.

Frozen cake of any sort—heated in the microwave with fruit, whipped cream, jam, pudding, even a touch of sherry and a handful of toasted nuts—makes a rapid trifle.

Shortcake is a snap made with prefrozen shortcake rounds. Use frozen fruit and whipped cream mounds for no-work shortcake.

Baked fruit, such as apples, pineapple, peaches, or pears, can be made when in season, spiced with various goodies such as brown sugar, nuts, raisins, cinnamon, nutmeg, butter and rum, brandy or sherry for extra dash, and frozen for simple but sumptuous fruit desserts.

Flamed fruits are oh-so elegant and yet easy using frozen fruit and the microwave. Thaw fruit in the microwave and add flavorings according to your favorite flaming fruit recipe. Warm the liquor, which must be at least 50% alcohol, for 15 seconds, then add to the warm fruit just before serving and flame. For elegance, place scoops of ice cream in sherbet glasses and serve flamed fruit over the ice cream. Or, you may prefer to use cake squares or even to "live it up" and use ice-cream-topped cake.

Tips on Beverages

Any type of beverage heats fantastically fast in the microwave. Each cup of beverage requires about 1 minute plus (depending on the size of the cup) to heat to boiling. If frozen, such as frozen tea or coffee, allow another ½ minute. Or if you wish to just take the iciness off a frosty slush, heat for 15 seconds per cup or until it reaches desired consistency.

RECIPES

Have fun creating the recipes that follow. Or use them as a guide for adapting your family's favorites. The use and care book that came with your microwave oven should offer many more recipe ideas too! *Listed thawing times are for regular or high power microwave ovens.*

CHILE CON QUESO

For a great-tasting Southwestern dip, keep a supply of this spicy cheese on hand. It's a super sauce too! Use it to top omelets, meats, vegetables, and bread or crackers.

Thawing and serving time: 3
minutes
Cooking time: 2 to 3 minutes
Yield: 1¾ cups

1 cup processed American cheese
½ cup Cheddar cheese

¼ cup light cream or
evaporated milk

221

1 medium fresh tomato, finely chopped	1 clove garlic, crushed
1 or more fresh, frozen, or canned green chiles or jalapeno chiles, finely chopped	2 green onions, chopped, or ¼ cup sweet red onion finely chopped
	Salt to suit taste

1. Combine all ingredients and heat until bubbly—about 2 to 3 minutes. Freeze if desired.

2. To serve, place frozen queso in serving dish, cover with cello wrap, then put in microwave oven for 3 minutes. Stir and give a quarter turn. Cook more if needed. Serve with tostados—crisp, deep-fried corn chips.

FREEZING HINTS: Package in quantities desired for serving; seal and label.

MAXIMUM RECOMMENDED FREEZER STORAGE: 2 months

SEASIDE CHEESE DIP

Cooking time: 6 minutes
Thawing time: 4 minutes
To serve: 2 to 3 minutes
Yield: about 2 cups

1 can (6½ ounces) minced or chopped clams	1 tablespoon Worcestershire sauce
2 jars (5 ounces each) sharp Old English cheese spread	½ medium green pepper, chopped (about ⅓ cup)
1 package (8 ounces) cream cheese	2 green onions, chopped (about 2 tablespoons)

1. Drain clams, saving juice. Place drained clams in 1½-quart casserole along with sharp cheese spread, cream cheese, Worcestershire sauce, pepper, and onion.

2. Place casserole in microwave oven. Cook 5 to 7 minutes, stirring every 2 minutes, until all cheese has melted smooth.

3. Add ¼ cup of clam liquid, stirring well, and reheat 2 to 3 minutes more. Freeze if desired.

4. To thaw, place carton of dip in microwave oven and heat for 2 minutes. Turn a quarter turn; stir. Heat another 2 minutes, stir, and turn another quarter turn. If still partly frozen, heat another minute or two.

5. Excellent served with fresh raw vegetables such as celery, radishes, and cauliflowerets.

FREEZING HINT: Package in desired serving or freezer containers. Seal and label.

MAXIMUM RECOMMENDED FREEZER STORAGE: 1 month

EGGS AND . . .

A fantastically fast dish. You can use any sort of frozen, refrigerated, or tinned fills or frills you have on hand.

Cooking time: 4½ minutes
Yield: 2 servings

4 eggs (thawed are fine)
¼ cup milk, beer, water, or wine
½ teaspoon salt
Few grinds of freshly cracked black pepper
Crushed herbs as desired—fresh or dried—rosemary, thyme, savory, basil, dill, or tarragon (choose one or two)

½ cup fill or frill—choose one (from the freezer, if possible)—sautéed mushrooms, cheese, cubed meat of any type including beef roast, cold cuts, tuna, leftover flaked fish or seafood, creamed meat, vegetable sauce, or undiluted soup
Garnish, optional: parsley, tomato wedges, fruit slice, or lettuce leaf.

1. Spray baking dish or 1-quart bowl with nonstick coating. Break eggs into dish. Add liquid and seasoning. Beat well with whisk or fork. Add filling such as cheese, meat, or mushrooms.

2. Cook on regular power for 2¼ minutes, stirring every half-minute. Turn dish a quarter turn and cook for another 2 minutes, continuing to stir every half-minute or until eggs are done. They will continue to cook after removed from oven—do not overcook or eggs will become dry and tough. If adding a frill (sauce), top eggs as you serve them.

Do not freeze after preparation. Leftovers can be saved a day or two and reheated for serving.

FISH FILLETS ALMONDINE

Microwave ovens are ideal for cooking fish because it cooks quickly, yielding tender, moist flesh. Standing time after cooking is critical for the heat to equalize. Cook fish or seafood covered so that the steam will be held in and cooking will be more uniform.

Cooking time: 12 minutes
Yield: 4 servings

¼ cup slivered almonds	White pepper
¼ cup butter	1 pound frozen
1 fresh lemon, cut in half	white-meated fish fillets
Salt	such as sole or perch
	Parsley and paprika

1. In a shallow 2-quart baking dish, combine almonds and butter. Cover with a paper towel. Cook until almonds are golden—about 5 minutes, stirring every minute. (Save time by having buttered, toasted almonds prepared and frozen ahead.)

2. Cut lemon in half lengthwise, squeeze half of lemon onto almond-butter mixture. Stir well.

3. Thaw fish by placing a frozen package of fillets in oven for 1 to 2 minutes or until package softens. Separate fillets and place in lemon-butter mixture. Season with salt and pepper. Turn and season other side. Garnish tops with buttered, toasted almonds.

4. Cook covered with a lid or cello wrap. Turn a quarter turn after 3½ minutes' cooking. Let stand covered for 2 to 3 minutes or up to 5 minutes. Meanwhile prepare four lemon wedges and dust top, thinnest edge with paprika.

5. Serve garnished with parsley and lemon wedges.

MAXIMUM RECOMMENDED FREEZER STORAGE: for fish before cooking, 6 months

SHERRIED SHRIMPS ROCKEFELLER

Cooking time: 25½ minutes
Thawing time: 10 minutes
To serve: 15 minutes
Yield: 4 servings

2 packages (10 ounces each) frozen chopped spinach	1 cup shredded sharp Cheddar cheese (4 ounces)
16 medium to large raw shrimp*	3 tablespoons cooking sherry
	2 medium slices fresh bread
1 can (10½ ounces) cream of shrimp soup	3 tablespoons butter
	Paprika

*If shrimp are frozen, defrost by placing in 2-quart casserole with 1 cup water. Cover. Place in microwave oven and cook for 2 to 3 minutes. Shrimp should still be firm and cold but no longer icy.

1. Place frozen blocks of spinach in large glass casserole or mixing bowl. Place in microwave oven and cook 3 minutes.

2. Break up blocks as well as possible and continue cooking 3 more minutes until just completely thawed. Drain well, squeezing out as much juice as possible.

3. Spread over bottom of 9½-inch-square casserole, or in four large, or eight small shells. (Place shells in glass baking dish.) Distribute shrimp evenly over spinach.

4. In 1-quart measuring cup or small glass mixing bowl, stir together soup, cheese, and sherry. Place in microwave oven and heat 3 minutes, stirring every minute, until cheese is melted. Set aside while preparing crumb topping.

5. Break bread in tiny bits into small glass bowl. Add butter to crumbs and place in microwave oven. Cook 1 minute, stirring after ½ minute, until butter is distributed among crumbs.

6. Pour hot sauce over casserole and sprinkle crumbs over top. Sprinkle with paprika.

FREEZING HINT: Chill; freeze until firm, about 2 hours; then package and label.

7. If not freezing, place dish in microwave oven. Bake large casserole uncovered for 15 minutes (check small shells after 8 minutes, large shells after 10 minutes), giving dish a half turn every 5 minutes. (If frozen, thaw covered for 10 minutes in large casserole, turning once, or 6 to 8 minutes for small to larger shells. Then cook as above.)

MAXIMUM RECOMMENDED FREEZER STORAGE: 3 months

SOLE FOOD
Clever as the title and mighty tasty!

Cooking time: 17 minutes
Thawing time: 6 to 8 minutes

To serve: 10 minutes
Yield: 8 servings

2 cups medium to large	1 cup milk*
frozen deveined shrimp	1 teaspoon salt
2 tablespoons butter	1 teaspoon parsley flakes
¼ cup chopped green onion	1 teaspoon grated lemon peel
2 tablespoons butter*	⅛ teaspoon pepper
2 tablespoons flour*	2 pounds sole fillets**

*One can cream of mushroom soup can be substituted for convenience.
**Thaw sole fillets by placing in paper package in microwave oven and cooking each package 2 to 3 minutes, turning package over every minute.

1. Place shrimp in 12x8x2-inch dish and thaw for 2 minutes. Cut in half lengthwise.

2. Add butter and green onion. Cook for 3 minutes, stirring after 1 minute. Let stand while making sauce, or substitute soup.

3. Place butter in 1-quart casserole. Place in microwave oven and cook until melted, about ½ minute. Add flour and stir until smooth.

4. Gradually stir in milk, keeping mixture smooth. Stir in salt, parsley flakes, lemon peel, and pepper.

5. Place in microwave oven and cook for 4 minutes, stirring smooth after 2 and 3 minutes.

6. Arrange thawed sole fillets over shrimp, putting larger ends of fillets near edges of dish and distributing shrimp throughout. Cover fish with hot sauce.

7. To serve, cover dish with plastic wrap and cook for 10 minutes, giving dish a half turn after 5 minutes. Allow dish to stand 2 additional minutes before serving.

DO NOT FREEZE AFTER PREPARATION.

MAINE CLAM SAUCE

A Maine favorite I loved making after clamming. A freezer and microwave oven preserve the succulence of freshly caught coastal bounty. A microwave oven will quickly steam the shells open.

Cooking time: 8 minutes
To thaw: 6 to 8 minutes
To serve: 2 minutes
Yield: 4 servings

2 cups clam meat	½ cup minced onion
2 cups wine broth	Parsley, minced, optional
1 teaspoon shrimp boil spice	3 cloves garlic, crushed
1 teaspoon salt or to taste	3 tablespoons flour
3 tablespoons olive oil	1 pound spaghetti
	½ cup or more grated Parmesan cheese

1. Steam clams in mixture of 1 cup white wine and 1 cup water sea-soned with salt, shrimp boil spice, and a sprig of seaweed placed in 2-quart bowl. Cover with plastic wrap.

2. Cook until the shells split open. Time varies according to the size of clams. Usually 3 minutes is about right for 2 cups. Let stand covered for 2 to 3 minutes. They should split open. If not, cook a minute longer and check; continue until just barely popping open. Overcooking toughens.

3. Shuck clams and chop coarsely if large. Strain wine broth and re-serve 2 cups.

4. Rinse bowl, add oil, and sauté onion and garlic for 2 minutes.

5. When these become transparent, add flour and stir until smooth. Add clams and broth and stir until smooth. Taste and adjust seasoning. Sometimes I have needed to add more broth if available; if not, add equal parts of white wine and water ¼ cup at a time. Cook 3 minutes longer, stirring every minute.

FREEZING HINT: Freeze at this point in cartons or jars. Seal and label.

6. To thaw, place in covered container or heat in freezer container if ovenproof and cook 6 to 8 minutes or until uniformly thawed.

7. Heat to bubbly hot. In the meantime prepare spaghetti or thin noo-dles in oiled, salted water until tender but not overly limp. Strain.

8. Place drained spaghetti on warm plates, top with sauce and cheese, and garnish with minced fresh or dried parsley. Dash with paprika if available.

MAXIMUM RECOMMENDED FREEZER STORAGE: 3 months

$5,000 FIESTA CHICKEN KIEV

Cooking time: 10 to 12 minutes
Thawing time: 6 to 8 minutes
Yield: 8 servings

4 whole chicken breasts, halved, boned, and skinned	3 tablespoons butter
	3 tablespoons Old English-style sharp cheese spread

2 teaspoons instant minced onion	1 cup Cheddar cheese
1 teaspoon salt	crackers, crushed
1 teaspoon monosodium glutamate	1½ tablespoons taco seasoning mix
2 tablespoons chopped green chiles	Shredded lettuce
¼ cup butter, melted	Diced tomatoes
	Chopped ripe olives

1. Pound each raw chicken piece with mallet or foil-covered brick to flatten.

2. Beat together butter and cheese spread until well blended. Mix in onion, salt, monosodium glutamate, and chiles.

3. Divide mixture equally among the 8 flattened chicken pieces, placing a portion toward one end of each piece.

4. Roll up each piece, tucking in ends to completely enclose filling. Fasten rolls with toothpicks.

5. Dip each roll in melted butter to cover, then coat with mixture of cheese crackers and taco seasoning mix.

FREEZING HINTS: Place the chicken rolls on a cookie sheet and freeze until firm. When solidly frozen—in about 1 hour—package in airtight vapor-proof freezer packaging; seal and label. If serving in just a few days and you can spare the dish, freeze the Kiev in the dish you intend to bake and serve from. To thaw, place Kiev in casserole, top with plastic wrap, and thaw in microwave oven, using defrost cycle if available for 6 to 8 minutes, turning once. Then cook as follows.

6. Arrange rolls in 12 x 8 x 2-inch buttered dish. Cover with waxed paper.

7. Place dish in microwave oven and cook 10 to 12 minutes.

8. Serve Chicken Kiev on a bed of shredded lettuce and diced tomatoes. Top with chopped olives. If desired, garnish generously with whole olives, tomato wedges, and favorite taco sauce.

MAXIMUM RECOMMENDED FREEZER STORAGE: 4 months

MALE EGO
(or "How to Cope in the Kitchen Casserole")

You don't have to be male to appreciate the great taste coupled with convenience in this casserole.

Cooking time: 8 to 10 minutes
Thawing time: 6 to 8 minutes
To serve: 8 to 10 minutes
Yield: 6 to 8 servings

1 can (10½ ounces) cream of chicken soup
1 can (4 ounces) diced green chiles
¼ teaspoon instant minced onion
½ cup water
2 large, firm, ripe tomatoes
1 package (6 ounces) corn chips
2 cans (5 ounces each) boned chicken, diced
1 cup shredded mild Cheddar cheese

1. In small mixing bowl, place soup, chiles, onion, and water. Stir until well blended.
2. Peel tomatoes and slice thin.

FREEZING HINTS: If you don't wish to freeze casserole in the dish, place criss-crossed pieces of wrap inside the dish.

3. In 2-quart buttered casserole, layer one-half of corn chips. Top with one can of diced chicken, then half of tomato slices. Pour half of soup mixture over chicken, sprinkle with half of cheese. Repeat layers in same order, ending with cheese. Freeze until solid—about 2 hours—then package for the freezer and label.
4. If not freezing, cover with paper towel, cook 8 to 10 minutes as follows, omitting defrosting time.
5. To defrost and serve, place covered casserole in microwave oven and defrost, using defrost setting for 6 to 8 minutes, turning once (5 to 7 minutes with regular setting). Then cook 8 to 10 minutes, giving dish a half turn after 5 minutes. Let stand 5 minutes before serving.

MAXIMUM RECOMMENDED FREEZER STORAGE: 3 months

COQ AU VIN MADE EASY

Convenience foods coupled with the microwave oven make this inexpensive dinner dish a real do-ahead favorite!

Cooking time: 15 minutes
Thawing time: 3 to 6 minutes

To serve: 4 to 6 minutes
Yield: 4 servings

2½ to 3 pounds chicken,
  cut-up or your favorite
  parts such as legs
½ cup flour
1 teaspoon salt
¼ teaspoon freshly ground
  black pepper
4 tablespoons dry onion soup mix
  Nonstick spray coating
4 slices bacon, cut in 1-inch pieces

¼ teaspoon garlic powder
1 tablespoon dried parsley
1 bay leaf
1 cup red wine
1 cup water
1 8-ounce can onions,
  drained
1 4-ounce can whole button
  mushrooms, drained
  Fresh parsley or scallions

1. Dredge chicken parts in combination of flour, salt, pepper, and 2 tablespoons onion soup mix. Spray 9 x 12-inch heatproof glass (or largest size your microwave oven will accommodate) baking dish with nonstick coating. Place chicken parts in baking dish.

2. Cover chicken with paper towel. Cook for 10 minutes in the microwave oven on full power. Add bacon and cook for 1 minute.

3. Add all ingredients but last three and cook for 2 more minutes, covering with plastic wrap and giving dish a quarter turn.

FREEZER HINT: Freeze, seal, and label. If baking dish is needed, transfer chicken and sauce to freezer container.

4. To thaw, place in microwave oven, using the defrost setting if available, and cook for 4 to 6 minutes, or 3 to 5 minutes on regular setting, turning a quarter turn every minute. Let stand about 10 minutes, then add mushrooms and onions. If not baking in dish transfer to it now.

5. Cook an additional 4 to 6 minutes or until bubbly. Serve garnished with parsley or fringed scallions made by finely scoring both the white onion part and the green tops.

SERVING SUGGESTIONS: Wild or long grain rice almondine and a tartly dressed green salad make this a fine French country dinner. French bread and a vegetable may also be desired.

MAXIMUM RECOMMENDED FREEZER STORAGE: 4 months

VEAL SCALLOPINE

Always a favorite for buffet or elegant sitdown dinners, scallopine can be created quickly à la microwave if the slicing and stirring are done ahead of time. The cooking as well as the serving time are mightily abbreviated with the microwave oven.

Cooking time: 9 minutes
Thawing time: 3 to 6 minutes
To serve: 5 to 6 minutes
Yield: 6 to 8 servings

2	pounds thinly sliced veal cutlets	¼	cup butter
2	tablespoons flour	½	teaspoon garlic powder
1¼	teaspoons salt	½	pound mushrooms, thinly sliced
¼	teaspoon freshly ground black pepper		Dash of salt (or butter salt)
		1	cup dry sherry or Marsala wine

1. Pound cutlets until very thin. Sprinkle lightly with mixture of flour, salt, and pepper.
2. Melt butter in 9 x 12-inch baking dish or largest size that will fit oven. Add cutlets to dish and sprinkle with garlic powder. Cover with paper towel and cook for 4 minutes.
3. Turn cutlets, add mushrooms, dash with a little butter salt, cover with paper towel, and cook 4 more minutes. Add wine and scrape bottom of pan and place juice on top of meat. Cover with plastic wrap. Heat for 1 minute.

FREEZER HINT: Freeze in baking dish or transfer to freezer carton. Seal and label.

4. To thaw, place covered dish in microwave oven for 5 to 6 minutes on defrost setting or 3 to 5 minutes on regular power, turning a quarter turn every minute.
5. Place in baking dish if in freezer carton. To serve, heat for 5 to 6 minutes or until bubbly, keeping covered with plastic wrap. Noodles, whole grain pilaf, or rice make a fine accompaniment.

MAXIMUM RECOMMENDED FREEZER STORAGE: 9 months

BEEF 'N' GREEN ONION QUICHE

A super-quick supper if prepared ahead and frozen.

Cooking time: 8 to 10 minutes
Thawing time: 12 to 13 minutes
To serve: 10 to 13 minutes
Yield: 6 to 8 servings

1 egg	1 teaspoon salt
½ cup cream or undiluted evaporated milk	1 cup sliced green onions, including tops
2 cups seasoned stuffing mix or croutons	3 eggs
½ pound lean ground round or chuck beef	1 cup shredded Swiss cheese
1 teaspoon Worcestershire sauce	3 to 4 drops Tabasco (hot pepper) sauce
	½ cup cream or undiluted evaporated milk
	Paprika

1. In large mixing bowl, beat egg slightly. Add cream and stuffing mix. Let stand a few minutes until most of liquid is absorbed.

2. Add beef, Worcestershire sauce, salt, and ¼ cup green onions. Mix only until combined.

3. Spoon lightly into bottom and sides of 9-inch pie plate and shape into crust. Sprinkle remaining green onions over beef crust.

4. In same bowl, beat eggs until foamy. Stir in cheese, Tabasco, and cream.

5. Pour over green onions in the meat crust. Sprinkle lightly with paprika.

FREEZER HINTS: Place in freezer and freeze until firm. If planning to store a long time, place criss-cross pieces of foil or plastic wrap in bottom of glass pie plate before adding meat crust. After firmly frozen, lift out of pie plate. Package in freezer wrap, seal, and label. To cook, peel off wrap and place in pie plate.

6. Place frozen quiche in microwave oven and cook 17 to 20 minutes, giving dish a quarter turn every 5 minutes. Filling should be almost set— if not, cook another minute or two. Remove from oven and let stand 5 to 10 minutes to firm before cutting into wedges. If not planning to freeze, cook 10 to 13 minutes, turning dish a quarter turn every 5 minutes. Allow to stand 5 to 10 minutes before cutting.

MAXIMUM RECOMMENDED FREEZER STORAGE: 2 months

SOUTHERN BARBECUED MEAT

Barbecue good old Southern style has long been a favorite at our house. I make it ahead several ways: from scratch in the microwave, or placing large, flat heatproof glass or casserole dishes of chunked ribs, chicken, beef, pork, and even ham right on the grill whenever barbecuing. Other times I place a baking dish of barbecue in the oven when baking a pie. This way I conserve energy and time and have the frozen convenience of yummy frozen barbecue, better-tasting than when just cooked and eaten. A spell in the freezer improves the flavor of barbecue and makes your evening so easy when you can just pull the barbecue out of the freezer and in a matter of minutes serve it piping hot from the microwave oven.

Cooking time: varies according to meat selected and method used: 1 hour in 400°F oven, 30 minutes on grill or under broiler. Check microwave manufacturer's directions for type of meat.
Thawing time: 4 to 8 minutes, depending on boniness of meat
To serve: 10 to 15 minutes
Yield: 4 servings

2 pounds lean to 3½ pounds bony meat (chicken, ribs, beef or pork roast, ham slice)

1 teaspoon salt
1 medium onion
1 18-ounce bottle barbecue sauce

1. Chunk or cut meat to serving size. Arrange single layer in bottom of baking or casserole dish. Season with salt and place a slice of onion on each piece.
2. Roast or grill according to times above or until golden and done. Drain fat. Drizzle one-half of bottle of barbecue sauce evenly over meat. Microwave for 15 minutes.

FREEZER HINTS: Place dish of meat in freezer until firmly frozen. Package in freezer wrap, seal, and label. If you cannot spare the baking dish in your freezer, remove meat to freezer carton, heavy-quality paper plate, or shallow foil pie plates.

3. To thaw, place covered meat in oven for 4 to 8 minutes, turning a quarter turn after half of cooking time.
4. To serve, remove packaging, turn meat over (placing onion slices aside), add about half of remaining sauce, and cook for 10 minutes or less. Turn meat over again, placing an onion slice on center of each portion. Add rest of sauce. Heat for another 5 minutes, placing casserole a quarter turn away from its position when you removed it from oven. Serve.

MAXIMUM RECOMMENDED FREEZER STORAGE: 3 months

SLOPPY JACQUES

A fun version of Sloppy Joes!

Cooking time: 18 minutes to
prepare
Thawing time: 5 to 6 minutes
To serve: 5 to 6 minutes
Yield: 6 sandwiches

1¼ pounds ground beef,
   crumbled
⅔ cup minced onion
½ cup diced celery
¼ cup diced green pepper
½ cup catsup

1 tablespoon Worcestershire sauce
½ teaspoon salt
⅛ teaspoon pepper
1 cup grated sharp Cheddar
   cheese
6 French rolls

1. In 1½-quart casserole place beef, onion, celery, and green pepper. Cover.

2. Place dish in microwave oven and cook for 6 minutes, stirring every 2 minutes. Drain meat well.

3. To cooked meat mixture, add catsup, Worcestershire sauce, salt, pepper, and cheese. Recover and cook 5 to 6 minutes, stirring after 3 minutes.

FREEZING HINT: Split the French rolls horizontally close to top crust. Pull out center of rolls to make hollow shell of crust, and fill each "shell" with meat mixture. Place on cookie sheet and freeze until solid, then package individually. Seal and label.

4. To thaw and serve, place all six sandwiches on a cookie sheet in microwave oven. Cover sandwiches with plastic wrap. Thaw for 5 to 6 minutes, redistributing sandwiches after 3 minutes. Cook for 5 to 6 minutes until hot. To prepare one sandwich at a time, heat each for 1 minute to thaw; turn, then heat each for 1 minute or until hot.

MAXIMUM RECOMMENDED FREEZER STORAGE: 3 months

MY FAVORITE LAMB CURRY

This recipe has got to be one of the best! It has never failed to please family and guests. I have lots of fun serving this curry with a wide range of condiments. Since the flavor actually improves with cooking ahead and freezing, you will discover the easy elegance of serving this without fuss at mealtime. Time-consuming chopping and preparation are done beforehand and the long simmering needed is shortened by the microwave.

Cooking time: 21 minutes
Thawing time: 6 to 8 minutes
To serve: 3 or more minutes
Yield: 6 servings

3 pounds lamb shoulder or neck
½ cup flour
2 garlic cloves, minced
4 medium onions, sliced
¼ cup butter
2 large apples, pared and
  chopped
3 tablespoons curry powder
4 tablespoons brown sugar
5 tablespoons raisins

2 tablespoons
  Worcestershire sauce
2 lemons or limes, sliced
  (seeds removed)
4 tablespoons coconut,
  shredded
¾ cup black walnuts
¼ teaspoon lime peel, grated
1 tablespoon salt
2 cups water

1. Cut meat into 2-inch cubes and roll in flour.

2. Meanwhile, add garlic and onion to butter in 2-quart ovenproof glass or ceramic casserole and cook for 1 minute. Add floured lamb and cook for 2 minutes. Stir and cook for another 3 minutes. (Cover with a paper towel to keep from spattering.)

3. Add remaining ingredients. Cook for 10 minutes, stirring once and turning dish a quarter turn. Cook for another 5 minutes and serve as below, or freeze, sealing and labeling.

4. To thaw, place in microwave oven covered and cook for 6 to 8 minutes on defrost setting, 4 to 5 minutes on regular power, using any heatproof glass bowl or dish. Stir; heat for another 3 minutes or more until bubbly.

5. Serve with a side dish of rice and several of the following condiments: sieved hard-cooked eggs. chutney, peanuts, coconut, raisins, grated lemon or lime peel, pineapple chunks, sliced bananas, chopped green peppers, chopped onions, pickled watermelon rind, or marinated cucumbers.

FREEZING HINT: Package in any carton or jar; seal and label.

MAXIMUM RECOMMENDED FREEZER STORAGE: 3 months

14
Single or Not

Travel, business, social, and school schedules frequently demand serving single meals. More and more people are living alone but that is no reason to eat boring or nutritionally inadequate meals.

One of the most gratifying frozen assets offered by a freezer is the variety of single servings that can be made and frozen to suit the desires of single diners.

Most important for a successful single meal plan is to keep this strategy in mind. Whenever you cook, prepare an extra portion or two for single meal packaging. Rather than putting bits of leftovers in the refrigerator, package them together for star billing at a single meal later.

When you gear your thinking to single servings, you can easily make great meals alone a regular happening. I like to keep a log of the "singles" so that when anyone in the family is home alone he can check out the menu and please himself. If you're a microwave oven owner, you can defrost, heat, and serve in a matter of seconds or minutes at most—a true no-fuss way to eat alone.

Love the ease of TV dinners, but are tired of the "vanilla" taste? You can have the best of all worlds—homemade flavor combined with TV dinner ease—by cooking at least one portion more of each dish whenever you fix a favorite meal. Or, you can deliberately prepare a number of "TV dinners" using your family's favorite menus. Either way, package the foods on a divided foil, plastic, or freezer-weight paper plate, seal, and label.

Always package the foods for greatest heating and serving convenience. For example, if you have a microwave oven, package as recommended on page 214. If you don't have a microwave oven, foil is the most convenient wrap because the foods can be heated in it right from the freezer.

Sauces such as spaghetti or enchilada packaged for single servings make meals super easy.

Salad Stuff

People seldom think of salads when eating alone, let alone think of them from the freezer! Actually, some of the individual ingredients for

236

frozen salads do not freeze and serve well—they wilt and get very limp—but combined in a frozen salad, they fare fine. Nuts, however, can discolor and become bitter.

When preparing a gelatin salad, use about one-fourth less liquid if it has whipped cream or evaporated milk, cottage or cream cheese, mayonnaise or salad dressing. For example, use 1½ cups liquid instead of the standard 2 cups.

In general, any combination fruit or vegetable salad with cheese, cream, or milk base freezes well. For serving, thaw in the refrigerator for a few hours—depending on the serving size—and serve while still well chilled. Mayonnaise, gelatin, and sour cream are definitely not recommended freezables yet when combined in a salad with any of the other basic ingredients and served chilled, they do quite well. Relishes, such as cranberry, store very well in the freezer.

Diced fruit combinations can be frozen together for quickie fruit salads. Mini-sized cans of fruit cocktail, or the large cans frozen and then sliced, make an attractive, no-effort frozen fruit salad served on lettuce, dolloped with mayonnaise.

Try any of the above ideas prepared in single servings ready for convenient serving!

Breads and Desserts

Freeze breads of various types in single serving quantities to add convenience. Frozen loaves of bread can be a real bother to try to slice for just one serving.

Satisfy your sweet tooth with various individually frozen sweets, varying from the always easy ice cream or fruit. The obvious ones—cookies, cupcakes, and tarts—are good, but why not be more exotic?

Freeze bags of cream puffs ready for filling or already filled, meringues, frozen individual fancy desserts such as chocolate soufflé, parfaits, or chiffon concoctions!

MENUS AND RECIPES

TV DINNERS

Prepare your own TV dinners using the following menus as a guide. I usually make several dinners at one time. To do this, I cook extra servings of each freezable food so as to have a surplus for my TV dinners. Holiday menus are fantastic for making TV dinners, and you can extend the fun of the holiday by eating another Christmas dinner three months later.

Use partitioned plates or trays for packaging these dinners. If heating in a microwave oven, check to be sure if the manufacturer recommends foil in the oven—if not, use heatproof plastic or heavy freezer-weight paper. Foil of course is great for conventional heating and whenever permitted in the microwave oven.

Menu

Tomato Beef Swirls
Parslied Rice
Green Beans with Sour Cream

TOMATO BEEF SWIRLS

2½ cups small bread cubes
2 cups grated Cheddar cheese
1 cup chopped green pepper
½ cup grated onions
1 tablespoon
Worcestershire sauce

2 teaspoons salt
¼ teaspoon pepper
1 can condensed tomato
soup
1 egg, beaten
2 pounds ground beef

1. Combine bread cubes, cheese, green pepper, onions. Worcestershire sauce, salt, pepper, and ½ cup tomato soup. Mix lightly, but thoroughly.

2. Blend ½ cup tomato soup and egg in with beef. Pat meat mixture out evenly into a rectangle ¼ inch thick.

3. Spread stuffing evenly over meat. Roll up as for a jelly roll and cut into 1½-inch slices.

4. Arrange in a shallow baking dish. Pour remaining tomato soup over meat slices. Bake at 325° F for 40 to 45 minutes. Cool before packaging. Package one serving in each partitioned plate.

PARSLIED RICE

4 cups cooked rice
2 tablespoons minced
parsely

½ cup melted butter or
margarine

1. Toss all ingredients lightly so that rice grains are well coated with melted butter. Cool before packaging.

GREEN BEANS WITH SOUR CREAM

2 packages frozen green
   beans, French-style
1 cup sliced mushrooms

2 tablespoons melted butter
   or margarine
1 cup sour cream
1 teaspoon salt

1. Saw blocks of beans into 8 individual portions. Sauté mushrooms in butter. Cool, mix with sour cream and salt, and pour over beans.

MAXIMUM RECOMMENDED FREEZER STORAGE: 3 months

To serve, place packaged dinner in 375°F oven for 30 minutes or until hot. To heat in a microwave oven, check for the manufacturer's recommendation.

Menu

Mushroom Stuffed Mini Steaks
Scalloped Cheddar Noodles
Lemon-Buttered Broccoli

MUSHROOM STUFFED MINI STEAKS

8 beef or veal cube steaks
½ cup melted cooking fat
1 teaspoon salt
1 cup mushroom slices

¾ cup chopped green pepper
¼ cup melted butter or
   margarine
½ teaspoon celery salt

1. Sear steaks on both sides in one-half cup hot fat. Sprinkle with 1 teaspoon salt. Remove from frying pan.
2. Cook mushroom slices and green pepper in ¼ cup melted butter or margarine for 5 minutes. Toss celery salt with cooked mushrooms and

green pepper; place 3 tablespoons mushroom mixture in the center of each cube steak.

3. Fold each steak in half and skewer ends. Cool before packaging.

SCALLOPED CHEDDAR NOODLES

2 tablespoons melted butter or margarine

1 package (8 ounces) narrow noodles, cooked and drained

½ pound Cheddar process cheese slices cut in strips

⅓ cup milk

½ teaspoon salt

1½ teaspoons Worcestershire sauce

1. Pour melted butter over hot noodles and toss until noodles are well coated. Add cheese slices to milk and cook over low heat, stirring occasionally, until well blended.

2. Add salt and Worcestershire sauce. Cool. To package for freezing, divide noodles into 8 portions and top each portion with cheese sauce.

LEMON-BUTTERED BROCCOLI

2 packages frozen broccoli spears

¼ cup melted butter or

margarine

1 tablespoon lemon juice

1 teaspoon salt

1. Use saw to separate spears. Arrange spears on plates. Combine remaining ingredients and pour over broccoli spears.

MAXIMUM RECOMMENDED FREEZER STORAGE: 3 months

To serve, place packaged dinner in 375°F oven for 30 minutes or until hot. To heat in a microwave oven, check for the manufacturer's recommendation.

SINGLE SERVINGS STARTERS

For quickie combo meals in solo, keep some of the following meats frozen handily in single serving amounts.

Cooked Cubed or Chopped Chicken

for salads
tacos

chow mein (combined with frozen package of Chinese mixed vegetables)

omelets
casserole quickies made by
combining with a favorite

soup and instant pasta,
rice, chips, or whatever

Cooked Sliced Roast Beef

for sandwiches of
unlimited types (layered
with other ingredients and
sauced or grilled or served
plain)
sukiyaki
tacos

Chinese beef and
vegetables (made with
frozen Chinese vegetables
of your choice)
main dish salads
casseroles

Cooked Sliced or Chopped Ham

for jambalayas
omelets
salads

casseroles as above or with
vegetable and cheese
layers

MAXIMUM RECOMMENDED FREEZER STORAGE: 4 months for chicken and beef, 2 months for ham

MAIN DISHES

ITALIAN RED MEAT SAUCE

Italian food a favorite? Never be caught without this savory sauce, packaged in various quantities. For variety and convenience, package the sauce separately in different quantities for single, family, and company cooking.

Temperature: medium and
simmer
Yield: serves 8

2 *tablespoons olive oil*
1 *cup minced onion*
1 *pound ground beef and 1*
    pound ground pork, or 2
    pounds ground beef or
    other substitute such as

   Italian sausage
4 *cloves garlic*
1 *tablespoon salt*
½ *teaspoon freshly ground*
    black pepper
2 *teaspoons oregano*

1 teaspoon each of the
following: thyme,
rosemary, marjoram, basil,
savory
6 tablespoons snipped
parsley
2 bay leaves

2 #303 cans of tomatoes
Optional: 1 #303 can
mushrooms
2 6-ounce cans tomato paste
1½ cups water
¼ cup grated Parmesan cheese
Optional: ½
cup Burgundy wine

1. Put olive oil in large pan and sauté onion until clear and slightly browned. Add meats and stir into small pieces.

2. Press garlic with salt and add to meat mixture with remaining spices, tomatoes, tomato paste, and Parmesan cheese.

3. Simmer sauce until flavors are well blended—about 1 hour—add wine if desired during last 5 minutes of cooking. Cool and package.

FREEZING HINT: Package in wide-mouth jars or cartons for a variety of uses.

MAXIMUM RECOMMENDED FREEZER STORAGE: 2 months

To serve, cook your favorite pasta, such as spaghetti, rigatoni, or shells, and serve topped with lots of fresh-grated Parmesan. Or use sauce as the basis for lasagna or manicotti.

MEAT LOAF MIX

Meat loaf is one of the most versatile of all meat main dishes. On less busy days, prepare a large batch of basic meat loaf. Then shape it into individual or large loaves, family- or company-sized rings, and pat crusts into pie pans for vegetable or bread stuffings.

Temperature: 350°F
Baking time: 1½ hours for loaves,
less for smaller servings
Yield: 12 servings

3 pounds ground beef (can
substitute 1 pound or less
of ground pork, veal, or
lamb or any combination)
2 cups cereal, flake or
oatmeal, or wheat germ or
bread crumbs (can use part
potato or corn chips)

2 eggs, beaten
1 medium onion, chopped
1 tablespoon salt (use less if
salted chips are used)
½ teaspoon each black
pepper, dry mustard, and
thyme
¼ teaspoon each garlic

powder and rosemary
2 *tablespoons*
  Worcestershire sauce
  Dash of hot pepper sauce

Optional toppers: cheese
strips, catsup, green pepper
rings

1. Combine all ingredients thoroughly until well mixed. Shape in any of the ways mentioned above. Garnish as desired with any of the toppers.

FREEZING HINTS: Freeze individual servings on a waxed-paper-lined cookie sheet. When solidly frozen—in 1 hour or more—package in freezer wrap and label.

MAXIMUM RECOMMENDED FREEZER STORAGE: 3 months

HUNGARIAN STUFFED CABBAGE ROLLS

For another easy one-dish meal prepare Hungarian stuffed cabbage rolls and freeze them in individual servings. Crusty bread and wine make this into a gourmet's delight!

Temperature:300°F
Cooking time: 1 to 4 hours
Yield: 6 servings

1 *large cabbage head*
1½ *pounds ground meat*
  (mixture of ⅓ pork, ⅓
  beef, and ⅓
  lamb preferred)
1 *egg, slightly beaten*
1 *cup rice (regular or quick*
  cooking, depending on
  length of time to be cooked)

1 *medium onion, diced*
1 *teaspoon salt*
½ *teaspoon freshly ground*
  black pepper
½ *teaspoon garlic salt*
1 *#303 can sauerkraut*
1 *46-ounce can tomato juice*
½ *pint commercial sour*
  cream, optional

1. Core cabbage, remove outer 10 to 12 leaves. Dip leaves in and out of boiling water until bright green and drain.
2. Combine meat, egg, rice, onion, and spices.
3. Make nest of sauerkraut in bottom of large, heavy pan, electric fry-pan, or deep-fat fryer. Pressure cooker is fine, especially if you're in a hurry.
4. Place 2 tablespoons of meat mixture in center of each cabbage leaf and start rolling from the stem end and secure with a toothpick.

5. Alternate layers of stuffed cabbage and place on top. Pour tomato juice over all and simmer on low heat for 1 to 4 hours.

FREEZING HINTS: Freeze in cartons—two or three to a serving—spooning some sauce and cabbage-kraut mixture over top of each. To serve, top with sour cream, if desired, and heat until bubbly—about 30 minutes if frozen in a 350°F oven.

MAXIMUM RECOMMENDED FREEZER STORAGE: 4 months

Stews

Any hearty stew is fantastic for single serving since it is so easy and satisfying. A variety of favorite stews stored in single serving quantities is a winner of an idea! Use any of your favorite recipes. Potatoes and rice get somewhat mushier than when served immediately, so you will have to decide whether the mushiness is tolerable or not. If not, then you can substitute noodles or other pasta or add potatoes or rice when heating to serve. Wedges of crusty bread coupled with a crisp salad combine to make for really good eating with any of these stews.

ARMENIAN LAMB STEW

Serve this savory stew with warmed pita bread and a mint-sparked, tossed green salad garnished with Greek olives.

Temperature: 450°F reduced to 325°F
Baking time: 4 hours
Yield: 8 servings

3 pounds bony lamb, cut into small pieces with bone in
4 cloves garlic, minced
2 tablespoons salt
1 large eggplant, sliced ½ inch thick
4 yellow summer squash, sliced ½ inch thick

2 green bell peppers, sliced into rings
2 #303 cans whole or sliced tomatoes
1 6-ounce can tomato paste
Freshly ground black pepper

1. Turn oven to 450°F while cutting lamb. Heat large stewing kettle or casserole briefly in oven with the garlic and olive oil—just until the garlic begins to sizzle.

244

2. Add the lamb and cook while slicing vegetables. Cook until browned, turning every 10 minutes. Should not take over 30 minutes. Drain off fat and discard.

3. Add the eggplant slices in a layer, then the squash and green pepper rings. Season with the salt and pepper. Add the tomatoes, cover and bake, reducing the heat to 325°F. Do not stir as stew cooks.

4. Stew can be held for an indefinitely long time in a warm oven if need be. To serve, sample and adjust seasonings. Take stew to the table without stirring, that is, if you are serving several. Otherwise, just serve in soup bowls with the pita bread and salad.

FREEZING HINTS: I like to serve the stew the first time to family or guests because it makes such an attractive entree. Then I package the remainder for the freezer in single servings. Or you can package the entire amount if you wish.

MAXIMUM RECOMMENDED FREEZER STORAGE: 2 months

TEX-MEX CHILE

Chile Tex-Mex style is almost everyone's favorite on chilly evenings. Few Texans or Southwesterners agree on the ingredients, quantities, or method of preparing chile. In fact, various Texas cities have regular chile festivals, with the best chile recipe winning great awards. This recipe is an easy and well-tested one that can be varied to your own taste.

Temperature: 300°F
Cooking time: 30 minutes
Yield: 6 to 8 servings

2 tablespoons shortening	2 cups pinto or kidney beans
½ cup chopped onion	(1 1-pound can)
¼ cup chopped green pepper	1 teaspoon salt
1 pound ground beef	½ teaspoon garlic salt
2 cups tomato sauce (2	1 teaspoon chile powder (or
8-ounce cans)	more to taste)

1. Heat fat in skillet or electric deep-fat fryer at 300°F.

2. Add onion, green pepper, and beef; reduce heat and simmer until meat is lightly browned, stirring as needed.

3. Add tomato sauce and simmer for 5 minutes.

4. Add pinto beans, salt, and garlic salt. Simmer for 5 minutes.

5. Stir in chile powder and simmer for 30 minutes.

6. Ladle chile into soup bowls and serve with crackers, tortillas or corn-bread, and dill pickles.

FREEZING HINT: Cook chile and ladle into one-serving-size cartons. Seal and label.

MAXIMUM RECOMMENDED FREEZER STORAGE: 2 months

CUCUMBER DELIGHT

This crisp, cool-tasting salad is one of those freezables that shouldn't be, according to the ingredients, but in fact works well.

Yield: 16 servings

1 3-ounce package lemon gelatin
1 3-ounce package lime gelatin
2 cups hot water
1 cup sour cream

1 cup mayonnaise
2 cups grated cucumber with peel (2 medium cucumbers)
3 tablespoons grated onion

1. Combine lemon and lime gelatins in water. Cool until consistency of egg white.
2. Combine sour cream and mayonnaise with gelatin. Add remaining ingredients. Pour into 1¼-quart ring mold or individual molds. Freeze until firm.

FREEZING HINTS: For single servings, freeze in individual small sealable containers. Small yogurt cups, plastic or waxed cups, or short glasses sealed with foil or plastic are ideal. Label.

MAXIMUM RECOMMENDED FREEZER STORAGE: 4 months

To serve, place salad on a bed of lettuce or fresh cucumber slices.

FROZEN FRUIT MEDLEY

Yield: 16 servings

¼ cup sugar
½ cup water
2 10-ounce packages frozen sliced strawberries
1 cup crushed pineapple

2 to 4 bananas
1 #2 can peeled apricot halves (drained and cut into quarters)

246

1. Boil sugar and water. Place strawberries in a bowl, then pour hot liquid over unthawed strawberries.

2. Arrange pineapple and sliced bananas in 1½-quart ring mold.

3. Arrange cut apricots on bananas. Pour first mixture over fruit in mold. Freeze.

FREEZING HINT: Salad mixture may be made in paper muffin cups placed in muffin tins.

MAXIMUM RECOMMENDED FREEZER STORAGE: 4 months

To serve, allow frozen salad to stand in refrigerator about 1 hour before serving. Serve on a bed of lettuce with a light salad dressing if desired.

15
Calorie Counting Convenience

The desire to be trim, healthy, and on the go has become a national pastime! Sagging waistlines, "middle-age spread," and "fat at forty" are no longer accepted fates. Complementing this is an increasing interest in learning more about the relationship of health to diet.

Calories and cholesterol are now recognized as potential causes of severe health problems. Lighter foods, decalorized sauces and desserts, and more fresh meat are growing diet trends.

After several years of expense account traveling and elegant entertaining, my avoirdupois increased noticeably. Upon studying food chemistry, I found that sumptuous foods can be had at no sacrifice in flavor when you really commit yourself to that goal! I began a series of diet cooking classes to help others get and stay skinny. I find this new way of cooking and eating very exciting. It's like finding a new Eden.

Your freezer can be an invaluable assist in holding down your calorie consumption. Why? How? Simply by serving as a larder for decalorized foods. Many foods require longer preparation time due to low-calorie substitutions, but they are worth the effort. For instance, sauces thickened by egg, homemade soups and stocks simmered for hours to gain flavor without thickening, and meats poached in low-calorie concoctions all save calories. Also, meats can be frozen in the exact portions for dieting (see table on page 250). Quick eating doesn't always mean pizzas, spaghetti, fried chicken, French fries, and milk shakes—not when you have a freezer stocked with low-calorie goodies.

From my years of thinking thin when cooking and eating, I've collected many low-calorie ideas which I'd like to share with you.

SUCCESSFUL SLIM TIPS

Experimentation can yield slenderizing results. Here are some general guidelines to help direct you.

Decide what food habits you feel you really don't want to forego. For example, if you like desserts, don't give them up, but direct your efforts to various low-calorie versions. Blended fruit ices have great flavor, for example, and save you the hundreds of calories there are in ice cream. Like sauces? Try decalorizing vegetable sauce, using pureed vegetables instead of rich, heavy cream sauces. Like to drink wines and liquors? Learn the calories and use low-calorie mixers. Extend wine by serving with one-third soda water over ice. The dilution created by the soda and ice gently shaves off one-third of the calories, almost harmlessly.

Eat less. Try fancy low-calorie garnishes of parsley, radish roses, celery curls, fruit slices, or a bed of lettuce to fill up the space formerly occupied by a more generous portion. Limit yourself to the portion served.

Broil often. Broiling trims off calories, especially when you carefully remove most of the fat before cooking, and then remove the balance as you eat.

Include eggs and milk in your diet, but try using the lowest-calorie forms. Diet or uncreamed cottage cheese and yogurt are very versatile—blended, they can substitute for sour cream. Plain yogurt made from skimmed milk saves at least half the calories of whole milk varieties. Skimmed milk or buttermilk supplies protein with many fewer calories. For cooking, use nonfat powdered milk—you will greatly save on convenience, cost, and calories.

Experiment using more egg whites in soufflés, omelets, scrambled eggs, etc., and save about 75% of the calories gained when whole eggs are used.

Keep low-calorie nibbles on hand such as pretzels, fruit ices, wafer thin crackers, or whatever low-calorie foods you like best. Your freezer will keep them fresh.

Use a sugar substitute, buy low-calorie products, and drain or trim out extra sugar sources wherever you can to save many unneeded calories.

Water-packed fish contains many fewer calories than oil-packed. If you accidentally get the oil-packed and time prevents returning it, drain as much of the oil off as possible.

A blender is your greatest creative implement—use it! Pureed vegetables and fluffed sauces stretched with low-calorie extenders are but two examples. Frankly, the blender provides a creamy texture without the benefit of cream—a great feat!

Use seasonings generously. Herbs and spices go a long way toward spicing up blah foods reduced of their high-calorie flavorings.

Vegetables are great sources of vitamins—they are filling and flavorful. Do not add extra calories to them with sauces and frying. A microwave oven is super if you have one—just rinse, slice or dice the vegetables, season with herbs, and cover with a lid or a tight wrap to seal in the steam and cook to a barely done stage. In just minutes you will surely be pleasantly surprised with the superb flavor. Lacking a microwave oven, try steaming or stir-frying. Steam well-rinsed and prepared vegetables in heavy pots utilizing just the water clinging to the vegetable and cook by using a flash of hot heat, followed by finishing on very low heat, well covered. Stir-frying finely chopped vegetables is the Chinese technique of cooking. Use a large, well-seasoned frying pan or wok over medium-high heat. Or, wrap the vegetables in foil or in a well-sealed casserole and bake or broil if meat is being prepared that way. Either broil in direct heat for a quick-cooking vegetable such as tomatoes, or cook in a packet of foil or covered dish. Butter salt is another great way to trim calories. Use it instead of butter.

Get ideas for low-calorie eating from diet cookbooks, magazines, diet clubs, skinny restaurants, health food stores, and even the low-calorie counter in your favorite grocery.

Acquire good-quality nonstick coated utensils to save on the calories from fats and oils. When necessary to assure nonsticking, use the spray can variety of no-stick shortening.

MEAT PORTIONS FOR REDUCING DIETS

For weight reduction, adults should eat 3 ounces of lean cooked meat for lunch and 4 ounces for dinner. Single portions of meat packaged to yield either amount, when cooked, are very convenient. The following guide reflects the amount to package for either size serving.

Meat as Purchased	Parts Weighed	Amount to Package Uncooked	Weight of Cooked Servings
Chops or steaks for broiling or frying:			
• With bone and relatively large amount of fat, such as pork or lamb chops; beef rib, sirloin, or porterhouse steaks	Package lean only	½ pound	2.5 to 3.5 ounces
• Without bone and with very little fat, such as round of beef, veal steaks	Package lean only	⅓ pound	3 to 4 ounces
Ground meat for broiling or frying such as beef, lamb, or pork patties	Patties	⅓ pound	3 to 4.25 ounces
Roasts for oven cooking (no liquid added:			
• With bone and relatively large amount of fat, such as beef rib, loin, chuck; lamb shoulder, leg; pork, fresh or cured	Package lean only	½ pound	3 to 4.5 ounces
• Without bone	Package lean only	½ pound	3.5 to 5 ounces

Cuts for pot-roasting, simmering, braising, stewing:

- With bone and relatively large amount of fat, such as beef chuck, pork shoulder

Package lean only ½ pound 3 to 4 ounces

- Without bone and with relatively small amount of fat, such as trimmed beef, veal

Lean with adhering fat ⅓ pound 3 to 3.6 ounces

Information courtesy of National Livestock and Meat Board and National Research Council

RECIPES

Appetizers and Snacks

Frozen low-calorie snacks can save many a bulge, especially if you are given to compulsive eating. Many of the fresh vegetable, dill pickle, and hard-cooked egg variety of low-calorie treats are not freezable but they can quickly be combined with low-calorie dips from the freezer.

ROQUEFORT SKINNY DIP

If you usually cut Bleu or Roquefort cheese out of your diet, don't from now on. This dip is not only great with fresh vegetable dippers, it is also great on hamburgers, baked potatoes, and other cooked vegetables.

Calories: 21 per tablespoon
Yield: 1½ cups

2-3 *tablespoons skimmed milk*
1 *teaspoon Worcestershire sauce*
1 *teaspoon lemon juice*
1 *cup (8 ounces) diet cottage cheese*

3 *ounces Roquefort cheese, crumbled*
¼ *teaspoon paprika*

1. Combine all ingredients in electric blender container and process until smooth.

251

2. Serve with assorted relishes as an appetizer (celery stalks, radish roses, carrot curls and frills, scallions, etc.)

FREEZING HINT: Freeze in small quantities for greatest convenience; seal tight, labeling each. Thaw overnight in the refrigerator.

MAXIMUM RECOMMENDED FREEZER STORAGE: 1 month

CHEESY TUNA BOATS

My uncle used to talk about minus-calorie foods, which required more energy to eat than they supplied. I am not certain this recipe would qualify totally, but the mushroom part surely would!

Calories: 23 each
Temperature: 400°F
Baking time: 10 to 15 minutes
Yield: 30 appetizers

30 large fresh mushrooms	2 tablespoons lemon juice
1 can (7 ounces) water-pack tuna	1½ tablespoons grated onion
	1 teaspoon Worcestershire sauce
2 ounces shredded Cheddar cheese	½ teaspoon paprika
½ cup diet cottage cheese	3 drops liquid hot pepper sauce

1. Rinse mushrooms in cold water. Dry mushrooms and remove stems. Chop stems finely.
2. Drain and flake tuna.
3. Combine the two cheeses; add seasonings, mushroom stems, and tuna.
4. Stuff each mushroom with about 2 teaspoons of the tuna mixture.

FREEZING HINTS: If freezing, placed stuffed mushrooms on cookie sheet. When firmly frozen, package with freezer wrap, seal, and label. Thaw overnight in the refrigerator or cook frozen. To serve, place mushrooms on a baking sheet. Bake at 400°F for 10 to 15 minutes or until lightly browned. (Bake twice as long if frozen.)

MAXIMUM RECOMMENDED FREEZER STORAGE: 2 months

LOW-CALORIE MARINATED MUSHROOMS

This low-calorie snack has always been especially popular. It is a non-freezable, but leftovers can be frozen for inclusion in tossed salads or with cooked green beans.

Fresh or canned
mushrooms, whole or
quartered

Low-calorie Italian
dressing

1. Rinse mushrooms well. If very large, quarter. Prepare the dressing if the packet variety.
2. Combine and leave on counter for 2 hours, stirring frequently. Chill and serve.

LOBSTER DUNK

Though rather expensive to prepare, this luscious low-calorie treat seems worth the cost.

Calories: 11 per 1½ teaspoons
Yield: 3¼ cups

¼ cup chopped green pepper
¼ cup chopped onion
1 can condensed mushroom
  soup
½ cup skimmed milk
2 egg yolks, beaten

2 cans (5 ounces each)
  lobster meat
2 tablespoons dry sherry
¼ teaspoon cayenne pepper
¼ teaspoon nutmeg
3 ounces shredded Cheddar cheese

1. Cook green pepper and onion in pan with nonstick coating using medium heat for about 10 minutes, adding a teaspoon or so of water, if desired.
2. Add soup, milk, and egg yolks; blend well.
3. Add lobster, sherry, cayenne, and nutmeg. Stirring constantly, cook until mixture is smooth and thick.
4. Add Cheddar cheese; stir until cheese is melted.
5. Serve the dunk warm in a chafing dish, standard or electric fondue pot, or saucepan. Serve with bite-sized crackers, celery, or cucumber sticks.

FREEZING HINT: Freeze in a sealed carton and label.

MAXIMUM RECOMMENDED FREEZER STORAGE: 1 month

Snacking Platters

Snacking platters can be very low calorie. Wrap thinly sliced luncheon meat, cheese, or roast meat of any kind around large pretzel rods, dill pickle spears, or quartered hard-cooked eggs. Boiled shrimp served with the usual catsup-lemony horseradish sauce is another low-cal treat. Paper thin crackers such as the Scandinavian varieties are great slimmers too. Serve them alongside meats and wafer thin sliced cheeses.

Instant Bloody Marys

As a snack, salad, or a central garnish for a platter of hors d'oeuvres, these are a fun nibble and so easy! Rinse cherry tomatoes, leaving the stems on. Place in attractive bowl that has three smaller matching side bowls. Place vodka in one, a packet of dry Bleu cheese or garlic salad dressing mix (seasoned salt can be substituted) in the second, and toothpicks in the third. Have guests dip a tomato on a toothpick in the vodka, then the seasonings. Each tomato, depending on its size, is only 5 calories or less!

Slimming Soups

Soups, especially the brothy types, are great fillers for light lunches or suppers. When served with a bulky salad or low-calorie lean meat, egg, or seafood open-faced sandwich, and a simple fruit-based dessert, not only do you have a tasty meal, but also a nutritious one.

MEAL-IN-ONE VEGETABLE SOUP

Calories: 121 per serving
Cooking time: 3 to 4 hours
Yield: 12 servings

1 pound lean beef, in 1-inch cubes	¾ cup diced raw turnip
1 tablespoon shortening	2 teaspoons salt
1 large soup bone, cracked	½ teaspoon celery salt
¾ cup chopped onion	½ teaspoon pepper
7½ cups boiling water	¼ teaspoon monosodium
1 cup sliced raw carrots	glutamate, optional
1 cup uncooked green beans	4 cups cooked tomatoes
cut in 1-inch pieces	¼ cup chopped parsley

1. In a large kettle, melt shortening and brown beef cubes evenly.
2. Wipe soup bone and add, along with onion and water; cover and bring to a boil. Skim off any foam and reduce temperature; simmer for 2 or 3 hours. Remove soup bone.
3. Add raw vegetables, salt, celery salt, pepper, and monosodium glutamate to kettle. Cover and simmer for 30 minutes. Remove from heat, cool, and skim off fat.
4. Force tomatoes through a sieve or mash with a fork and stir tomatoes and parsley into soup.

FREEZING HINT: Freeze in sealed cartons, packaging some single servings. Label.

MAXIMUM RECOMMENDED FREEZER STORAGE: 3 months

Slimming Condiments

WHIPPED BUTTER

Though not too freezable, this version of calorie and cost-extended butter can be made from frozen butter in quarter or half-recipe amounts.

Calories: 58 per tablespoon
Yield: 2 pounds

1 tablespoon unflavored gelatin	1 pound butter, fresh or
1 pint cream or evaporated milk	frozen, softened

1. Soften gelatin in ¼ cup cold light cream. Heat very slowly just until gelatin is dissolved.
2. Gradually whip the remaining cream and the dissolved gelatin into softened butter with electric mixer or in electric blender container.
3. Additional salt may be added, as well as yellow food coloring. If whipped butter should separate, continue beating until thoroughly mixed.
4. Chill until firm. (Freezing breaks down the emulsion.)

LOW-CALORIE SOUR CREAM

This version of sour cream does lose some of its creaminess when frozen. For cooking, though, there is no appreciable problem with the slightly grainier texture.

Calories: 13 per tablespoon
Yield: 1 cup

2 tablespoons skimmed milk
  or buttermilk
1 cup (8 ounces) diet cottage

cheese
¼ teaspoon lemon juice
Pinch of salt

1. Combine all ingredients in electric blender container. Blend until smooth, completely eliminating all lumps.
2. Refrigerate and serve.

NOTE: This does not stand up under heat as well as regular sour cream.

FREEZING HINT: Package in sealed cartons of sizes most frequently used.

MAXIMUM RECOMMENDED FREEZER STORAGE: 1 month

LOW-CAL PEACH JAM

Want your jam and eat it too? Other fruits can be substituted.

Calories: 10 each tablespoon
Yield: 4 half-pints

2 teaspoons unflavored
  gelatin
1 tablespoon cold water

3½ pounds fresh peaches
4 tablespoons liquid
  sweetener
8 teaspoons lemon juice

1. Soften gelatin in cold water. Peel, pit, and cut peaches into pieces or blend coarsely a few at a time. Sterilize 4 half-pint jars or glasses in boiling water.
2. Place peach pieces in heavy, large saucepan. Cook over medium heat, stirring occasionally, until peaches are soft; crush lightly if not previously blended.
3. Measure fruit, add water, if necessary, to measure 4 cups pulp.
4. Add sweetener, lemon juice, and softened gelatin. Return to heat and continue to cook for 1 minute. Remove from heat and ladle into sterilized half-pint jars or glasses. For immediate use, can be stored in refrigerator.

FREEZING HINT: Cover and seal if freezing.

MAXIMUM RECOMMENDED FREEZER STORAGE: 12 months

Skinny Central Themes

Without slaving to be slender, you can freeze many low-calorie, tantalizing main dishes. Lean, simply prepared meats are well-known waistline helpers. Broiled, baked, or steamed meats flavored with herbs and seasonings can be great. Freezing servings of meats broiler-ready, already roasted and sliced; or portions of meats ready for steaming, as well as some already steamed, makes for limitless variety. The following sauced and more complicated meat or main dishes will add to this variety. The low-calorie cooking habit, once developed, is easily continued as a way toward more attractive and healthful "looking."

FISH STEAKS WITH LEMON PARSLEY SAUCE

Calories: 165 per serving
Temperature: broil
Broiling time: 14 to 16 minutes
Yield: 4 servings

> 1 pound halibut fillets or
>   other white fish, thawed
> ½ cup lemon parsley sauce

> Cherry tomatoes and
> parsley sprigs for garnish

1. Lightly oil or spray with nonstick vegetable spray the rack of broiler pan. Place fish on broiler rack about 6 inches from broiler. Broil fillets for 2 minutes, then brush with lemon parsley sauce and broil an additional 4 to 6 minutes.
2. Turn fillets and broil 2 minutes on second side, then brush with lemon parsley sauce and broil an additional 4 to 6 minutes or until fish is flaky and well done.
3. Remove fillets to heated platter. Garnish with fresh parsley sprigs and cherry tomatoes.

Sauce:

Calories: 15 per tablespoon
Yield: ½ cup

> ½ cup parsley sprigs
> 1 medium onion, quartered

> 1 lemon, peeled, seeded, and
>   quartered
> ½ teaspoon salt

257

1. Combine all ingredients in blender. Cover and process until smooth.
2. Brush on fish while baking, broiling, or barbecuing.

MAXIMUM RECOMMENDED FREEZER STORAGE: 6 months

SHOYU CHICKEN

I discovered this dish in Hawaii one summer and found it almost as pleasing to the palate decalorized. Skinned breast meat is only 135 calories for a 3½-ounce serving if you really want to trim down!

Calories: 283 per serving
Temperature: medium, low
Cooking time: about 45 minutes
Yield: 4 servings

2 cloves garlic, crushed
1 piece ginger root
1 3-pound chicken, cut up
⅓ cup soy sauce
1 cup water

1 tablespoon dry sherry
Artificial sweetener
equivalent to ¼ cup sugar
2 teaspoons cornstach

1. Preheat skillet with nonstick coating on medium heat; add garlic and ginger. Add chicken pieces and brown slightly.
2. Pour soy sauce, water, wine, and sweetener over chicken; reduce temperature to low; cover and simmer until tender, about 30 minutes. Turn chicken occasionally to assure even browning. Taste and adjust seasoning if desired. Remove ginger root.
3. To serve, thicken gravy with cornstarch; serve with rice.

FREEZING HINT: Freeze in sealed carton; label.

MAXIMUM RECOMMENDED FREEZER STORAGE: 6 months

SLIM STYLE SHISH KABOB

Use a tender, well-trimmed leg of lamb so you can have your shish kabob without calorie worries! Keep the marinated lamb chunks frozen ready for those "I feel fat" days!

Calories: about 166 per serving
Temperature: broil

Broiling time: 15 to 20 minutes
Yield: 4 servings

½ cup low-calorie Italian
  salad dressing
2 small bay leaves
1 pound lean, boneless leg of
  lamb cut into 1-inch cubes
1 green pepper, cut into
  1-inch squares

4 cherry tomatoes
4 large mushroom caps
¼ cup catsup
1 teaspoon Worcestershire
  sauce
⅛ teaspoon monosodium
  glutamate, optional

1. Combine bay leaves and salad dressing in freezer container. Add lamb and marinate 2 to 4 hours, turning occasionally, at room temperature or overnight in the refrigerator.

FREEZING HINT: Freeze now, sealing in carton. Label.

2. To serve, thaw overnight or about half a day on the counter. Prepare vegetables. Combine remaining ingredients to make a sauce.

3. Alternately, thread lamb and green pepper squares on four skewers. Broil about 4 inches from heat for 9 minutes, brush with marinade, turn, and broil 6 more minutes.

4. Place a mushroom cap and a tomato on end of each skewer. Brush generously with sauce. Continue broiling for about 2 minutes on each side or until lamb is of desired doneness.

MAXIMUM RECOMMENDED FREEZER STORAGE: 6 months

VEAL PAPRIKA IN SOUR CREAM

Here is a skinny version of that famous Hungarian main dish, paprikash. Save mealtime preparation by freezing ahead.

Calories: 212 per serving
Temperature: 350°F, 200°F
Total time: about 60 minutes
Yield: 6 servings

2 pounds veal cutlets, cut
  ½-inch thick
1½ teaspoons paprika
1 teaspoon salt
¼ teaspoon pepper
2 medium onions, sliced

1 beef bouillon cube,
  dissolved in 1½ cups water
1 teaspoon prepared
  mustard
½ cup Low-Calorie Sour
  Cream (see page 255)

1. Pound meat until ¼-inch thick. Cut into serving-sized pieces.
2. Sprinkle meat with paprika, salt, and pepper.
3. Set electric skillet with nonstick coating at 350°F, or heat nonstick skillet on medium heat of range. Cook onion until transparent, adding a teaspoon of water, if desired. Remove onions.
4. In same skillet, brown veal pieces at 350°F, or medium heat.
5. Add bouillon broth, onions, and mustard. Cover and reduce heat to 200°F, or low heat. Simmer 25 minutes, or until veal is tender.

FREEZING HINTS: Place in freezer carton with drippings; seal and label. If not planning to freeze, place meat on warm platter immediately and proceed with next step.

6. To serve, heat meat, then remove to warm serving platter; add sour cream to liquid in skillet and blend. Spoon over meat and serve immediately.

MAXIMUM RECOMMENDED FREEZER STORAGE: 4 months

SKINNY TIME SAVER'S LOAF*

Ideal for the individual calorie counter! Prepare loaves ahead of time and freeze separately. Pop one in the oven for a real quickie or for a night when everyone else is having a calorie-laden dish!

Calories: 249 per loaf
Temperature: 450°F
Baking time: 20 to 25 minutes
Yield: 6 servings

1½ pounds ground round steak	1 cup chopped onions
1 1-pound can tomatoes, drained	1 teaspoon leaf basil
	1½ teaspoons salt
1 tablespoon Worcestershire sauce	1 teaspoon pepper
	1 teaspoon garlic powder

1. Preheat oven to 450°F.
2. Combine all ingredients together in medium-sized bowl.
3. Shape into 6 mini-loaves and place on a rack in 9x13-inch baking pan.
4. Bake at 450°F for 20 to 25 minutes. You can serve immediately or freeze them.

FREEZER HINTS: Package each individually in freezer wrap. Seal and label. To serve, thaw and heat for about 20 minutes in a 350°F oven.

*A sugarless barbecue sauce may be served over the top.

MAXIMUM RECOMMENDED FREEZER STORAGE: 3 months

Salads

Salads are well known for their low-calorie characteristics, though many fall down when it comes to the dressing. Knowing that a nice crisp head of lettuce is only about 60 calories, don't drown it in rich dressings. Instead, keep a variety of low-calorie dressings on hand.

A freezer is very handy for this, although if you are a regular diet salad eater perhaps you won't want to freeze them. If you are not, the freezer adds greatly to variety and convenience.

Some dressings may be a bit grainy after freezing—however, they have always been acceptable to me. I store them in mini-size containers which thaw quickly and are ready for a fast whisk with a fork before tossing in with the greens. Individual plastic cups for coffee cream, airline containers, or any other portion control serving containers work very well.

FRENCH DRESSING

Calories: 9 per tablespoon
Yield: 1¼ cups

1 cup water	1 tablespoon salad oil
1 tablespoon cornstarch	¼ teaspoon dill weed
1 teaspoon paprika	¼ teaspoon basil, crumbled
½ teaspoon dry mustard	Noncaloric sweetener
½ teaspoon salt	equivalent to 1 teaspoon
¼ teaspoon garlic salt	sugar
¼ cup red wine vinegar	

1. Combine water, cornstarch, paprika, mustard, plain and garlic salts in small saucepan. Cook, stirring, until mixture boils and clears. Cool.

2. Turn into a jar and add all remaining ingredients. Cover and shake well to blend.

FREEZING HINT: Freeze in one-serving sealed containers. Label. Shake again just before using.

MAXIMUM RECOMMENDED FREEZER STORAGE: 3 months

MEXICALI DRESSING

Calories: 19 per tablespoon
Yield: 1 cup dressing

1 cup water
2 beef bouillon cubes
2 teaspoons instant minced
  onion
1 teaspoon cornstarch

¾ teaspoon salt
2 tablespoons vinegar
2 tablespoons salad oil
1 teaspoon bottled Mexican
  seasoning

1. Combine water, bouillon cubes, instant onion, cornstarch, and salt in small suacepan. Cook, stirring, until mixture boils and thickens.
2. Remove from heat, cool, and turn into small jar. Add vinegar, oil, and Mexican seasoning.
3. Cover and shake well to blend. Freeze in one-serving sealed containers. Label. Shake again just before using.

MAXIMUM RECOMMENDED FREEZER STORAGE: 3 months

LOW-CALORIE THOUSAND ISLAND DRESSING

The yogurt base makes this dressing more perishable than some; if frozen, it keeps much better in single-serving containers.

Calories: 13 per tablespoon
Yield: 1½ cups

1 container (8 ounces)
  low-fat plain yogurt
¼ cup catsup
1 teaspoon prepared
  mustard

½ teaspoon prepared
  horseradish
½ teaspoon onion salt
⅟₁₆ teaspoon pepper
3 tablespoons chopped dill pickle

1. Stir yogurt, catsup, mustard, horseradish, salt, and pepper together. Mix in pickle. Freeze in one-serving sealed containers. Label.

NOTE: If not freezing, you can add one hard-cooked, diced egg for about one calorie more per serving.

MAXIMUM RECOMMENDED FREEZER STORAGE: 3 months

Vegetables

MUSHROOM BAKED TOMATOES

Tomatoes are a very versatile low-calorie vegetable—tremendous for dieting. For variety, try these! For convenience use fresh rather than frozen tomatoes, speeding up preparation by having the topping frozen.

Calories: 51 per serving
Temperature: 400°F
Total time: about 25 minutes

½ cup chopped onion
½ cup soft bread crumbs
1 cup sliced mushrooms
1½ tablespoons minced parsley

Salt
Pepper
4 medium tomatoes

1. Cook onions until limp in skillet with nonstick coating. Add bread crumbs and cook 1 minute.
2. Add mushrooms, parsley, salt and pepper to taste. Mix well and cook for 2 to 3 minutes.
3. To serve, cut tomatoes in half and place in a 9-inch-square baking dish. Sprinkle with salt and pepper, top with mushroom mixture.
4. Bake at 400°F, for about 15 minutes.

FREEZING HINT : Freeze topping in sealed carton. Label. Topping thaws quickly under hot water.

MAXIMUM RECOMMENDED FREEZER STORAGE: 6 months

ASPARAGUS ORIENTAL

Calories: about 38 per serving
Yield: 4 to 5 servings

2 teaspoons butter or
  margarine
1 teaspoon seasoned chicken
  stock base
⅛ teaspoon celery
  salt

⅛ teaspoon ginger
  Dash of white pepper
1 10-ounce package frozen
  asparagus or 1½ pounds
  fresh asparagus
1 teaspoon soy sauce

1. Melt butter in skillet; add seasoned stock base, celery salt, ginger, and pepper, and mix well.
2. Add asparagus; toss gently. Cover and cook using high heat for 2

minutes or until tender-crisp, stirring two or three times. Add soy sauce and mix well. Serve piping hot.

Calorie Cheating Desserts

One of the best calorie cheaters is fruit. Fruits baked in low-calorie soda, sparked with spices, or blended to a puree and frozen as ice are two simple variations to fresh fruit. Substitute low-calorie sweetener for the sugar in freezing fruits. Unsweetened fruit juice, substituted for the sugar, is even better!

FRUIT ICE

I always try to have some fruit ice in the freezer. It is easy to make gobs and it's so great tasting. If you can spare the calories, compatible brandies or liqueurs dress it up!

Calories: 36 per serving
Yield: 4 servings (2¼ cups)

1 pint sliced strawberries, raspberries, watermelon, other melons, apricots, or other fresh or processed fruit without sugar

Artificial sweetener equivalent to ¼ cup sugar
2 tablespoons lemon juice
8–10 ice cubes

1. Combine fruit, sweetener, and lemon juice in electric blender container. Process until smooth. Add ice cubes a few at a time until a very thick consistency is obtained.
2. Freeze until firm, for at least 3 or 4 hours—or for months.
3. Place scoops of the ice in sherbet dishes and serve plain or top with low-calorie topping, if desired. Parfaits can also be made by alternating layers of fruit, fruit ice, and topping in parfait glasses, or drizzle with liqueur.

NOTE: This dessert freezes quite hard. When serving, remove from freezer about 15 to 20 minutes ahead of time.

MAXIMUM RECOMMENDED FREEZER STORAGE: 2 months

CHILLED LEMON SOUFFLÉ

Frozen uncooked eggs work well in this soufflé which is amazingly flavorful and the missing calories seem like no loss at all.

Calories: 88 per serving
Yield: 10 servings

2 envelopes unflavored gelatin	½ teaspoon salt
½ cup cold water	2 teaspoons grated lemon rind
8 eggs, separated	1 cup lemon juice
Artificial sweetener equivalent to 2 cups sugar	½ cup dry milk solids
	½ cup ice water

1. Fasten a 6-inch band of foil around a 2-quart soufflé dish, allowing 4 inches to stand above top of dish. (Or, use any 3-quart baking dish.)

2. Soften gelatin in cold water.

3. Combine egg yolks (thawed, if frozen), sweetener, salt, lemon rind, and lemon juice in top of double boiler. Cook over hot water, stirring occasionally, until thick.

4. Remove from heat; add softened gelatin, stirring to dissolve. Chill until mixture begins to set.

5. Beat egg whites (can be thawed, if frozen) until stiff but not dry; fold into gelatin mixture.

6. Combine dry milk and ice water; beat on high speed of electric mixer until stiff, about 10 minutes; fold into gelatin mixture.

7. Gently spoon into soufflé dish; chill several hours until set; or freeze, then package, seal, and label. Remove foil before serving.

MAXIMUM RECOMMENDED FREEZER STORAGE: 2 months

16
Frozen Assets

Many clichés have been penned about saving little bits and pieces, such as Ben Franklin's famous pennies and feeding the poor starving children of the world from needlessly wasted scraps. Though we have rightfully earned the title wasteful Americans, the shortages and worries about ecological unbalances are beginning to be felt all the way to the grass roots and to our kitchens. Some highly respected world food supply experts have cited 1973 as the year of the food famine turn-around. In 1973 we lost our battle for plentiful foods and now must resort to ever more resourceful and frugal food habits to feed the world's growing population.

If your main concern is your own family's food bill and your limited time, a freezer offers many opportunities for plentiful dividends adding up to great assets. The result: less waste, better eating, more variety, and more time for other activities.

Following are some fun and exciting ways to maximize your own resources.

Save Money—Shop in Season

This is an especially good idea for big-ticket items such as meats. Unless you have a very large freezer, you may find, as I have, that snatching up great buys when you see them makes a lot of sense. For me, this is smarter than buying a part of a carcass although of course your freezer and your family's meat appetites may be different. At any rate, buy when the meat is at its best price. Meat bargains can be found almost any day if you have a liberal attitude to the cut and the cooking required. Check the best seasonal buys in many newspapers and from the County Extension office. Farmers strive to have continuous availability of meats and avoid shortages and oversupplies—yet most of the hoofed animals are most available toward the end of the year, in November and December. Turkeys are often cheapest around holidays, usually just before the actual season. The price of chicken is not usually seasonally based.

Fruits are best at the peak of their ripening season and the same is true for vegetables—meaning summer and early fall are the best times to buy. Keep your eyes open for bargains and take advantage—when your time and freezer space allow, that is!

Take Stock and Make Stocks

Beef, fish, and chicken stock are the most common stocks and can easily be squeezed in during most mealtime preparations when your freezer "stock" corner says "it's time." Save up for stock making—I never scrap good-looking bones, especially raw ones I've trimmed out of a roast or carcass of any sort. When shopping, inquire if there are extra bones available. Especially be sure to take them when they are rightfully yours, such as when you had the fish man behead fresh fish or the butcher specially prepare a roast. Reserve gravies and pan juices—even deglaze pan brownies when not making gravy and save the rich, tasty stock in an eternal jar, one for each kind of stock you wish to prepare. Save chicken skins and innards too.

Scraps from carrots, onions, and celery should also be frozen and saved for the stock taking or making time. The stocks I make combine the bones, gravy and pan drips, carrots, onions, and celery, plus bay, salt, and pepper and an occasional herb such as thyme and sometimes wine. I add the tail end of marinades sometimes, if compatibly flavored. Use your imagination and the joy will be yours many meals over!

Use stock to flavor meats, basting them as they roast; to cook vegetables in; to make gravies; to create quick soups; and to serve as the basis for an occasional bullshot—a brunch cocktail made of beef stock. Save scraps of meats for use in soups, stews, creamed and curried casseroles, meat loaves, sandwiches, croquettes, omelets, soufflés, quiches, and foreign favorites such as tacos and chow mein.

Save bones for trivets for roasted meats and for long-simmering meat and vegetable combinations. For example, I always save lamb bones to use as a base for steaming stuffed grape leaves. As you can guess, they impart a rich flavor.

Vegetable scraps and juices can be conserved for the same uses—soups, stews, combination casseroles, salad flavorings, and garnishes. Never toss out the tops of celery—they're excellent in stock as well as sauces and soups.

Savory "Saves"

I've often plundered the Saturday-afternoon "Too Ripe and Blemished" baskets at friendly local vegetable stands and come home with great goodies. Such delights as red ripe tomatoes for sauces and very ripe fruits for pureeing and freezing for toppings and jam have been frequent finds.

Too ripe bananas can be mashed and frozen for use in baking. Just sweeten the quantity of bananas required with the amount of sugar you use in your favorite bread, cake, (or muffin recipe and stir in ascorbic acid to prevent darkening. Be sure to label the intended use! When you use the exact quantities your recipe calls for, results are great on baking day. And so are banana daiquiris if baking day never seems to happen!

Freeze citrus rinds whole for flavoring flaming fruit sauces, hot or cold wines or ciders. Grate some too, and package in 1-teaspoon packets for use in cooking. Bundle the individual packets together in a larger bag or carton.

Soured milk, buttermilk, and yogurt—frequently considered nonfreezables—freeze fine for cooking use and this saves on waste! Package in frequently used amounts of ½ to 1 cup.

In the never, never waste category, breads of any kind should always be salvaged and frozen for many delightful recyclings. Save a bag of bread ends for use in making crumbs in the blender.

White bread is particularly good made into croutons, especially if it's the substantial homemade variety. Save bits and pieces for this. When you have accumulated a worthwhile amount and the time is available—preferably when the oven is already warm and in use—cut the bread into uniform pieces, about ½ inch square. Then spread them in a single layer on a cookie sheet and place in a warm oven, up to 325°F. Actually you can start the toasting process at higher temperatures, if for a short time, and finish with the heat completely off. Toast triangles are whimsical garnishes made from extra toast. Assorted breads can be used in French toast, bread pudding, and stuffings. Just save up ends in a bag in your freezer.

Ends and pieces of crackers make good crumbs too. Any of these can serve as casserole toppers, or as an extender in meat loaf.

Rice is too good to waste. Save in a bag or carton, accumulating until you have enough to make fried rice, to use as a base for a meat or fish sauce, or to use in pudding or soup.

Cheeses should never be thrown out. Keep a close watch on their quality and when they are fading, grate or crumble them. Freeze commonly used amounts, such as ½ or 1 cup quantities, in little bags. Or, freeze the entire quantity in a large carton.

When You Go Away

Vacation time need not mean wasted food. First, anticipate going away. Buy fewer perishable foods, and more canned, dried, or frozen foods.

Many perishable foods can be frozen for later use. Even lettuce, as I mentioned in the vegetable chapter, is good in soups, French peas, and the like. Eggs can be frozen raw; so can dairy products, meats, vegetables—even crackers, cereals, and chips.

If you live in a humid climate and don't freeze everything, long trips can be disastrous. I know—once when I left for three weeks I did not have room in my freezer for my gigantic storehouse of grain products and came home to utter chaos: bugs of all small descriptions were crawling over everything. Prevent this! Freeze any food to prevent infestation. (More about control of infestation later in this chapter.)

Another great idea is to have someone check your freezer every other day to be sure it is running well. This prevents problems should it fail for any reason.

Sandwich Serendipity

Sandwiches are much more interesting when you are a creative freezer user. Bologna on whole wheat all week can be varied with a different bread and filling each day. Some ideas that are great freeze-aheads are:

- Breads of all varieties made from any grain or mixture, or flavored with cheese, herbs, onions, olives, fruity or even nutty, add spark and interest.
- Spread or brush the bread with soft butter or margarine to protect the bread from absorbing the filling.
- Create a storehouse of fillings, adding a new one whenever time or the mood allows. Good roast meats are ham, beef, pork, lamb, chicken, turkey, game, fish, or shellfish. Spread with favorite sauce such as mustard, mint jelly, or meat sauce. Instead of the many paper-thin sliced meats, use thicker slices for more moist frozen sandwiches.
- Or try—Deviled ham mixed with pickle relish and just a bit of mayonnaise, dried beef mixed with horseradish to taste, or . . .
- Mashed chicken livers flavored with sherry and thyme and layered with thin butter-fried mushrooms
- Pimiento cheese made yourself from Cheddar and perhaps a blend of other on-hand cheeses, pimientos, and cream
- Cream cheese mixed with herbs to make your own Continental cheese
- Peanut butter and jelly become exotic flavored with cream cheese, cinnamon, and nuts or raisins

269

- Curried or barbecued meats are good
- Grind extra frankfurter and sauerkraut, drain well, and place in a rye roll—then season with your favorite mustard
- Baked beans layered with cheese, relish, and bacon bits
- Feta cheese, chopped Greek olives, tomatoes, and pickled cherry chile peppers blended together and stuffed in a pita bread served warm

Other Goodies

Butter balls, curls, and flavored butters are a grand treat for adding subtle variety. Flavor butter with orange or lemon rind, herbs, garlic, anchovy, curry, barbecue spice, or other favorite addition. Garlic and anchovy butters are great for bread spreads and as condiments for beef fondue, so you may want to make bigger batches.

Create sauce sorcery instantly with a supply of sauce cubes in your freezer. Never throw out sauces; instead, pour into ice cube trays, freeze, then bag. Examples are tomato, cheese, lemon butter, curry, wine, Chinese mushroom, Mornay, and Bearnaise. Leftover coffee and tea can be frozen into cubes for iced teas and coffee on simmering days.

And speaking of ice cube trays, you may wish to treat guests to special cubes with cherries frozen in the center for punch or frosty Manhattans; fruit or syrup-flavored cubes for the small fry; colored cubes for punches and fanciful serving of cool foods such as shrimp, canapes, and the like. Pureed fruits such as applesauce are handy in cubes too, for single servings or garnish.

Pureed fruits made with a blender and a few larger chopped pieces, sweetened and treated with ascorbic acid mixture, make cobblers, sundae sauces, jams, upside down cakes, fruit crisps, and pancake or waffle toppings. Last-of-the-season fruit or windfalls are expecially good for this use.

When Amy was a baby, I don't really know what I would have done without a freezer. I wanted her to have only the very best foods—so I cooked and pureed them. Also I wanted her to know and love varied cooking, not just bland foods. It was well worth the effort. She shifted quite easily over to table food with hardly a wrinkled nose.

Oil stays dependably fresh-tasting when frozen. Used oil that you like to keep for deep-fat frying is much fresher than when stored at room temperature or even in the refrigerator. Freezing prevents rancidity in olive oil too.

Fresh-ground and whole-bean coffee, and nuts, keep much better frozen.

Home-grown fresh herbs are very easy to freeze and have more flavor than when dried. Just snip off young leaves or ends of stems and rinse well, chop, and package in rounded teaspoon cello packets. A rounded teaspoon of fresh equals about 1 teaspoon of dried as used in most recipes.

Other frequent flavorings–chopped onion and chopped pepper–make lots of sense to prepare when the vegetables are in season in late summer. Package in large bags, cartons, or frequently used quantities. No blanching is needed.

On Keeping Your Spirits Cool

You can quick-chill beers and wines—but don't forget about them as I once did. A large bottle of wine exploded in the freezer and the waste and mess was awful—broken glass all over and wine in all the crevices was almost too much!

After a beer keg party, or whenever there is any beer left opened, save some for immediate cooking use. Freeze the rest in plastic or glass jars, allowing generous head space—about 4 inches between the top of the beer and the lid. You're wondering—just how do I cook with beer? Beer is a great tenderizer for steaming meats from shrimp to beef. A glaze of beer and honey is my favorite for hams and turkeys lazily turning on a spit. Beer as the liquid in omelets imparts a unique flavor. Cheese sauces are smoother with at least some beer as the liquid.

Wine that seems to be borderline sour can be frozen for cooking use, keeping it from souring all the way. Freeze in often used amounts such as 1-cup quantities.

Marinades and bastes keep their freshness much better when frozen. After they're used they get some blood mixed in and will spoil quickly—hence freezing is the only really dependable method for keeping them.

Strange and Wondrous Uses

Many unusual uses for the freezer have been developed through ingenuity and necessity. Those I know of and have tested I am delighted to share with you—perhaps they'll inspire even more from you.

Demoth woolens by packaging in heavy plastic wrap, sealing well. Chill the woolens for 72 hours in your freezer, then place on a shelf or in a drawer for storage.

Debug precious herbs, meals, and cereal products by freezing. Sometimes if freezer space does not permit storage, I place the foods in the microwave oven for about 1 minute per pound. This is an added insurance that the bugs and larvae are killed by subjecting them to both ends of the temperature spectrum. Seal foods well in freezer wrap and freeze. A minimum of 72 hours is required for debugging and if the bugs are of the hard-shelled variety, sometimes indefinite freezing is the only sure preservation. The bugs can then be sifted or sorted out. The best method is to prevent infestation in the first place by freezing.

"Stuck-on" freezer packaging comes off quickly and easily in the microwave, after a few minutes in a moderate oven, or when placed in hot water a moment.

Quickly dry glass, such as a sugar bowl, by placing the just washed bowl in the freezer. In a few minutes, once it warms, it will be dry.

Ever get too much candy, or make too much for the holidays? It freezes beautifully when packaged airtight while it's still fresh. Airtight packaging prevents oxidation, which shows as whiting on chocolate, and preserves the freshly made flavor.

Ever quit smoking or buy more special tobaccos or cigarettes than you can quickly use? If so, packaging in good-quality freezer wrap, sealing, labeling, and freezing them will keep them fresh as can be, for use when the time is right.

Appendix

MAXIMUM STORAGE TIMES

Times are for optimum storage at 5° F or below. Much shorter storage times must be used for freezers at higher temperatures. Foods must be properly packaged in moisture- and vapor-proof packages (see Index for packaging instructions for specific foods). Foods stored longer than recommended will become less flavorful and less nutritious—they do not become harmful!

FOOD	MAXIMUM STORAGE PERIOD
APPETIZERS (canapés, hors d'oeuvres)	½ to 1 month
BREADS	
Quick	
Baked muffins, waffles, biscuits, and simple quick breads	2 to 3 months
Richer, fruited, nutted, or spicy quick breads	1 to 2 months
Unbaked doughs	Up to 1 month
Yeast	
Baked bread and rolls	3 months
Spiced, fruited, or nutted rolls or loaves	2 months
Danish pastry	3 months
Doughnuts, either cake or yeast	3 months
Half-baked (brown 'n' serve)	2 to 3 months
Unbaked	Up to 1 month
CAKES	
Any type of butter cake, frosted or unfrosted	4 to 6 months
Angel or chiffon	2 months
Fruitcake	12 months
CANDIES	12 months
COOKIES	
Baked cookies	6 to 8 months
Meringue cookies	2 to 4 weeks
Unbaked refrigerator cookies	6 months

273

COOKED COMBINATION DISHES

Casseroles, pasta or rice base	2 to 4 weeks
Cooked meat and meat dishes	2 to 3 months
Pizza	2 to 4 weeks
Sauces and stews	1 to 3 months

DAIRY PRODUCTS

Butter	6 months
Margarine	12 months
Cheese	
Cottage cheese, uncreamed	2 to 3 months
Cream cheese, for use as an ingredient	2 months
Natural cheese, small portions	1 to 1½ months
Natural Cheddar (all forms)	1½ months
Natural Swiss	1½ to 2 months
Process cheese products (Process cheese is identified on the label. If not so designated the cheese is natural.)	4 months
Shelf-stable cheese products	4½ months
Veined cheese, blue, Roquefort	3 months
Cream	
Whipping cream	2 months
Whipped cream	1 month
Half and half	2 months
Sour cream, for cooking purposes	1 month
Yogurt, for cooking purposes	1 month

DESSERTS

Cream puffs or eclairs	1 to 2 months
Fruits, baked, or fruit desserts	2 to 4 months
Steamed pudding	6 months

EGGS

Whole, yolks or whites separated	12 months

FATS

Oil from cooking	4 months
Lard, rendered	4 to 6 months

FRUITS

Fresh fruits, sugar or syrup-packed (except as below)	12 months
Dietetic pack	4 to 6 months
Dry pack	4 to 6 months
Citrus fruits	4 to 6 months
Melons, plums, prunes	8 to 12 months
Pears	6 to 8 months
Juices	
Citrus	6 months

Other fruit	12 months
GRAINS	12 months
ICE CREAM	
Any type, including ice milk, sherbet	1 month
JAMS, JELLIES, and MARMALADES	12 months
MEATS, COOKED	
Red meats	
Meat dinners, dishes, pies	3 months
Meat gravy, broth	2 to 3 months
Meat loaf	2 to 3 months
Poultry	
Dinners, pies	6 months
Dry meat, not covered with gravy or broth	1 month
Fried chicken	4 months
Stuffing	1 month
Whole, unstuffed	6 months
Seafood	
Fried or sauced fish or seafood	3 months
Seafood main dishes	3 months
MEATS, PROCESSED	
Frankfurters	Up to 3 months
Bologna and luncheon meats	Not recommended. Up to 3 months— only in emergencies

MEATS, RAW
note: When portioning, refer to meat yield chart, page 250

Beef	
Steaks, roasts	8 to 12 months
Ground beef	2 to 4 months
Stew meats	2 to 4 months
Corned beef	2 weeks
Liver, heart, kidney, tongue	3 to 4 months
Brains, sweetbreads, tripe	2 to 3 months
Game, most types, including birds	8 to 12 months
Lamb	
Roasts	6 to 9 months
Chops	3 to 4 months
Ground or stew meat	3 to 4 months
Pork, Cured, such as bacon, ham	Up to 2 months
Pork, Fresh	
Roasts	4 to 8 months
Chops	3 to 4 months
Sausage	1 to 3 months

Ground pork, unseasoned, or stew meat	2 to 3 months
Liver, heart, kidney, tongue	3 to 4 months
Brains, sweetbreads, tripe	2 to 3 months
Veal	
Cutlets, chops	6 to 9 months
Roasts	6 to 9 months

POULTRY

Chicken	
Cut-up	9 months
Whole	12 months
Livers	1 month
Giblets	3 months
Duck, whole	6 months
Goose, whole	6 months
Turkey	
Cut-up	6 to 9 months
Whole	12 months

SEAFOOD, SHELLFISH AND FISH

Shellfish	
Clams, shucked	3 months
Crabmeat, Dugeness	3 months
Crabmeat, King	10 months
Oysters, shucked	4 months
Shrimp, raw unpeeled	12 months
Shrimp, cooked	3 months
Fish	
Lean fish (bass, cod, perch, pike, sunfish, etc.)	6 to 8 months
Fatty fish (catfish, herring, salmon, mackerel)	2 to 3 months

NUTS

Salted	6 to 8 months
Unsalted	9 to 12 months

PASTRIES

Pastry Dough	
Unbaked	1½ to 2 months
Baked	6 to 8 months
Pies	
Unbaked	2 to 4 months
Baked	6 to 8 months
Chiffon	Up to 2 months
Meringue topped	Up to 2 weeks

SALADS

Fruit, vegetable, cream or mayonnaise combinations	4 to 6 months

SANDWICHES

Meat, poultry, cheese, jelly or jam mixtures	1 to 2 months

SAUCES
    Dessert or meat   3 to 4 months
SOUPS
    Includes concentrates and stocks   1 to 3 months
VEGETABLES
    Most vegetables with following
        exceptions   8 to 12 months
                                              depending on quality

    Exceptions:
        Asparagus   6 to 8 months
        Mushrooms   Up to 6 months
        Potatoes, baked, fried, or mashed   2 to 3 months

Index

Recipes appear in boldface type.

278

280

282

283

286